Bark and Lunge:

Saving My Dog from Training Mistakes

A memoir by Kari Neumeyer

How do you make sure the dog you love never bites anyone (again)?

I need to look great for all patrons,

so please keep me away from food,

drinks, pets, ink, pencils, and other

things that may harm me.

ISBN 978-0-9904664-0-6
Interior book design by www.booknook.biz
Cover designed by Debbie Glovatsky
Photos by Kari Neumeyer and Rob Eis

KariNeumeyer.com
BarkAndLunge.com

As a work of nonfiction, the events depicted are true.
Some names and identifying details have been changed.

Dedicated to all the dogs still wearing aversive collars and the owners who don't know any better. And of course, to Isis, my Smiley Bird.

Contents

The Turning Point

Isis sleeps at my feet, chin resting on her paws and green leash stretching across the floor. I reach down and stroke her head where the black marks from puppyhood have faded but still frame her face in a widow's peak.

She doesn't open her eyes.

"You are the most beautiful girl in the world," I murmur.

Glancing out my office door, I lock eyes with a man passing by. Before I can utter the first syllable of "Hello," Isis springs to her feet, a black-and-tan blur, barking and bolting out the door.

"Isis! Hey! No!" I scramble for the green leash, but too late. Isis is beyond my reach. Snarling, she backs the man into a corner, gnashing her powerful German shepherd jaws against his leg. "Isis! No!"

Eyes wide, the man holds his hands by his face like this is a stickup. I leap toward him and grab Isis's leash. Yanking her away switches off her "attack" button. The vicious beast is gone; Isis is herself again.

She looks up at me, bright-eyed and panting. *Hey, Mom, what's up?*

I stand gaping in the middle of the room, stunned into paralysis, feeling powerless and guilty. I'm out of words. I can't excuse Isis's actions as rambunctious or reactive. A dog doesn't attack a man unprovoked unless she is a dangerous dog. Aggressive.

The kind of dog that gets confiscated and euthanized.

I never imagined that Isis would go after someone like that, yet after it happened, I couldn't pretend the signs weren't there. Over the previous year, her behavior had grown increasingly volatile.

But none of her previous misdemeanors came close to what she'd just done.

Of course, it was my fault. I never should have brought her to work when she'd rather be at home anyway, playing in the backyard with her soccer balls. She carried one in her mouth at all times, releasing it only to nudge it down the hill with her nose so we could throw it to her again. She could jump higher than six feet in the air. Long and lean, she sprang off her hind legs, her black-and-golden body vertical in midair, catching the ball, then spinning and flipping before landing on her feet. I watched from the kitchen window sometimes as Rob, devoted dog poppa, kicked the ball over and over, until Isis's tongue hung out the side of her mouth. Then he'd lean over and wrap his arms around her, because for some reason he thought she needed to catch her breath and bring her heart rate down.

She took the hug standing up, and even from the kitchen—even with a ball in her mouth and her tongue hanging out—I could tell she was smiling. But if he chased her, she sprinted away, her tail sliding through his hands and out of his grasp.

Limiting her adventures to our own yard didn't seem fair, though. A few months earlier, I took Isis to the beach during a weekend getaway. Wearing that same green leash, Isis pranced ahead of me in the low waves. I scanned the long stretch of beach, weighing the odds that she might run away. Just under two years old, Isis was not entirely trustworthy off-leash, but hardly anyone was around, and there were no other dogs. I dropped her leash, letting it drag in the water. When Isis realized she was free, she zoomed away, galloping in the knee-deep water.

My shoulders tensed as I wondered how far away from me she might run.

"Isis!"

Turning at the sound of my voice, she ran back in my direction. I lifted my camera to capture the sheer joy on her face as she frolicked in the waves, shaking the salt spray from her face. That photo shows Isis at her most carefree, reveling in the waves, wild and uninhibited.

After she bit the man at my office, in the car ride on the way home, she didn't look much like she had a care in the world, either. How could she do that? Go from mindless attack mode to smiling at the view outside the car window? I carried for both of us the shame of what she'd done. How she'd violated my trust.

Could I ever take her anywhere in public again?

Isis had bitten someone, and there was no going back.

Chapter 1: Smiley Bird

A mob of black-and-tan puppies fought for position against the chain-link kennel gates, wailing a high-pitched chorus.

A litter of nine German shepherds on one side of the room, a second litter of twelve on the other. Among the litter of nine, one puppy stood back from the ruckus, her head cocked to one side, checking out the strangers on the opposite side of the gate.

I mirrored her expression, tilting my head to admire the tan markings on her face. Her siblings' faces were darker and their ears were floppy. This puppy's ears stood straight up, disproportionately large compared to her face. I didn't have to look at any of the others. She was the one I wanted. Maybe I was projecting, but I could see in her eyes a depth of intelligence the other pups didn't have.

Technically, we had no plans to get a dog that day. My boyfriend, Rob, and I were in Southern California for a late November wedding, visiting from northwest Washington. The puppies were merely an interlude. My brother's wife, Quin, lured us here to her parents' property, where they trained bomb and drug dogs. She promised Rob he could try on the sleeve used to teach dogs to clamp onto a bad guy's arm and not let go. As a martial artist and juvenile corrections officer, Rob was into that sort of thing. I was more interested in the puppies; I'd dreamed of getting one since Rob and I first started shopping for houses the previous spring.

We had arrived in two cars: Quin and my brother, Andy; their miniature Dachshund, Zoe; my mother and her husband, Roy; their Lhasa apso, Barney; and Rob and me. The dogs waited in the cars while the humans gathered in a white-carpeted living room where Quin's mother, Pip, welcomed us. I may have let on to Quin how much I wanted a dog, because Pip seemed to think that's why we were there.

Playing along, I expressed a preference for a female. Pip confirmed that female dogs were better for home protection. "There's a reason they call them bitches."

Why else would we seek a German shepherd from renowned police-dog trainers, if not for home protection? Rob and I both had small dogs growing up, but liked the idea of having a big one. German shepherds in particular appealed to me because of their intelligence. Perhaps I should have considered more carefully the breed's potential for ferocity, protective or not, and the sheer strength of their jaws.

Instead, I focused on the dogs' ability to scent out explosives and drugs, not the prey drive that led to the invention of such a thing as a bite sleeve.

We never got around to seeing the bite sleeve that day. Pip and Quin led us across the sunny back patio past several fenced-in yards. A majestic German shepherd watched us from behind the chain link. My brother pointed him out as the family dog, Portos, retired from the police force and father to both litters of puppies.

Pip invited us into a small concrete building divided by chain-link panels separating the litters. Quin, gregarious even with small animals, opened the gate to let a few puppies out. She plopped down on the floor and slapped the ground around her thighs to encourage the puppies to run around her in a circle. None of the rest of us shared her ease among a herd of puppies—Quin grew up here, after all—so we stood around and watched.

In the interest of customer service, Pip felt around the pile of puppies. "There's a penis, there's a penis. Oh! Here's a girl."

A glint in Rob's smiling brown eyes said *Might as well check them out,* so we waded into the herd, feeling soft fur brush our bare legs. We were dressed for late fall in Southern California, meaning cargo shorts for Rob and capri pants for me. My white T-shirt, given to me at a martial arts convention, identified me as the ALPHA FEMALE, which struck me as appropriate for the occasion.

The puppies nibbled on our fingers and ears, and wriggled out of our arms when we tried to hold them. Their sweet puppy smell was masked by a faintly unpleasant aroma; bits of poop clung to their backs as a side effect of their confinement and lack of bowel control.

The tan-faced puppy captivated me. I picked her up and held her in my arms like a toddler, upright, with her head near my shoulder. She licked my face and had no discernible crusty patches of feces on her fur.

"Let's get this one," I teased. "Her name's Isis!"

Months of puppy fantasies meant that I already had a name picked out. Isis was how Rob's last name, Eis, sounded in the plural. She also was a winged Egyptian goddess representing motherhood, protection, and fertility.

"Okay," Rob said, as if telling a car dealer that yes, he has decided that this model meets his needs.

"Really?" I was shocked. I'd tried to get him to go with me to adoption events at our local pet store, and he'd refused to go with me. Now he was willing to impulse-buy a puppy in California? Maybe he was just going along because he could see how much I wanted a puppy, but I didn't care.

We were getting a dog!

Rob aimed his video camera to capture me holding our new baby, my oversized sunglasses holding back my hair as I nuzzled her soft tan face. Her legs were light tan too, although the rest of her body was black.

"I love her and she loves me."

My mother and brother exchanged perplexed glances, silently asking each other if this was always part of the plan. While Pip went inside the house to get our puppy's papers, I sat with Isis on a brick wall on the back patio, Rob still recording.

We were joined by another adult German shepherd, sleek and golden, with black markings around her muzzle, a saddle pattern on her back, and what looked like the femur bone of a large animal in her mouth. Her eyes were the same light gold as her fur. The dog, introduced to us as Duxa, our puppy's biological mother, dropped the bone momentarily to lick Isis from head to toe, plastering the black fur against her head.

"You can't have her," I told Duxa. "She's my baby now."

In a maternal instinct I didn't understand, Duxa wrapped her massive jaw around Isis's head.

"We're giving her back if Duxa eats her," I said.

Let out of his yard, Portos approached calmly and gave his prodigal daughter a final sniff. His face was dark and he was much larger than I expected of a German shepherd. A nervousness tickled the back of my brain. Somehow I had persuaded Rob into getting this dog, and we knew nothing about German shepherds.

Should we tell someone we had no idea what we were doing?

Pip invited us back inside, where her husband, Dave, gave Isis her second round of vaccinations against parvovirus and distemper. The smaller dogs could come in from the cars, but Portos and Duxa had to stay out back, Pip insisted. "I just cleaned up so much black fur."

Barney, my mother's dog, was old, blind, and indifferent to other canines. He ambled around the room, his fluffy white coat stirring up something in Isis's DNA. She bounced over to him, startling the poor old dog.

"She's seen her first sheep," said Dave, smirking behind his white mustache.

We all laughed; Barney did resemble a very small sheep.

"I hardly think of German shepherds herding sheep," I said, watching Isis continue to patrol the living room.

"Why would you? It's only in the breed name," my brother said.

"I know it's what they were originally bred for," I defended myself. "But in movies, you always see border collies herding sheep. German shepherds are cast more often in search-and-rescue roles."

"Rin Tin Tin," Mom offered.

While we contemplated what our puppy's future might be in showbiz, Pip bagged up some kibble so we wouldn't have to buy food before returning to Washington.

Officially, Quin's parents were charging a thousand dollars each for Portos's puppies, but I qualified for the family discount. I wrote them a check for six hundred dollars, and Rob and I were the proud owners of a new puppy.

Roy drove us back to my childhood home in North Hollywood, with Barney on Mom's lap up front to make room for Isis in back with me and Rob. Barney had been something of an impulse purchase himself. During my freshman year of college, Mom bought him from a guy selling puppies out of the trunk of his car in a 7-Eleven parking lot. Barney was small enough to fit in a coat pocket, white with brown around his eyes and a black nose. Mom thought he looked like the Pokey Little Puppy from a children's storybook. He had fleas and worms and parvovirus, but after hundreds of dollars of veterinary care, he thrived and had lived a rich thirteen years.

Because Barney was a small dog, Mom never had to do any formal training with him. It didn't matter to anyone if he could sit or lie down on cue, because he came when you called him, and knew his name and the word "outside." He was too small to climb on the furniture without assistance and never strayed past the boundaries of the front lawn. As he got older, he developed back pain and startled easily.

He was mostly blind, so if you tried to pick him up while he was sleeping, he'd growl and snap at your hand. He'd broken the skin a few times, but nobody held it against him. He was otherwise gentle and everyone loved him. As far as my family was concerned, he was the perfect dog.

If Rob and I hadn't gotten Isis, I would have spent the drive home from Quin's parents' with Barney on my lap. "Hey, Mom," I called to her in the passenger seat. "Can I get a puppy?"

"Oh sure, now you ask me." I thought she'd laugh, but she didn't, and actually seemed irritated that we'd gotten the dog. Probably that was my fault. I just assumed she'd be thrilled for us. I realized too late that the considerate thing would have been to ask if she'd mind hosting an un-house-trained puppy.

I kept my tone light. "You don't mind having another dog around, do you, Barney?"

"Barney doesn't like other dogs," Mom snapped. From my vantage point in the backseat, I could see only the side of her fair-skinned face framed by short gray curls, but I pictured her lips pressed tightly together.

"Barney doesn't know he's a dog," my stepfather said jovially. It was one of his regular riffs: Barney never interacts with any other dogs, therefore he doesn't know he is one.

"Well, I'll do my best to keep Isis out of Barney's way then." I petted Isis's head as she slept between me and Rob.

Before I started bringing Rob home with me to Los Angeles, Mom had my full attention. During my visits now, time I spent entertaining Rob detracted from time I used to spend with her. On this trip, Rob would be flying back to Bellingham a few days before me, because he wasn't able to get Thanksgiving off from his job. No doubt Mom had been looking forward to mother-daughter time later in the week.

Except now I had this puppy.

I felt torn between Mom's disappointment and Rob's enthusiasm. Why couldn't she just share in our excitement?

Like my mother was to me, Rob's mother, Alice, had been his best friend until I came along almost three years earlier. He called Alice from the car. "Guess what we just got? A puppy!"

Through the cell phone, I heard her say, "You did not!" But her words floated atop a smile.

Rob responded with a laugh that was practically a cackle. He beamed behind his broad grin, which sported an overgrown soul patch of dark beard stretching from his lower lip to his chin. His short dark brown hair stuck straight up in a style I called the Bart Simpson. As laid back as Rob was, I tended to be wound a little tight, which made him my ideal match. Yin and yang. His calm energy was so contagious that we rarely fought. No matter what got under my skin, especially if it was something Rob himself did, he had a way of shrugging it off with such good humor that I never mustered up any real anger in his direction.

While he talked to his mother in the car, my nervousness festered into a panic. Even if my mother wasn't super-pumped about the new addition, I knew I could take care of Isis the rest of Thanksgiving break. But what the hell were we going to do with her once we got back home? Rob and I both worked full-time. Where were we going to put her? For that matter, how were we going to get her from California to Washington? My rational mind reminded me to take things one step at a time. No matter how overwhelming the task, experience had taught me that I could accomplish anything if I broke it into smaller parts.

After we got back to Mom's house, step one was to call the airline to find out the requirements for traveling with a puppy. While on hold, I came up with Plan B to rent a car and drive the twenty hours north to Bellingham, but that didn't wind up being necessary. I made arrangements to pay seventy-five dollars to check Isis in the heated cargo hold on my return flight Friday.

That problem solved, I joined Rob and Isis on the front lawn where Isis danced in the fallen yellow leaves under Southern California's autumn sunshine. From behind, because of her size, black head, and pointy ears, our seven-week-old puppy looked like a cat as she climbed into Rob's lap.

"She seems to know she's ours," I said.

Rob's face lit up when he held her. "I'm your poppa!"

In the span of a few hours, Rob went from *We're not ready to get a dog* to *This dog is my daughter,* and I felt a warmth in my heart, realizing that I hadn't persuaded him to do anything. The reason he refused to look at dogs before was that he knew he wouldn't be able to resist bringing one home. He'd fallen in love with Isis as easily as I had.

Isis needed a bath, Rob insisted. We drove Isis to the pet store to buy puppy shampoo, an ID tag, and a book on what to do with a brand-new puppy. We hadn't yet read anything telling us not to take a puppy anyplace where she could get sick before her vaccinations were complete, so we proudly showed her off by pushing her around in the shopping cart. Everyone in the store fed our parental pride by oohing and aahing at her fuzzy black-and-tan cuteness.

I set her on the floor near a toy aisle, where she pounced on a plush pink-and-purple soccer ball.

"Good job, Isis. You just picked out your first toy."

We also bought a plastic airline crate and a gerbil-style water bottle so she'd have access to water on the flight. Back at Mom's, we put Isis in the kitchen sink and ran warm water over her. Rob was right. Brown water pooled in the bottom of the sink. We sudsed her up and rinsed until the water ran clear. The water plastered her fur along the side of her face and top of her head.

Isis responded by speaking to us for the first time. Her voice came out as a whimper with the decibels cranked up.

"Aaaahh-roooooo! Aaaaah-roooo!" *Help! I don't like this. Please stop.*

Feeling enormously guilty over subjecting her to this torture, I scooped her out of the sink and wrapped her in a beach towel. Rob wiped up the water we splashed all over the blue-and-white tiles of Mom's kitchen floor, and I sat down with my swaddled baby on an overstuffed couch in the living room, comforting her as water seeped from her fur into the towel.

That night we slept in my brother's old room, which had a bigger bed than mine and hardwood floors instead of carpet in case Isis had an accident. We tried putting her in the plastic crate, but it was too small. Had she grown since we brought her home? I removed the crate's beige top with the idea of putting towels in the bottom half and using it as a bed. Each of the puppies of my childhood slept in a plastic laundry basket beside my bed, whimpering through the night. Isis was no different. She woke me every hour or so, and I rushed her outside to see if she had to go potty while Rob slept undisturbed.

★★★

Although Rob had surprised me with his enthusiasm about getting a puppy, he had no intention of letting this life-changing event interfere with our plans for the last two days of his trip.

We would still go to Universal Studios, but first we took Isis to the vet to get a health certificate so she could fly. After she was pronounced healthy and we exchanged the too-small crate for the next size up, we brought her back to Mom's and strategized what to do with her while we were at the theme park and Mom was at work. We had no luck trying to get her into the new crate of her own free will, so we shoved her inside.

She responded with the same horrified wail she cried during her bath.

"She'll probably calm down after a few minutes," I said, latching the metal door. Isis thrashed so violently that the plastic crate rocked back and forth.

"We can't leave her like that," Rob said. "Let's just close her in the kitchen."

When I called midday from Universal Studios, my cheerful stepfather told me Isis had escaped through the swinging kitchen doors by the time he got home from work. Otherwise, everything was fine. Roy, a dog person, was perfectly happy to watch Isis until we got home.

Before we became parents, our plan for the evening had been to go out to dinner with my friend Kelda and see her recently redecorated kitchen. I thought probably she'd come over to see our new puppy instead, but no, she still wanted me to see her place. After a few margatinis at dinner, I accidentally left my cell phone in the car at Kelda's.

All night, I had the nagging feeling we should get home to our baby, but reassured myself she was just fine at home with my parents. Back in the car, however, I discovered several missed calls, along with one stern voicemail message from Mom: "You need to come take care of your dog."

Everything seemed perfectly under control when Rob and I walked back through the front door. Mom was watching television with Isis lying underneath the coffee table in front of her.

Mom let out an exasperated sigh as soon as she saw us. Rob quickly said goodnight and headed for my bedroom.

"What happened?" I asked, sitting beside her on the overstuffed blue couch and tucking my feet under me.

"I couldn't leave the room without Isis following me. She kept trying to herd Barney."

"She tried to hurt him?"

"No, *herd*. She tried to herd him."

I marveled at the little creature sleeping on the terra cotta tiles, sheltered by the wooden coffee table. "I would have liked to see that, her genetic heritage at work," I said. "Do you think shepherding is so ingrained in her DNA that she instinctively knew how to herd the first fluffy white animal she met? Even though her particular line was bred for police work, not shepherding?"

"That does seem to be the case," Mom said.

The late-night conversation eased the tension between me and Mom. I should have known better than to impose on her. Better to insist that Kelda come to us, but I hadn't wanted to disappoint my friend. Instead I inconvenienced my mother, who was trying to be helpful, despite her lukewarm attitude the day before. Worse, I felt guilty for putting old Barney through the stress, and vowed to make it up to both of them.

After Rob returned to Bellingham, I kept Isis with me at all times. Unfortunately, Barney wound up neglected as a result. The day Isis and I flew home, I was so preoccupied that I forgot to say goodbye to him.

Although Isis had not gotten used to the crate by then, the airport noises in the cargo area were so loud her whining was barely audible. I fretted and fidgeted in my seat with my copy of *German Shepherds for Dummies* until a stewardess brought me a card with Isis's name that said, HI, JUST WANTED YOU TO KNOW THAT I MADE IT SAFELY ON BOARD. The card had its intended effect and I relaxed just a little. Even so, the two-hour flight felt longer than usual.

I pictured my puppy howling all by herself in the dark cargo hold. She must have been so scared, not knowing that I was coming back for her.

Rob had to work late that night, so his parents picked me up at Sea-Tac Airport. Alice found me in the baggage claim area where they unload special cargo. About five feet tall with closely cropped silver hair, Alice's gusto could fill a room. She smiled broadly, as eager to meet Isis as any grandmother waiting in a hospital maternity ward. For what felt like an interminable number of minutes, we waited for my puppy to be delivered. Finally we heard her wails from behind the metal door. Alice wanted to get a look inside the crate right away, but I was worried about my baby's bladder. She hadn't peed at the Burbank airport before I put her in the crate, so she probably really had to go. I hustled her to the airport curb, set the crate down, and let her out.

"Ohhh," Alice murmured as I snapped on a leash and urged Isis to pee on the sidewalk. "She's much littler than I thought she would be."

I felt around the towels in the crate, which all seemed to be dry. "I guess she can hold it longer than I gave her credit for."

"Hi, Isis." Alice crouched. "I'm Grandma."

Isis sat on the sidewalk and used her hind leg to scratch at the blue collar I'd stolen from Barney. Then she tilted her head, looking from Alice to me.

Rob's dad, Jerry, pulled the van up to the curb and we climbed in. He drove us to a patch of grass where Isis finally relieved herself. On the two-hour drive home, Isis lay with the back half of her body inside the crate and her head in my lap. I tapped the metal ball inside the water bottle and let her lick the droplets.

"Sweet little girl. You weren't too traumatized by your first airplane ride, were you?"

Rob waited eagerly for us at home, having prepared for Isis's arrival by setting up baby gates and buying a squeaky monkey toy, two sets of food and water dishes, poop scoopers, and a dog bed. The dog bed probably was designed for an adult beagle, about the right size for Isis at eight weeks.

I hoped Rob knew she was going to get a lot bigger, fast.

I set Isis down in the front hall and watched her explore. Our single-level house had two long rooms we used as living areas: one was for TV watching, the other was a library lined with mahogany bookcases. Two of the home's four bedrooms were off the library; Rob stored and watched martial arts videos in one, and the other was the guest bedroom I used as my home office. The front hall led to our bedroom and Rob's computer room.

Isis padded on her little tan feet from the TV room to the kitchen, where Rob opened the sliding glass door to the patio and backyard, saying, "Isis! This is your home."

We woke the next day delighted to see a layer of white coating our backyard. Our first snow in the new house. Isis's initial steps in the snow were tentative. *Where did the grass go?* With just a few more steps, she decided she liked it and pounced in the snow, mouthing and play-bowing to it.

Rob dressed Isis in the coat he'd bought her during his shopping spree: light brown faux suede with a shearling lining. I looked at the two of them and wondered whether Rob realized that he had picked out a miniature dog version of his own coat. Like the dog bed he bought, I knew the coat wouldn't be big enough for long. I assured Rob the bed was wonderful, and she could sleep on that in our room for now, but we also needed a bigger bed to line the extra-large crate we set up in the kitchen.

At least that was something we didn't have to buy; I already happened to own a black metal dog crate. It had been home to the first beloved pet of my adult life: a five-foot-long iguana named Emerald, who died shortly after I moved in with Rob.

Despite all the money Rob spent before Isis came home, we kept thinking of more things we needed. I thought we could temporarily use Barney's old collar until Isis got bigger, but Rob didn't like the way it had to be threaded through a buckle and fastened. He wanted one we could release with the click of one hand, so we made another family trip to the pet store to buy a pink collar and matching sparkly pink leash.

★★★

The snow stayed on the ground all weekend, and the temperature dropped so the roads were icy by Monday morning. The news people kept saying, "If you don't have to leave the house, don't."

Had I still worked as a newspaper reporter, I would have been expected not only to leave the house, but also to experience the inconvenience and hazards of the bad weather so I could write about them. Lucky for me, I didn't work for a newspaper anymore. About a month earlier, I'd started a public relations job out of a satellite office of an environmental organization based in the state capital, Olympia. Working from home was an option in the best of weather, but I was so new at my job that I didn't have any actual work to do at home.

That morning, I sat at the kitchen table in my pajamas and watched the weather reports in a loop on Northwest Cable News. Isis still cried every time I left the room without her, so I never even took a shower. She poked around my feet, then napped on the plush tan bed in her crate while I repeatedly clicked CHECK MAIL on my laptop.

When the sun came out, I slipped my boots and parka over my pajamas and snapped a leash on Isis. She waded beside me through snow as high as her fuzzy black belly. Nosing the terrain, she dusted her muskrat face with white flakes, her oversized pointed ears as long as her muzzle.

We walked around the side of the house to the front yard where Isis sat down in the snow and assessed her surroundings. The neighbors, college kids who rented the house next door, had built an igloo. A blue sky framed our plowed street, nearly devoid of cars, and Rob's tire tracks had carved trails in the layer of snow covering our long driveway shaded by a canopy of cedar branches. A creek ran along the other side of our house, where icicles formed underneath blackberry brambles. I walked Isis up the stone steps to our front porch, past our little garden with a heavenly bamboo plant bent in half from the weight of the snow.

"This is a magical place where we live," I told Isis.

The second day, I put Isis in her crate while I showered. She cried her head off for the first several minutes, but had quieted down by the time I returned. Was I really supposed to leave her alone for eight hours a day while I went to work? How did people with jobs do this? I called Rob at work and asked him to pick up teriyaki for me on his way home. Then I felt like a total jerk. Unlike me, Rob was considered essential personnel at his job. He had driven to the county juvenile detention facility in a car without four-wheel drive, while my SUV sat in the driveway under a paltry four inches of snow, and I couldn't even be bothered to pick up food down the street. I felt worse when I realized the folks at the teriyaki restaurant had made it to work, while I had not.

By day three, I was restless and suspected myself of using the bad weather as an excuse to stay home and play with my puppy. The news kept showing abandoned cars by the sides of roads, warning of trees falling on the freeway, but I wasn't getting any work done at home. What was I supposed to put on my timesheet? By mid-morning, I figured the roads must have thawed some, so I ventured to the office, a half-hour drive from our house, with Isis in the passenger seat of my red Honda CRV. I crept along my icy street, testing the four-wheel drive and anti-lock brakes. Isis howled her favorite song, the one she sang whenever we tried to crate her.

What's happening? Where are you taking me?

"Silly, you've been in this car before. You're fine."

She calmed down once we hit a steady speed on the freeway. I wasn't sure if anyone else would be in the office, but when I pulled into the strip mall across the street from the Skagit River, I saw my co-workers Al and Julee smoking on the sidewalk outside the front door of our office. While we all worked for the same organization, each of us worked for a different department. Without consulting either of them, I considered our office to be the kind of workplace where it was appropriate to bring one's dog. Very casual, sparsely populated, and with parking spots directly by the front door.

I pulled into the space carved into the snow by a previous car and brought Isis out on a leash. "I got a puppy!" Al and Julee were both appropriately smiley and friendly, but

17

paranoia weighed on me. I didn't want them to feel in the slightest inconvenienced by Isis's presence.

Pulling open the glass front door, I led Isis inside. My office was closest to the entrance and had a window with a view of the parking lot. I set Isis up with toys and a dish of water, shut my office door, and turned on my computer to check my e-mail. Nothing new since I'd checked from home. Still, I felt better having come into the office. More productive. I looked at the clock on my computer. Eleven thirty. Another snowstorm was supposed to hit that afternoon, so I better leave around two. Seemed a perfectly reasonable amount of time to spend at the office. On a regular day, I sent e-mails, monitored online news sites, checked in with biologists, and wrote stories about salmon habitat restoration. Ideally, I'd go out in the field a couple of times a week, taking pictures of restoration work. But the snowstorm had put the whole region on hold, and I couldn't think of anything to do.

For the most part, I loved the freedom and flexibility of my new job. My boss left me to my own devices, satisfied that my work got done. No one hovered over my shoulder supervising me. The tradeoff was that I suffered from loneliness and boredom, not having much in common with Al, a middle-aged biologist, or Julee, the office manager.

Isis whimpered at my feet. Worried that her cries would disturb Julee through the walls, I lifted her up and put her on my lap, letting her chew on the zipper of my hooded sweatshirt as I typed. Advice from a dog book rang in my ears: *You get what you pet and raise what you praise.* Nice job, Kari. Way to reinforce her behavior. Now she knows all she has to do is whine and you'll pay attention to her.

After about twenty minutes, I took Isis outside. We crossed the slick parking lot to a stretch of lawn buried under hardened snow. I shivered in my parka as Isis sniffed around me in circles. Circling and sniffing was supposed to be a sign that a dog is about to go to the bathroom, but Isis circled and sniffed quite frequently without actually eliminating.

Julee poked her head out the office door and called out that my boss was on the phone. Uh-oh. Would he mind that I'd brought my dog to work? Probably not, but I didn't want him to know if he didn't have to. I came back inside and opened up a bag of peanut butter treats called Better than Ears before picking up my headset to take his call.

"Hey, just checking in," he said.

I handed Isis a piece of the rubbery, pig-ear-shaped confection. "Hi," I said. "I made it to the office."

"Anything going on?"

"Nothing much, it's pretty quiet around here."

Isis swallowed and looked at me cheerfully. *More please?*

I tore off another piece and put it in her mouth. "Hey, is it okay if I leave early? It's supposed to snow again up here."

"Sure."

That was easy. I hung up the phone and drummed my fingers on my faux wood desktop, realizing how nervous I'd been during the call. Since I was still so new at my job, I really didn't want to get in trouble for bringing my dog to work.

Isis twitched her eyebrows expectantly toward the bag of Better than Ears.

"I think you've had enough for now." I stashed the bag behind my phone to get it out of her line of vision. "You did very well, baby girl. I'm proud of you. But you're going to have to stay home by yourself sooner or later."

The next day, I tossed a couple of treats on the plush bed in the crate, let Isis follow the trail, and closed the door behind her. She didn't mind going in, but didn't like to be left there alone. I could still hear her howling from my car before I started the engine, and was plagued with guilt for putting my baby in a cage. I could only bear to leave her because I knew Alice and Jerry would come by to visit her.

Alice immediately bonded with Isis, treating her like the four-legged granddaughter she was. Jerry, who enjoyed affecting a "grumpy old man" persona, was slower to commit. Alice told me that the day Isis came home with me, Jerry worried how big she was going to get, because a bigger dog would be harder to manage. Evidently, he intuited how much pet care would fall to him and Alice.

But deep down, Jerry was a softie, and he fell for her, too.

Rob and I, of course, were hopelessly smitten. We played with her every second we weren't at work. We discovered the discarded soccer balls of former residents in the blackberry and juniper bushes that bordered our sloping backyard. Isis pierced the skin of the balls with her pin-like puppy teeth, deflating them just enough that she could comfortably carry one in her mouth while running around the yard.

Indoors, she held one neon-colored tennis ball in her mouth, concentrating very hard on pushing a second ball around the wood-laminate floor with her tan paws. We watched her for hours, finding her far more entertaining than anything on TV. Capable of occupying herself this way for long stretches, Isis's face lit up when Rob joined her. He threw the tennis ball down, introducing her to the wonderful world of things that bounce. She jumped in the air a few seconds too late, not quite agile enough to catch the airborne ball, but thrilled with the new game.

Isis trotted devotedly after Rob, her tongue hanging out happily, as he retrieved another toy that resembled a baby's rattle, or barbell, made of two squeaky tennis balls connected by a straight piece of the same material. He squeaked and bounced the toy for Isis and she scrambled to catch it. She latched onto the barbell while Rob tugged. When she had a tight hold on one end, Rob put the other side in his own mouth so Isis would feel like she was playing with another dog. After about five seconds, Rob made a face and released the toy, not enjoying the feel of tennis ball between his teeth.

He was so childlike with her, sometimes I wondered whether we were parenting the puppy together, or if I was now a single mother taking care of two children. Between rounds, Rob lay beside Isis on the carpet of his computer room. She stretched a front leg toward him, and he kissed her paw.

Whatever the dynamic, I loved my little family.

Puppies were known to burn off bursts of energy by racing wildly, an act termed "the zoomies." Isis got the zoomies at least daily, sometimes after I thought we'd settled down for the night. I sat under the covers reading in our queen-sized bed while Isis ran circles around and underneath me on the carpet. She finally came to a rest dead center under the bed where I could hear her wrestling with a toy.

"Soon you won't be small enough to fit under there, Baby Boo."

Of all the nicknames we gave Isis in those early weeks, Baby Boo was a favorite. Rob coined another charming yet short-lived moniker when he blew raspberries on her smooth stomach, calling her his Pink Belly Girl. Once when she poked her pointy nose in Rob's dinner, he said, "Get your beak out of there."

I laughed. Her muzzle did look like a beak. And then one day when she sat looking happily at us with her mouth open, I asked, "Whatcha doing over there, Smiley Bird?"

That one stuck.

Chapter 2: Basic Training

Rob and I decided to exchange only small gifts that Christmas, because we'd spent so much money on toys and other accoutrements for the puppy. In Isis, we had the best gift of all. She made us a family, and neither of us could remember, or wanted to remember, the time before she came into our lives.

Rob was the first single man I'd known who decorated his own home for the holidays. Alice was a big-time holiday decorator, and apparently Christmas spirit is genetic. For the Eis family, Christmas was more than an exchange of gifts and a festive dinner. It was a state of mind. As soon as the weather turned cold and the sun set before five p.m., Rob started looking forward to seeing lights on trees. He loved driving past elaborately decorated homes and strolling past downtown businesses festooned with white twinkle lights. When his mom pulled boxes of decorations down from the attic, she said it was like opening presents, a sentiment Rob shared. He loved being reunited with a favorite reindeer or Santa Claus he hadn't seen in a year.

We drove nine-week-old Isis up snowy Mount Baker Highway to a Christmas tree lot to browse the lanes of evergreens and pose our little Muppet Baby in front of our chosen Nordmann fir. As a child, I never realized there were different species of Christmas trees, let alone farms where you could cut down your own tree. U-Cut lots had become a key ingredient in Rob's and my holiday tradition, ever since I learned he'd been cutting down Christmas trees his whole life. He singlehandedly sawed through the trunk and heaved the tree over one shoulder as he carried it to the bed of his dad's pickup truck, with Isis and me walking beside him.

At home, Rob cleared the piles of unopened bills from a table in the front room, where he merrily arranged Christmas CDs, a board game based on the movie *A Christmas Story*, a battery-operated singing reindeer, and an animatronic caroling Mickey and Minnie Mouse. Charming as the decorations were, I felt like Rob was just adding more clutter to a house already crowded with his martial arts memorabilia.

"Do we really need to put that board game on display? Can't we just bring it out when we're going to play it?" I left unspoken the unlikelihood that we ever would play the game.

Rob shook his head. He knew when to pick his battles. "I like looking at it."

My irritation evaporated. Playing the game was irrelevant. Just seeing the decorations made Rob happy. That was enough for me.

He blew up a giant inflatable snowman in our front garden, and strung lights across the Japanese maple and heavenly bamboo. Inside, I worried that Isis would pull ornaments off the tree or chew the strands of lights, but she was an incredibly well-behaved puppy. She didn't mess with any of our decorations. We had only one near miss, which was Rob's fault for accidentally tossing a tennis ball right onto the tree skirt. Isis trotted after it and wrapped herself up in the tree lights.

"Wait. Hold on, baby." He disentangled her as Isis waited patiently.

Although Rob and I celebrated all season long, we didn't have traditions locked into Christmas Day itself. I had a standing engagement to spend a few days with my mother in Los Angeles, and Rob couldn't always get the time off from work. That year, he stayed home with Isis. I missed them both, of course, so I redirected all my affection onto Barney.

The day before Christmas, Mom dropped me off with Barney at the vet for him to have his ears cleaned. In the waiting room, he sprawled across my lap like a fluffy white throw pillow. Several people walked by, making sympathetic sounds and saying, "I hope your dog feels better." I smiled and said thank you, but wondered what they were talking about. Barney recently had a cancerous part of his jaw removed, and was down from fourteen pounds to about eleven, but he felt fine. The ear cleaning was routine.

After the vet technician finished and brought Barney back out to me, I decided to bask a little longer under the warm blue sky by walking home instead of calling Mom to come get us. Since Barney refused to walk on a leash, I carried him the four blocks home past the green lawns and single-family homes of my mother's neighborhood.

The next day, while snuggling him, I noticed a foul odor. "Mom, Barney's breath smells really bad. I'm surprised the vet didn't say anything."

"Well, they muzzle him."

"Oh yeah, because of that habit he has of snarling and biting people who try to pick him up."

"The smell could be necrotic tissue from the cancer." Mom's mouth twisted. "I'll have Roy take him to the vet after the holiday."

Sweet Barney. At thirteen years old with cancer, I knew he might not be around much longer. Despite his stinkbreath, I gave him some extra kisses on his soft white head and little black nose, preparing myself for the worst-case scenario, in case I didn't see him again.

After Christmas, I drove myself home from the airport and peered through the front window where Rob watched TV with Isis lying on a pillow at his feet. She heard me and stood, stretching her long, fawn-like legs. Bursting through the front door to reunite with my little family, I exclaimed, "Isis! You got taller while I was gone!"

★★★

In mid-January, Mom called with a report from Barney's vet. His cancer was back and he wasn't expected to live more than a few weeks. I held my phone to my ear as I paced the backyard with Isis, tearing up as I remembered what a loyal friend Barney had been. Even though I already was in college when

Mom got him, he slept on my bed whenever I came home. Mom said he always snuffled around my room looking for me after I left.

Not long after we got the bad news from the vet, Barney started bleeding from the mouth and wasn't living the quality of life we wanted for him. My brother, Andy, made a slide-show of Barney's last day, with photos of our fluffy white dog eating cooked chicken and walking to the edge of the driveway and back. Andy used Cyndi Lauper songs for the soundtrack, because once, years earlier, he watched the singer perform on a show while house-sitting for Mom. When Cyndi sang, Barney perked up and looked directly at the screen, which he'd never done before or since.

We decided this meant that Cyndi Lauper was Barney's favorite artist.

Mom took Barney into the back room at the vet's office by herself. My stepdad couldn't stand to watch him die. Mom stood beside her dog as the vet euthanized him. In true form, Barney snarled and barked at the needle before slipping away.

"He did not go gentle into that good night," Mom reported.

Although I said a heartfelt goodbye at Christmastime, Barney's death hit me hard. I watched my brother's video at work and bawled at my desk. I stared at a photo of myself sitting in an overstuffed chair at Mom's house, with Barney at my feet and my iguana Emerald looking over my shoulder. My grief for Barney echoed my loss of Emerald, who died unexpectedly less than a year earlier. Fewer people related to my grief over losing a pet iguana, because he wasn't soft and cuddly, but he had been my companion for seven years. His death was my first loss of a pet who had been entrenched in my everyday life.

Looking at the picture of Emerald and Barney, I grieved not because Barney died—he was thirteen years old with cancer; we all saw it coming—but because things would never again be like they were in that picture. I wanted those days back, reading in my pajamas in the comfy chair, with Southern California sun streaming over my shoulder, and my two little buddies napping beside me. But now, Emerald was gone. Barney was gone. Even the house would soon be gone; my mother sold it a few months later.

I took comfort in knowing that Isis's whole life was ahead of us, and I had someone to share the love. I'd fully expected most of the work of raising Isis to fall to me, and while that turned out to be true, Rob's complete adoration of our new baby was an endless source of delight. We were in agreement that she was the smartest and most beautiful puppy in the whole world. So far, her only annoying quality was her incessant nipping. Totally normal, the dog books said, especially among teething German shepherds. The books offered helpful advice like soaking a rope toy in chicken broth and sticking it in the freezer. Isis's favorite chew toys, however, were Rob's feet. I could hear him yell in pain from across the house.

Joining them in the TV room where Rob sat on the floor with Isis, I offered another tip from the dog books. "Try redirecting her to one of her toys."

In Rob's opinion, the only training Isis needed was in dog martial arts. He deflected her nips with a couple of air kicks near her face. She pounced on the moving target like a cat on a ball of yarn.

He squealed. "Her teeth are like needles!" Sure, he enjoyed the game now, but how would he like it when those puppy teeth were replaced by big-dog teeth? As secure as I was in my own relationship with Rob, I had a secret fear that

Isis might do something really bad and he'd fall out of love with her.

Fortunately, she was done with her vaccinations and ready for obedience school. I'd started researching schools as soon as we got her, and liked the sound of a place called Firgrove, because it featured German shepherds on its website. The trainers there employed the choke-chain method. When I was a little girl, my brother and I were horrified by the idea of a collar meant to choke a dog. We had enrolled our first dog, a black-and-white Springer spaniel named Fritzi, in an obedience class where they showed us how to use a chain collar. I remember attending exactly one class and being astonished that we didn't walk away with a fully trained dog. I didn't get that we, the owners, were the ones who were supposed to do the training. I must have been too young at the time to understand the merits of a chain collar, but I was mature enough to handle it now.

I understood that dogs' necks were strong and that choke chains were widely accepted.

Firgrove's owner was Walter, a white-ponytailed, bearded, and bespectacled codger who entertained people before class with rope magic tricks. He wore a plaid shirt with a pocketed utilitarian vest, and had a German shepherd named Chief who helped demonstrate obedience commands. Walter held the class in a barn-type outbuilding on his residential property. A gravel driveway and parking area separated his house from the class building and fenced dog kennel.

For the first Saturday morning class, we left the dogs in our cars while Walter opened with a long explanation of his training philosophy. He didn't believe in using treats to lure dogs into obedience. If you used treats to get a dog to behave, he said, the dog wouldn't behave when you didn't have a treat in hand. Rob and I, and six other dog parents, shivered inside the concrete and steel building warmed only by space heaters. A small area in the front of the room served as the stage where we'd practice our new skills. Pictures of proud owners with dogs of all sizes and breeds decorated the bulletin board. I expected a photo of me, Rob, and Isis to grace that board in no time. Maybe we could even get into competitive obedience. Walter gave us a three-ring binder with lesson plans for the eight-week course, and we bought an extra-durable green leash sewn by Walter's red-haired wife, Shelley.

Classes began with the humans practicing the commands on each other. I held the person-end of the leash while Rob held the snap, walking beside me as if he were the dog. When he pulled ahead, I was instructed to "zing pop" the leash, pulling it so that the chain collar (if Rob were wearing one) constricted quickly, then released. Once the humans had the choreography down, the puppies had their turns. Among our classmates were another shepherd named Sirius, a Great Dane named Lexis, and a golden retriever named Tucker who was so little and fluffy he looked like a stuffed animal. Tucker endeared himself to us all on the first day when he squatted on the concrete floor of the classroom and peed.

During basic puppy training, Walter had the dogs wait in the car and take turns practicing each new skill. Multiple puppies would never be able to concentrate if they were all practicing in the same room at the same time, he said. When it was our turn, Rob waited inside while I went out to the car. We couldn't leave the training collar on Isis unattended, lest she choke, so my first task was to slip the chain over her pointy little face. At the sight of me, she wriggled around, desperate to get out of the car. I struggled to hold her silky black body still enough to get the collar on properly.

If the chain didn't circle her neck in just the right way, my zing pops would not register.

Walter advised us to practice heeling on our way to the classroom from the car, but Isis pulled ahead, thrilled to explore the exciting new surface of gravel and dirt. In the classroom, we didn't have any time to adjust or calm her down. Isis couldn't focus at all, dragging me over to Rob and jumping up on him, placing her front paws on his lap. *Here I am, Daddy! What are we doing here? Hey, I smell something.* Then she darted out to the end of her leash to sniff all the interesting pant legs carrying the odors of various other unknown dogs.

"Isis! Come on, baby, let's do this," I chirped, trying to appear the consummate dog trainer, unfazed by my puppy's flightiness. I urged her to join me in the practice area in front of the class. Isis knew how to sit; we'd taught her (using treats) long before we started Firgrove. But I couldn't even get her to do that during the few minutes allotted to us. My dreams of winning first place at an obedience show circled the drain.

Not that the other dogs were such exceptional students, either. Certainly they weren't smarter than Isis. For some reason, she was too excitable to focus in class. Unwilling to give up on my goals of scholastic achievement, I was determined to follow Walter's lesson plans and homework to the letter. We were supposed to work with Isis at least twice a day for a few minutes at a time. Before each training session, Walter instructed, we needed to put Isis in her crate for a fifteen-minute "time out" to get her ready to learn. After the brief session, she went back in the crate for another fifteen minutes to process what she'd learned.

Sounded easy enough, but we got stuck on step one of the assignment. Instead of lying quietly, Isis whined and cried when I put her in the crate, completely defeating the purpose of having relaxing time to herself. Was I supposed to leave her in there until she was quiet for a full fifteen minutes? By the time I let her out, she was so worked up, all she wanted to do was race around the backyard and play, not work on our exercises.

Our homework was to practice leash control with a twenty-foot lead. Walter's well-rehearsed setup was, "Most people say, 'I can't control my dog on a six-foot leash, how am I supposed to control them on a twenty-foot leash?' " He then explained that twenty-foot leash control would lead to six-foot leash control. We were supposed to attach the long leash to the chain collar and let the dog run ahead of us. Before the dog got to the end of the leash, we should turn the other direction. The "correction" of the chain tightening around the dog's neck would teach her not to try to run twenty feet and one inch in the wrong direction. Therefore, she would learn to keep her attention on me so she would know where she was supposed to be.

I wasn't able to teach Isis this lesson because she never went more than twenty feet away.

When I tried walking her in the backyard, she got ahead of me. I whirled around and walked the other way. She came with me obediently enough before the leash went completely taut, so she didn't receive the correction of the jerked collar. Then she'd pull ahead and I'd change direction again. A two-minute training session was dizzying, exhausting, and left both of us confused. Discouraged, I shoved her into her crate for fifteen minutes to ponder the meaning of the jerking and twirling that had transpired.

"Aaaaaa-roooo. Aaaaaa-rooo." Isis's howler-monkey cries echoed through the house. I walked into Rob's den where he sat at the computer.

"I don't get it," I said to his back. "Does it count as a time out if she's crying the whole time? Am I supposed to start the countdown after she settles down? I can't let her out while she's crying, because that would only reward the crying. But what if she doesn't stop crying?"

"Just let her out," Rob said. For a disciplined martial artist, Rob had a hard time being militant with our puppy. Already he rebelled against one of Walter's fundamentals, which were listed on a pumpkin-colored page in our lesson book:

1. There are no stupid questions.

2. Say the command one time.

3. Make sure you understand the lesson completely before executing.

4. Do not be a littermate. Your dog will not be inclined to take direction from a littermate. Be a Parent Figure. The love and respect between a parent and child is what we are striving for, not the rowdy disrespect shown by children to each other.

Even if he didn't consider himself a littermate, Rob definitely saw Isis as a jiu-jitsu partner. He let her out of her crate and sat on the floor in front of her. She crawled into his lap, licking and biting his ear. He lifted her up by her front paws and she twisted and chewed on his hand.

"If you don't want her to do that, what you have to do is hold her mouth closed …"

Isis let go of his hand and engaged him with a play bow. They were both still for a moment before Rob batted at her paw and she wrapped her tiny teeth around his hand again. "See, Rob, what you're doing there is encouraging her … Wait, are you enjoying this?"

Rob smiled and screamed in pain at the same time. "I can't help it. She just gets me so excited!"

Silly me, I thought it was the other way around. But their joyous, carefree play was infectious, filling me with love for the family we'd created. Isis made Rob happy, which made me happy. If only he'd take the training more seriously. The books said that puppies were supposed to learn bite inhibition from their littermates, so if Rob insisted on playing with Isis like a littermate, the least he could do was teach her to mouth softly.

We tried a variety of techniques to curb her biting: ignoring it, getting up and leaving the room, yelping "Ouch!"—anything anyone suggested. Firgrove endorsed some aversive methods, including forcing your hand into the dog's mouth to "feed her that which she bites" until it became uncomfortable to her. Rob tried this one; I didn't have the heart. I did attempt a technique of folding a bit of her lip in her mouth while holding it closed, so she could see how much her nipping hurt. She cried when I aggravated a loose and bleeding baby tooth, and Rob accused me of being abusive.

Nothing seemed to make any difference, anyway, probably because we didn't do any one thing consistently.

"For a smart dog, she sure hasn't learned the consequences of biting." I watched Rob energetically rub Isis's belly, sticking his face in hers and waving his hands near her mouth. Rob was as poor a student, because he hadn't learned, or didn't care, that his behavior only led to more biting.

My shoulders grew tight as I debated whether to let the two of them have their fun, or to act as stern schoolmarm to keep Isis's studies on track. Wasn't Rob's version of play effectively training her to bite our hands and feet? Rob complained loudly when Isis attacked his feet unprovoked, which hurt my feelings worse than Isis's. All I wanted was to have a well-behaved dog, but Rob refused to follow my instructions about how to get her to stop chewing on him.

From our failures with the twenty-foot leash exercise, we moved onto the basic heel with a six-foot leash, which perplexed us even more. On a shorter leash, at least Isis pulled enough for the chain to tighten around her neck and deliver the correction, but she barely noticed. If I let her, she'd pull hard enough for the chain to cut off her airway until she gasped for breath, still trying to get to whatever was just out of reach. Again, we found ourselves bewildered and walking in circles. I asked Walter what he recommended for keeping her in line.

"Some dogs try to get us into play mode when we are trying to get them to go to work," he said. "It sounds like you are doing the right thing. Be careful not to get excited. That's exactly what she wants you to do." As if Isis were an elementary school student trying to keep a substitute teacher from getting through the day's lesson plan. As much as I trusted Walter's expertise, I seriously doubted my puppy was trying to pull one over on me.

One Saturday, Shelley watched as I "zing popped" Isis's choke chain, demonstrating her failure to respond. Shelley recommended a pinch collar, a medieval torture device with two rounded prongs sticking out of each chain link. When yanked, the pinch collar constricted so the prongs poked into the dog's neck. Shelley compared it to "power steering."

"I'll show you." Shelley fitted Isis with the collar, took hold of the leash, and strode away from me. When Isis ran ahead, Shelley gave a mighty jerk and Isis let out an anguished squeal. I felt a stabbing pain in my chest, but the horrible cry lasted only briefly. Isis changed direction and walked beside

Shelley quite cheerfully. "See? She forgives me." Shelley handed the leash back to me and Isis jumped up, putting her front paws against my legs.

"Off," Shelley and I said in unison.

Pinch collars weren't completely foreign to me. I'd noticed them hanging on the wall at Firgrove and had the same attitude that I assumed all conscientious dog parents had: I would *never* use that on my dog. But I'd already accepted the choke chain as an acceptable training tool; how much worse could the pinch collar be? Some dog websites argued that the pinch collar was more humane than a standard choke chain, even though it looked much scarier. I rationalized that Isis already weighed forty-five pounds and had a neck so strong that she felt nothing when I jerked the regular chain collar. We were getting nowhere in our training sessions because she had no idea what I was asking of her. Her education was suffering.

I thought Rob would reject the pinch collar outright, but he too accepted it as a necessary evil. If the dog trainers said we needed to use this thing, we figured we needed to use this thing. They were the experts.

For her everyday look, we upsized her little pink collar with a purple one, accessorized with a beaded necklace. We won the necklace from a humane society drawing I entered because we happened to have her spayed during National Spay and Neuter Month. Our prizes were a T-shirt (for me) and a necklace of plastic flower beads in bright shades of lime, tangerine, rose, and lavender. Four beads spelled out ISIS. I considered it Isis's signature piece of jewelry. At first glance, lots of people mistook it for a candy necklace.

★★★

On a frigid, almost raining February afternoon, Rob and I took Isis to a seaside park. Rob took the extra-sturdy green leash in his gloved hands to practice walking her on the path between the grassy park and the choppy gray waters of Bellingham Bay. He wore an army green jacket with frayed cuffs and I had the hood up on my black parka. I coached Rob on handling techniques because he had forgotten the confusing choreography from the first class. He'd tired of Firgrove already and stopped going with us, turning me into the nag that constantly parroted what I'd learned in school, trying to keep him on board. Despite Rob's imperfect handling, Isis walked beside him pretty well, her sleek back as high as his mid-shin. I trailed behind them along the rocky shore, taking pictures.

Rob asked Isis to sit and stay, and took a few steps away before walking back. She alerted to passing birds and squirrels, looking every which way while in the stay, but her butt remained rooted to the ground.

"Good girl, Isis," Rob cooed, returning to her. We were both proud of her for mastering sit and stay, although we were having trouble getting her to lie down on command. Following the instructions from our handbook, Rob knelt beside Isis on the boardwalk and wrapped his arms around her ribs, putting weight on her with his chest to show her that he would like her to lie down. Some dogs resist lying down, Walter had told us, so this is how we should teach her. Isis splayed her tan legs and squirmed, but eventually submitted, flattening her body. Rob released her and repeated the process. Isis's soulful brown eyes grew wide and she curled her pink tongue over her nose.

"Why does she keep sticking out her tongue? So weird," I said. "I don't get why she doesn't do better in class. Why isn't she catching on to this stuff faster?"

"Don't worry about it," Rob said. "She's fine. She's great at home and that's more important anyway."

He had a point. I was an educated woman with a great career. No one cared if my dog failed obedience school. Except I had this fear she'd reach full size and take over the house. What if we couldn't control her?

We fell so far behind on our lessons that I started missing classes out of embarrassment. The expectations were too high. Reviewing the manual, I read Walter's words: *This is the time to correct any mistakes. Your performance should be perfect.*

For real? My six-month-old puppy was expected to be perfect with just a few months of training? I was on the verge of giving up entirely, except after a few weeks of doing nothing obedience-related, Isis whined at us more often and chewed on furniture she had never chewed before. I worried that she was developing bad habits without the structure of class.

Upon my return to Firgrove, I learned about a "tune-up" class that I wished someone had told me about sooner. For eight dollars a session, we practiced commands outdoors for an hour alongside other dogs, instead of bringing the dogs out one-by-one for five minutes each. I loved this remedial obedience school. The first time we went, we worked with two German shepherd males about Isis's age. One was white, the other dark. We were no longer pariahs; the other dogs wore prong collars too, and exhibited way worse attention spans than Isis. One snarled. The other whined.

The only discouraging part was learning that I was the one doing everything wrong. Shelley criticized me for handling the lead wrong and not correcting hard enough. This was the slap in the face that all parents must feel. My dog had obedience problems, and I was responsible. But in a way, this revelation renewed my hopes for Isis's academic career. She only underachieved because I had not trained her correctly. Now that I knew what I'd done wrong, I could fix it, and she'd do better.

I enjoyed socializing with the other dog owners at the tune-ups. Separating the dogs in the basic class had a way of separating the people too; we interacted very little. A woman named Chelsea had sat beside me in puppy class, but we never spoke until we worked side-by-side in the tune-ups. Her dog was a Great Dane named Lexis, and like Rob, Chelsea's husband lost interest in attending class. Lexis had about doubled in size since the first day I saw her, and I felt like she and Isis were friends.

At the beginning of one evening session, Shelley warned us that a pit bull was working in the adjacent parking area with Walter. The dog was muzzled, she said, because he was aggressive. "This is a life-or-death case. He's a rescue, and if his owner can't handle him, it's gas-chamber time. Should anything go wrong, if the pit bull charges us, use your body as a shield to protect your own dog."

As a jaded, macabre journalist, I thought to myself, *Now, that would be exciting.* The pit bull thrashed on his lead, and we moved our dogs farther away from him, closer to the classroom building. I saw him sit calmly beside the young woman on the other end of his leash.

The tune-up class walked in a circle, stopping, sitting, heeling, and reversing direction as guided by Shelley. Isis heeled calmly beside me, not quite flawlessly—she certainly wouldn't earn the top score in an obedience trial—but I was enormously proud of her progress. Firgrove should have made the tune-ups part of the regular class.

We put our dogs in a down-stay and walked to the ends of their leashes. I glanced over at the pit bull and noticed that he didn't have his muzzle on anymore. *Cool,* I thought. *They've taken him off his leash. He must be making progress.*

Suddenly, the pit bull scrambled from a seated position and launched toward Lexis, who happened to be nearest. He latched onto the Great Dane's haunches, snapping and snarling. Isis and I, along with the other people and dogs, stood frozen as Lexis's mom and Shelley clumsily tried to move their bodies between the two dogs, and wound up falling on top of each other on the ground. I watched detached, probably in shock, grateful that Isis hadn't been the target.

She remained in the down position, apparently oblivious to the violent confrontation just fifteen feet away.

Shelley finally got hold of the pit and said breathily, "We're done."

Still not quite grounded in the moment, I almost laughed with relief that it was over. *Boy, Shelley, you really called that one. Good thing you prepared us for what to do if the pit bull charged us.*

The pit bull returned to his handler, Shelley took Lexis and her teary, shaken mom inside the classroom building. I followed with Isis, feeling like I wanted to be there for my friends, realizing that I was shaken too. Shelley found three puncture wounds on Lexis, who was handling the situation better than the humans. I stood there while Shelley and Chelsea discussed whether to take the dog to a more expensive all-night clinic or wait until morning to go to the vet. I didn't know what else I could offer, so Isis and I left, walking past the despondent owner of the pit bull, who was crying and talking to Walter.

Before I put the key in the ignition, I called Rob, who didn't answer. My hands quivered as I tried to make sense of what happened. Shelley said something about the pit bull "somehow managing to get off his leash," but that's not what I remembered seeing. Shelley and Walter were supposed to be these big dog experts, and under Walter's supervision, a pit bull had gotten loose, bitten another dog, and now probably would be put to sleep. I felt sorry for everyone involved: Chelsea, Lexis, the pit bull, and his mom.

Isis sat in the passenger seat, her ears flat against her head as I stroked her face with both hands and kissed her beak. "That was scary, huh?"

Isis's wide eyes glanced from me out the car window, seeming unfazed by the whole thing. I couldn't believe she stayed lying down during the pit bull attack.

"You were really, really good tonight, Baby Bird."

If Isis's worst trait was pulling ahead of me on a leash, we had it pretty easy.

★★★

Sometimes after the tune-up sessions, Shelley let us unleash the dogs in a big field behind the outdoor kennel. Seeing Isis romp with her classmates made me long for her to have more doggie friends, so I took her to Bellingham's only fully fenced dog park. The off-leash area was beside some ball fields at a park that encompassed a small lake and included wooded trails. The dog park itself was nothing fancy, just dirt and grass with some bushes in the middle. Spring rains collected in the uneven patches, creating mud pits that delighted the dogs, if not the owners who had to bathe them.

During our first visit, two Jack Russell terriers raced up to greet Isis as soon as we got there. At six months old, she already was twice their size, yet the black fur between her shoulders stood straight up in terror, like a Halloween cat. She reared back her head and widened her eyes, elongating the distance between her nose and the points of her ears, which she pulled back so far the tips touched. She looked ridiculous. The Jack Russells circled her, sniffed, and ran away. Isis relaxed the fur on her back. Another dog approached, this one closer to her size. Isis took off running, but not in a playful way. She tucked her tail between her legs and screeched as she jetted across the field. Slightly embarrassed, I avoided eye contact with the other owners and listened to my precious creature's high-pitched, agonized cries.

Isis had no idea anyone, especially another dog, might find her frightening. Rather, she feared lots of things herself. Since she'd gotten bigger, people's reactions had changed from "Aww, isn't she cute?" to a trepidatious "Is she friendly?" She didn't look any scarier to me. Sure, her jagged back teeth resembled mountain ranges, but when she smiled, her flapping tongue softened the look. The markings on her face had faded, so she had tan eyebrows with black around her eyes like Cleopatra, and an Eddie Munster widow's peak. The pattern on her forehead resembled the Bat Signal.

I heard the other dog park people murmur appreciative comments.

"Oh, honey, look at the German shepherd."

"Where'd you get your German shepherd?"

"She's a beautiful German shepherd."

Aside from the Jack Russells, most of the other dogs looked like mixed breeds. Their owners marveled at Isis's hips because her hind legs were as long as her front legs. Many lines of American German shepherds had been bred so that their hind legs were shorter, giving them an exaggerated sloped look. Isis's back, on the other hand, was parallel to the ground and she was lean and long. Her back was still mostly black, but blonde streaks had developed, highlighting her haunches and the muscles of her shoulders. Compared to the grassy sea of black, brown, and white dogs, Isis stood out with an elegant beauty. Her fur wasn't strictly tan, but had a hint of red to it. Practically strawberry blonde.

After a few more visits to the park, Isis stopped crying when other dogs chased her, and started enjoying herself. She preferred to be pursued, not the pursuer. The wind blew her lips back slightly as she ran, her ears lay flat, and her eyes widened maniacally. When she picked up speed, her hind legs worked together, instead of in opposition, propelling her off the ground in a gallop.

"Are you sure she's not part greyhound?" a man asked. "That dog can run!"

Oh yes, we knew how fast she could run. Even Rob, a natural athlete, couldn't catch her if she didn't want to be caught. Her speed, combined with newly developed skills of reasoning, caused a problem when we needed her to come inside the house. Ordinarily, treats motivated her, but she learned to rationalize: *Boy, I really love that freeze-dried chicken breast Mom's holding by the back door, but I'm not ready to come inside, so I'll resist it for now. Better yet, maybe I can get Mom to give it to me, and then I'll run away really fast so I get both the treat and twenty minutes more with my soccer ball.*

Most days, she ran around the yard by herself while I got dressed. On a morning when I had a work appointment, I called Isis to come inside around nine, but she refused to come down the hill. I threw treats in her direction, trying to create a trail for her to follow like Hansel and Gretel. She nibbled the treats as far as the gate to the chain-link dog run we'd installed around the patio, then dashed back up the hill to the yard. I moved to grab her, and she raced away from me.

Oh, the chase game, I love this one.

I couldn't leave her out there because our yard wasn't fully enclosed. Exasperated, I tried reverse psychology and went inside, sliding the glass door closed behind me. She tiptoed down to the dog run, stepped through the gate, then turned around and raced back up the hill. I went outside and she walked toward me slowly, so I cooed, "Good girl. Good puppy," and reached for her. She bolted in the other direction like a cheetah. At nine thirty, I called to cancel my appointment. I was tied up, I said, unwilling to admit that my dog refused to come inside the house. Who had such little control over a dog?

Meanwhile in the backyard, Isis chased her tail. Then she started a couple of excavations, for which I sharply reprimanded her, although part of me wondered if I'd be better off showing no emotion at all. I'd read that scolding was negative attention that rewarded misbehavior. Or should I yell at her really loudly to let her know that I wasn't playing anymore? At about ten fifteen, she got bored and came in. I wasn't even angry at that point, just guilt-ridden because she had sent me a message loud and clear: she needed more exercise.

I'd been hearing this message for weeks already from celebrity trainer "The Dog Whisperer" on his television show. Marathon episodes had taught me his number-one rule: *Walk your dog, early and often.* Letting Isis run around our backyard wasn't enough, I knew, but I had the hardest time walking her. She pulled ahead so much that the leash chafed my hand.

Rob initially had fantasized that Isis would be a jogging partner, but he had given up trying to get her to run beside him. Like Isis, he had unlimited energy. He could run on a treadmill for long periods without tiring, but he never made walking Isis part of his exercise program. I couldn't understand why. Giving up on anything was unlike him. Decades of martial arts training made him a model of determination and discipline, just not where dog training was involved.

Apparently, he thought Isis was perfect the way she was, which made me the one overly obsessed about the need for training.

Rob's obsession was martial arts, which left him with not a lot of free time. He rented space at a yoga studio where he ran a small martial arts club three nights a week. When he wasn't at his day job or training, he was thinking about martial arts. On class nights, he liked to lie down after work for about half an hour. It pissed me off to no end to come home and find him asleep with the bedroom door closed, and Isis in the backyard by herself. Our puppy needed exercise and stimulation! She should be more of a priority than his afternoon nap, but I couldn't force him to work on her training when he got home from work.

I tried nagging. "The least you could do is let her nap with you!"

"I played with her outside for a little bit. She didn't want to come in."

How could I argue with that?

Before we got Isis, I helped teach beginners in Rob's class, as a sort of assistant, but I felt too guilty leaving our puppy home another couple of hours after she'd been alone all day, so I started skipping his classes to be with her.

I made up my mind to be the kind of owner who walked her dog every day. After a week of hitting the snooze alarm until the dog-walking window had closed, I managed to get myself out of bed early. The Dog Whisperer assured me that the walk would be even more effective if I put a backpack on Isis, so I strapped on a green Outward Hound pack and weighted it with a can of soda on each side. The extra weight would tire her out that much more, the Dog Whisperer said. Isis shook a few times to get the unfamiliar thing off her back, shifting the pack lopsided. The backpack gave her an assistance-dog vibe that countered the severity of her prong collar. She still pulled ahead of me, but she looked awfully pleased with herself as she did, looking back to check on me. I congratulated myself and was motivated to continue the morning walks. Not only would they benefit Isis's training and overall mental fitness, but they'd also allow me to eat ice cream every day without gaining weight. When I left for work after that first walk, Isis was in a great mood, cheerfully bounding into her crate.

I solved her backyard game of keep-away by clipping the twenty-foot leash to her collar and letting it drag on the ground as we played outside. If she didn't come inside willingly, I stepped on the leash. She conceded the battle and started responding to the words, "Let's go inside," by racing to the back door ahead of me. I always knew she was smart. She just had to be good and ready before she learned anything.

Chapter 3: Perro! Perro!

My company held a summer picnic at Twanoh State Park on the shoreline of Hood Canal, quite a long drive and a ferry ride away. The potluck was a strongly family-oriented affair, and we were encouraged to bring spouses, children, and grandchildren. I looked forward to socializing with the co-workers I interacted with only over e-mail. None of them had met Isis, although I'd certainly told them a lot about her, so I decided to bring her. She was a delight on car rides and this was an outdoor event, after all. I had replaced my sport utility vehicle with a bright blue Honda Fit, a hatchback that looked quite small from the outside, but had plenty of room for Isis when the backseats were folded down.

During our hour-long wait for the ferry from Whidbey Island, I walked Isis along the beach. August was the one month when you could count on warm weather in northwest Washington. Puget Sound shimmered underneath a perfectly clear sky as Isis raced circles around me in the sand. I transferred her leash from hand to hand behind my back. A few loose dogs ran up, sniffed hellos, then ran back to their owners. I was tempted to unhook Isis's leash too, but I didn't trust her in such an open space around so many people.

The drive took longer than I anticipated. As we crossed the bridge over Hood Canal's glittering water, I glanced at my car's clock and realized we were an hour late to the party. When we arrived, I sauntered over to the picnic area with a blackberry cobbler in one hand and Isis's leash in the other. Good thing I'd brought dessert, not a main dish, since everyone already was eating. I carefully set down the cobbler at the end of the table, trying to keep Isis an appropriate distance from the food.

Was everyone looking at me funny because I had a German shepherd with me, or because they didn't know who I was? Self-conscious, I sought out a familiar face and found Tiffany, who was close to my age and also worked in a satellite office. She was speaking to Craig, a friendly fish biologist. Both seemed pleased to meet Isis. Handy, since I hadn't anticipated the challenge of getting food from a buffet table with a dog on my arm. I left Isis with Tiffany and quickly loaded up a plate while Isis whined at my back. Rushing back to the table, I discovered that another co-worker had brought over her two-year-old grandson to meet the doggie. Isis lurched forward, her long nose brushing his, bringing her mountain-range teeth dangerously close to the boy's face.

Hi, my name is Isis. What's yours?

The dark-haired boy burst into tears.

"She didn't bite him, did she?" I knew she hadn't, but wanted everyone around me to know that I was a conscientious dog owner. If it were up to me, I wouldn't have let Isis get that close to a toddler's face, but I couldn't control everything.

Grandma scooped the boy into her arms and smiled warmly at me. "No, no. She was just giving him a kiss. He's fine."

Isis was quite well behaved after that, sitting at my feet as I chatted with Craig and Tiffany about the life cycle of salmon. Then the party seemed to be breaking up. What an anticlimax. So much for my high hopes of making more of a connection with my co-workers. Of course it was my own fault for being late, but I'd had to drive so far. Not ready to get back in the car and go home, Isis and I used the park's two and a half miles of trails to practice walking on a leash.

We ambled uphill through cedar and alder trees, enjoying the view of Hood Canal as we ascended. Isis hardly pulled on her leash, maybe because she was enjoying the scenery as much as I was. When she did get a few steps ahead, she looked back over her shoulder to check on me, eyes bright and tongue hanging out.

"Oh, Smiley Bird. Who needs work friends when I have you? I'm so glad I brought you with me."

We drove back up the Olympic Peninsula to Port Townsend to catch the ferry back. I parked my Honda among the rows of vehicles and took Isis down some rocky steps to a small beach. This time we were the only ones there. Steep rocks and concrete walls shielded us from the road and the parking lot, so I unhooked her leash and watched her cavort knee-deep in the water. She didn't like it when her feet couldn't touch the ground, so she wasn't much of a swimmer, but she sure did like to splash.

Taking a break, she found a nice spot in the sand, hunched her back, and pooped. Shoot, I didn't have any plastic bags on me. Intending to grab one from the car and come back for the poop, I made my way to the steps, expecting Isis to come alongside me so I could put her leash back on. She pretty predictably stuck by me in new environments.

Isis raced up to me, and then past me, running up the rocks out of my sight and into the line of ferry-terminal traffic. Feeling like my heart had stopped, I scrambled up the steps after her, hoping we'd both wind up next to my car and she would just jump in. Instead, she bolted across the open lot toward a woman smoking a cigarette. Horrified that my loose German shepherd might scare the woman, I called out, "Isis, come!" She ran in my general direction, then blew by me as I said to the woman, "Sorry, was she bothering you?"

The woman looked at me apologetically. "Oh, no. I love dogs."

Dammit! Had she actually beckoned Isis? If I hadn't called my dog back, she might have stopped long enough for the woman to pet her, which would have given me a chance to catch up.

Isis moved on to weaving between the parked cars. She dashed behind a Subaru, pausing to make sure I saw the glint in her eye before she bolted behind another car. As far as she was concerned, we were playing a game. I tried, "Isis, come!" and "In the car!" and luring her with a cookie. Nothing worked, and my terror that she was going to get hit by a car competed internally with my complete public humiliation.

Other drivers called to her from the open windows of their cars, but she ignored them. Finally, a few people got out of their cars to box her in, enabling me to grab her collar and lead her back to my car. During our walk of shame, a woman rebuked me, "You shouldn't have taken your dog off-leash."

Yes, thank you. Wonderful advice. I'll be sure to remember that.

I kept my eyes straight ahead as I drove onto the ferry, not wanting to face any of the witnesses to Isis's reckless adventure. I was a crazy, irresponsible dog owner, and all those people knew it. Worse, Isis could have been hit by a car and killed. Turning off my engine, I sank down into my seat, closed my eyes, and wished I could turn back time by half an hour. What was all our obedience training for if I couldn't trust her not to run off?

I had to work harder. Despite my dogged adherence to Walter's training manual, Isis failed the basic obedience class and we had to retake it. The failure was a bitter pill, but I held onto the hope that we'd do better next time since she already knew the basics, and the tune-up classes were helping to reinforce the lessons. Even so, I must not have worked her hard enough the second time around, either, because she passed the final exam by only a slim margin.

My work was not yet finished; she was not a perfectly behaved dog. We enrolled in the next level at Firgrove, which focused on off-leash behavior. The key to this training was a "light line," a thirty-foot thin length of rope clipped to Isis's pinch collar that dragged on the ground as a safety precaution. In the event she bolted, I could step on the line to regain control. As the dogs progressed, we were supposed to cut the light lines shorter and shorter until all that was left was a little rope we could grab to administer corrections when the dogs weren't on leash.

The off-leash class was structured like the tune-ups and Isis was never the worst behaved in the circle. Her weakest skill was "drop on recall," which involved my leaving her in a stay, walking away, calling her to me, and then commanding her to "down" before she got to me. She was supposed to lie down immediately, about five feet away, but she always ran right up to me, and then I had to take her by the collar and walk her back several feet before guiding her down. I didn't know how to communicate to her that she was supposed to lie down before she got to me, but figured her version of drop on recall probably was good enough to score at least a few points.

When exam time came, we started out great. Isis stood perfectly still as Shelley patted her down during the "stand for examination" portion. Her stays were well executed too. But when it was time for drop on recall, Isis not only didn't lie down on command, she didn't even come to me. She broke free and raced around the testing ring, demarcated by cones in Firgrove's gravel parking lot.

Isis let out a few barks, pouncing playfully, picking up rocks in her mouth and chasing her tail. After she did that a couple of times, I was ready to stop the test. Obviously we had failed. But Shelley continued giving us instructions until Isis ran all the way out of the ring, behind the dog kennels, and out to the grassy field.

I'm outta here. Wild with freedom, Isis scampered, picked up sticks, and ignored my pleading to come back. I went through the motions of trying to catch her, entirely for show, knowing from experience that she couldn't be caught. Shelley's voice bellowing "Siiiiiit!" finally broke the spell.

Isis sat.

Why didn't you say so? No need to shout.

Shelley scored us sixty out of two hundred on that test. She checked the *unmanageable* box next to heeling off-leash, and of course we got zero out of forty for the drop on recall. At least Isis's stand for examination earned a perfect thirty out of thirty. I was surprised Shelley bothered to score us at all, but the failure didn't sting as much as Isis's sheer belligerence.

No chance she wasn't smarter than the other dogs in class. Isis was capable of acing that test. I knew she had it in her, but she didn't care. She blew off the test and ran away from me because she knew she could get away with it.

Nobody offered me any effective training tips for correcting what I called "canine belligerence syndrome." All the Dog Whisperer had to offer was, "Be calm and assertive and your dog will be calm and submissive."

Shelley suggested we retake the off-leash class. My sister-in-law, Quin, whom I considered to be an expert in German shepherds, said, "Try to sound pissed when she disobeys you like that. Once you catch her, make her lie down until you give her permission to get up." Quin didn't think I needed to spend the money to retake a twelve-week class, but I signed up for it anyway. Maybe brattiness was just something Isis needed to outgrow. Surely we could master the other stuff with practice.

Walter and Shelley advised me to take Isis places where she would be distracted enough to try to bolt, so I could train her not to by stepping on the light line. One of our regular training grounds was the parking lot behind the high school near our house. Some weekends when no one was around, I let her run loose on the expansive field.

One Sunday, I noticed a game in progress, so we worked at the other end of the mostly empty parking lot. I unhooked Isis's leash, clipped the light line to her collar, and put her in a sit-stay before walking about ten feet away.

"Isis, come!"

She performed the recall exquisitely, finishing with a perfect sit in front of me. "Fantastic, let's do that again." I asked her to sit, walked away, turned to face her and said, "Isis, come!"

This time, instead of coming, she curved around me and raced at freeway speed to the field. The light line zipped past me on the asphalt, just out of reach of my foot. She had premeditated the escape, deliberately moving far enough away that I didn't stand a chance of stepping on the line in time.

"Isis!" I didn't bother to say "Come" again. I knew she wouldn't. She was on a mission, racing toward the muddy ball field crowded with tanned men wearing shorts and knee socks. Children and wives sat with coolers on the bleachers and in folding chairs. I ran after my dog, dismayed to realize that the players weren't high school students, but a Spanish-speaking soccer league. Isis dashed between the players, intercepting the soccer ball and running with it.

"*Perro! Perro!*" the players shouted.

Mortified, I said, "Oh my god, I am so sorry."

I understood their words. *Perro, Perro* meant Dog, Dog, but whether the players understood me or not, they just looked at me and laughed. They tried to reach out and grab Isis, but she was too fast. I didn't know the Spanish words for, "Could you try to step on that string? It's the only way we'll be able to catch her."

She galloped through the mud, dropping the ball to pause and drink from a puddle.

"Now she's thirsty," the referee said in Mexican-accented English.

A child got hold of the ball and Isis bounded toward him. The child shrieked and threw the ball back. Every time Isis slowed down, a player reached toward her and she bolted.

"She's too fast," I said.

"She's no dummy," the ref replied. Another kid got the ball, and the ref told him to give it to me.

I took the ball and ran the other direction, trying to get Isis to follow me. Instead, she pranced right back onto the field.

"She's not falling for it," the ref said.

"Let's make a circle around her," someone suggested.

"How'd she get away from you?" someone else asked.

I burned with shame. "I was working on her training." Her goddamn training. I wanted them to understand, I was trying to cure her of this very behavior. I wasn't some negligent person who let her dog run loose through soccer games. And yet, here we were.

"She's never going to stand still if we keep moving," the ref said. "She'll tire out sooner or later."

I knew it would be a long time before that happened. I stood helplessly in the mud, repeating, "I'm so, so sorry."

Eventually, Isis decided she'd made her point and allowed me to catch her. She sat patiently, panting blissfully while I took off the mud-covered light line and fastened her green leash back on her collar. The soccer players cheered as we walked off the field. I waved back, humiliated. I hated for total strangers to think that I had this completely out-of-control dog, because she was such a good dog most of the time. We made our way down the narrow wooded trail that led home, Isis bouncing along beside me.

Best day ever.

"Pretty pleased with yourself aren't you, Smiley Bird? Well, what did I expect? We taught you to chase soccer balls."

I couldn't even be mad at her. Isis didn't know she was misbehaving when she ran onto the field. She had no idea she'd just botched her obedience exercises. Plus, some of those nice people passed her the ball, willing accomplices, smiling and laughing, not mad that a dog forced their game into a time-out.

Isis didn't strain against her leash to get ahead of me, because she didn't have anywhere special she needed to go. There was no topping the exuberant romp she just had. She'd followed her heart onto that field and had a grand old time.

I was eager to get home to tell Rob the story, because I knew he'd think it was hilarious and help me put it in perspective. But maybe it wasn't funny at all. Interrupting a soccer game was one thing, but her antics at the ferry terminal were dangerous. Other people had well-behaved dogs they could take anywhere. That's all I wanted, and I thought I was doing everything I was supposed to: taking obedience class, walking her almost every day. What more could I do?

Without any better ideas, I diligently kept taking Isis to obedience class. Our classmates in Intermediate Level, Take Two included two boxers named Franklin and Berta. Berta wore a smart brown coat to keep warm and refused to sit on the cold gravel in a blatant display of canine belligerence. To be fair, boxers have thinner coats than German shepherds, but when Isis refused to mind me, she always had something better in mind: *Why should I march around the testing ring like a soldier in boot camp when there's a huge grassy field calling my name?* Berta, on the other hand, was plain stubborn. Franklin wore Breathe Right nasal strips on his freshly clipped ears to keep them standing up straight. He was more obedient than Berta, but not as skilled as Isis.

Then again, Isis was the equivalent of a fifth-year senior.

A chocolate Lab named Cola struggled the most in class. She had too much energy and jumped up on her handler, a teenage boy. I felt bad for the kid, since I'd been in his place, and hoped he wouldn't give up. In the early weeks, I wanted to tell him, "Stick with it. Isis used to be like that too, and look how well she does in class now!"

While Isis's mastery of the lesson plans had improved, shortly before her first birthday she took an unhealthy interest in a sensitive black poodle named Genny, whose owner's curly black hair mirrored the dog's. Classes began with a warm-up where we practiced heeling our dogs in a circle. Genny must have gotten too close, or looked at Isis funny, because Isis lashed out, snarling and lunging.

I didn't think too much of it the first time it happened, and made a little joke. "Isis finds Genny particularly delicious today." My words didn't have the intended effect. No one laughed. Then Isis's outbursts became more frequent: at least once a class, sometimes several times in one session. Since the dogs were on leashes or light lines, no harm was done. I redirected Isis's attention elsewhere and moved her away. Stupidly, I kept trying to lighten the mood by quipping the same line about how delicious Genny was. *Come on, folks, these things happen, right?* As sympathetic as I was to the other dog owners' struggles, no one ever threw as much as an understanding glance my way when big scary Isis bared her enormous teeth at poor timid Genny.

Genny and Isis were the same size, but obviously not evenly matched.

Surely Shelley had seen this before; she had German shepherds of her own. She just advised me to correct harder. When Isis barked at Genny, Shelley told me to jerk her collar and scream "Out!" supposedly to mimic the sound of a momma dog reprimanding her young. Sometimes, this method put an end to Isis's tantrum of the moment, but it didn't effectively prevent another one from occurring. In my desperation to correct the problem, I had insane thoughts, like: *Was her prong collar not tight enough? Should I sharpen the points so she'd really get the message?* Of course, I would never do anything so drastic.

I trusted Shelley, so I kept following her methods.

Still, I was completely bewildered because Isis had never shown any aggression before. How could this be happening for the first time in obedience class? She played perfectly normally at the dog park, but after the Genny incidents, she started snarling at other dogs on walks. Her outbursts grew increasingly more intense and lasted until the other dog disappeared from sight. A person who'd never seen Isis smile or chase gleefully after a soccer ball might mistake her for a vicious dog.

Shelley didn't help me diagnose the problem, but I found lots of people online with similar problems. Dog behaviorists called it "leash reactivity," and Isis wasn't alone. Many dogs were perfectly well behaved off leash, but barked and lunged when they saw other dogs while on leash. Theories abounded about possible causes, from a bad experience in puppyhood to poor socialization, or something trainers called "barrier frustration." I didn't spend too much time trying to trace the problem to its origins. After all, I had been obeying all the rules since Isis was seven weeks old.

I just wanted to know how to make it stop.

One wet morning, Shelley and Walter's daughter Jane substitute-taught the class. Isis was in a particularly feisty mood and I was losing my composure, working up a sweat under my rain gear from struggling to outmuscle her. The first rule of dog training was to stay calm at all times. Easier said than done.

"Isis, this way," I sing-songed, hoping to refocus her attention. She ignored me and found a new mark, snarling at Franklin.

Jane stepped in. "You want to keep the lead loose. When you cinch up on it like that, the prongs in her collar make her think she's being bitten by another dog. That's why she's lashing out at the nearest dog."

I assembled this information on my mental recipe card. Reflecting for a moment, I attributed every leash-reactive moment in recent weeks to the damn prong collar. Whenever I saw another dog, I tightened up on Isis's leash, which apparently was the exact wrong thing to do. I had trained her to associate the pain of the pinch collar with the approach of another dog.

I felt like throwing my leash down and shrieking, "Why the hell am I hearing this for the first time now? Your mother prescribed this device and now you tell me it's the root of my dog's problem?"

I was still reeling when Jane threw another ingredient into the confused training stew. She told me that when Isis reacted to another dog, I should grab her by the face, look her in the eye and say "out" in my lowest, least emotional tone of voice. Was she kidding me? First of all, she'd seen how quickly Isis's switch flipped to ferocious. No one could grab hold of a German shepherd's face in mid-bark and calmly tell it anything. Even if I could, this was the opposite of what Shelley taught me to do. Whose directions was I supposed to follow?

Shelley was the supposed expert, but Isis certainly hadn't improved under her instruction; she was getting rapidly worse.

★★★

Based on Jane's analysis that the prong collar was triggering Isis's aggression, I bought a blue harness that fastened in the front and was designed to discourage pulling. During our first morning test stroll, a lady walked toward us on the sidewalk. I squared my shoulders and relaxed my grip on the leash, smiling pleasantly as we walked past her. Isis lunged at her—in a completely friendly way, not barking or anything. At the lady's frightened look, I said, "I'm so sorry," making a mental note not to let Isis get too close to pedestrians.

We turned off the main sidewalk onto a creekside trail, enjoying the lush greenery around us. I heard the jingle-jangle of dog tags and saw a person through the trees. No leash in her hands, though, so maybe the jingling was her keys?

Next thing I knew, a black dog about Isis's size bounded toward us. I futilely told Isis, "Sit," but the dog was upon us. Both dogs reared up on their hind legs, snarled, and gnashed their teeth near the other's face. No way to grab Isis to tell her "out" in a low voice. That wouldn't get rid of the other dog anyway, so I tried shouting, "Out!"

The other woman yelled, "Let your dog go!" I dropped the leash and let Isis run off the path, crying the high-pitched squeal that means she's terrified. After the woman caught up to her dog, Isis ran back to me. The other owner said something asinine about dogs being aggressive on leash sometimes, but at least she expressed appropriate concern whether my dog was okay.

To my surprise, Isis did not appear to be injured or even upset. She looked perfectly smiley and fine.

After our attackers moved along, Isis trotted ahead of me on her leash and I burst into tears, completely rattled, even though nothing truly terrible happened. Isis had plenty of times been the perceived aggressor, but she'd never gotten up in another dog's face like that.

I didn't want to blame the other woman, since I knew exactly how she felt, but dogs were supposed to be leashed on the trail. Obviously, if her dog were on a leash, or if it were walking by her side instead of up ahead of her, OR if her dog came back to her when she called, then the worst case would have been two dogs snarling and lunging at each other from a distance. I wasn't the world's biggest stickler to the leash law, but I felt violated.

This woman and her dog completely derailed our training.

That day, Isis learned that other dogs were terrifying and might attack. As if we didn't already have a leash-aggression problem, from that point forward, Isis's philosophy was: *When strange dogs approach, snarl and growl to keep them away.*

I refused to let one bad incident keep me off the beautiful and convenient trails in our neighborhood. When we weren't being attacked by loose dogs, I appreciated the enormous cedars and maples, majestic no matter what time of year. In the fall, some of the leaves turned bright red and yellow, making the trees look like they were on fire. Isis and I had lots of peaceful walks and sometimes she impressed me by handling unusual circumstances with poise. A few days after we got jumped, Isis and I simultaneously sensed movement on the trail. Suffering from a little post-traumatic stress, my first thought was: *Oh, no, a dog without an owner,* but then it turned and made eye contact. I ran quickly through the list of creatures I'd seen before on this trail: human, canine, rabbit. Then I breathed, "Ohhh, it's a deer." The doe took a few steps forward and watched us before stepping carefully into the woods, peering through the trees as we passed by.

Isis did not make a sound or move a muscle in the deer's direction.

The new harness wasn't working out, though. Isis charged ahead as much as ever, and the straps chafed her underarms, rubbing off her tan fur and leaving behind scaly red patches. Lining the straps with moleskin lessened the chafing, but didn't solve the pulling. Since we still were using the pinch collar in our classes at Firgrove, I went back to using it on our walks, too.

In class, I strove to stay positive about the things Isis did well, rather than get frustrated every time she turned into Little Miss Snarly Pants. At least she'd started to master the concept of the down-stay. Shelley had us leave the dogs in a row and walk about twenty feet away. For the advanced version, we went inside the classroom building, out of the dogs' sight but where we could still see them through the window. A few times, Isis army-crawled a teeny bit, but stopped when I poked my head out and told her, "You stay."

I considered this huge progress.

Determined to pass the final exam the second time, I got there early on test day and walked around the ring a few times. I trotted around the cones in a figure-eight pattern, and Isis followed happily. We worked the drop on recall several times, and she actually dropped without my having to correct her. Unfortunately, she still trotted all the way up to me before she lay down, but still, major improvement.

Isis and I tested first and I was astonished how well she did. I didn't have to jerk her collar once. First, we walked a pattern around the ring on lead, and then we did the same pattern off leash. She was right beside me as we walked forward, turned left, turned right, sped up, slowed down, and halted. She was a little slow to sit on the halts, so I scooted her butt toward me. At one point, she sniffed the ground, but I said, "No sniffing," and when I turned, she was beside me again. Franklin and Cola were standing just outside the ring, which a few months earlier could have tempted her to run away from me, but this time, she did not.

I put her in a sit for the drop on recall and walked to the other end of the ring, thinking: *Here's where it all went to hell last time.*

As test administrator, Walter said, "Recall your dog. When I put my hand down, drop your dog."

"Come!" Isis bounded toward me, and when I said, "Down," she slowed and took a few more steps, still standing. I rushed to her and eased her almost all the way down, pressing on her haunches to get her the rest of the way. "Stay." Isis smiled at me as I backed up to my place at the end of the ring. "Come!"

She ran at an angle slightly to my right, so I grabbed her collar, redirected her, and put her in a sit in front of me.

"Exercise finished," Walter said, and I praised Isis effusively. I was so proud; we might even have passed. Sure, she didn't drop on the recall, but she hadn't done anything embarrassing at all. How far we had come since the last time when she bolted out of the ring entirely!

When it was Franklin's turn, his handler had some trouble getting the dog to focus. Then Franklin slowed down and hunched his back. Marbles of poop plopped onto the gravel.

"Good thing this isn't American Kennel Club," Shelley commented from the sidelines. "They'd kick you right out of the ring."

Having soiled the test ring, Franklin got his groove back and moved around the figure-eight cleanly. I'd seen him practicing the drop on recall before the test and was impressed how fast he went down. In the test ring though, Franklin took a few extra steps.

I walked Isis around the parking lot to make sure she hadn't been sitting still too long, which might make her restless during the final part of the test: the long sit and down, which all of the dogs performed together. When it was time, I giddily trotted with Isis into the test ring, feeling like we were competing in a dog show. I put her in a sit-stay and went inside the building with the other handlers to hide from the dogs for five minutes.

About a minute in, Isis put her head down on her paws and settled into a down.

Damn. Her utter relaxation was going to cost us ten points. We probably were pretty close to passing; this could drag us down. I ran up to her and made a thumbs-up gesture with my hand, jerking it skyward to tell her to sit up. Although the hand signal meant nothing to her, she sat up when I got right in front of her. I returned to my post, but that clever girl made the connection that lying down made me reappear, so she rested her head down again. And again I ran out to her.

This time, I pinched her ear (as Shelley had suggested to me once) and said, "When I say sit, you stay seated."

Okay, Mom, sure, whatever. Isis sat up the rest of the time. After we came back outside and Shelley told us, "Exercise finished," we all praised our dogs.

Rather than bask in my attention, Isis whirled her head around and snarled at Cola, getting up in the Lab's face. The teenage boy spun Cola around to try to get her away from my aggressive dog. I tried to move between the dogs too, but Isis was fast. She pounced on Cola again and bared her gums.

She really looked like she might bite the other dog.

"Isis!" I said sharply. She backed up slightly, still showing Cola the whites of her eyes, her shoulder fur standing on end. I grabbed her collar and said "Out!" but by then, her ferocity had waned. She calmly returned to her position at my side in preparation for the long down. Cola's handler was stroking her head and checking her for bite marks. There were none.

"I'm sorry, Cola." I didn't know the teenager's name.

"Isis," Shelley scolded, not taking the outburst lightly. "What were you thinking?"

And because I had as many bad habits as Isis, I retorted, "She's thinking, 'Cola looks especially delicious today.' " *Ugh, seriously? That stupid line again?* Why did I care so much whether people knew how friendly and clever Isis and I were? More importantly, why did Isis keep doing these things? What was wrong with her, and how come the trainers hadn't helped me cure it?

We still had one more exercise on the test. The long down-stay. At least this time Isis lay down without my having to tug on her collar. I strode forward to my hiding place.

"Kari," Shelley warned and I turned to see Isis trotting toward me without a care in the world. Her movement distracted Cola, who ran after her owner too. I dragged Isis back and again put her in a down. Surely our score was in the failing range by now, especially if Shelley took points off for trying to eat Cola.

When Cola's handler made it back to the hiding spot, I joked, "Cola's saying, 'Don't leave me out here with the mean dog.' " The boy smiled wanly, not remotely amused. I withered from the familiar shame of having a troublemaking dog. Cola lost ten points for that move, completely Isis's fault. The Lab might have stayed in place if Isis hadn't gotten up.

Before the long sits and downs, I felt pretty good, like we had a shot at passing, but now I doubted it. Isis had let me down again. Lying down during the long sits wasn't such a crime. Even if that had cost us enough points to keep us from passing, I wouldn't have been too disappointed. No one really cares outside of the competition ring if a dog lies down instead of sits. But the outburst with Cola was horrible and I couldn't explain it. Isis had been acting so gentle all morning, and had done well in the earlier part of the test.

Had Cola done something to make Isis suddenly strike out at her? Was Isis just nutso?

"Well, folks," Shelley said after she tallied our scores. "That was not good."

Fine. I didn't mind taking the test again. I was sure Shelley saw how well Isis had done before the attack on Cola.

"There was only one passing score," Shelley continued.

Oh my god, really? We'd done it. She had to be talking about us, since Isis was the only one who heeled properly during the off-leash part.

"...and that's Franklin."

"Wow," I heard myself saying aloud. Franklin? No way he did better than Isis during the first half of the test. I bit my tongue to keep from making a crack about his crapping in the ring. Had they even taken points off for that? How could he have passed if he would have gotten thrown out of the AKC ring?

"Some of you will want to retake the test, I know," Shelley continued. She turned to Berta's mom. "Now, she's fine with you at home, so you may not want to stress out too much about passing the test."

Funny, all Shelley ever said about Berta was how disrespectful she was for blatantly disregarding her owner's commands.

"Cola has come a long way," Shelley said. "A long way. You can take the test as many times as you like. And Isis has come a long way too."

Thanks for noticing.

"But she still has those aggression issues," Shelley said. "You might want to consider getting her a shock collar."

"A shock collar? What is that, remote-controlled or something?" I didn't like the sound of it one bit.

"Right. You time your voice with the shock, so that when she acts up, you zap her while giving her a verbal correction, like saying her name in a harsh tone of voice, so that eventually, when you say her name like that, she'll stop whatever she's doing right away."

"Oh." Horrified, disappointed, and disillusioned, I took the page with our test results and got in my car with Isis, a deep frown settling into my face. I'd trained with Walter and Shelley for almost a year, but that day, I lost trust in everything they'd taught me. There was no way in hell I would put a shock collar on Isis. What possible effect would that have, other than to make her totally neurotic? Yes, it would be fantastic if I could just call Isis's name and she'd come right back no matter what the distraction. Maybe a shock collar would instill that, but at what cost? I pictured putting the device on her, activating it, and having her totally freak out, run in circles, or away from me, being afraid of me because I did that to her.

Nothing Isis could do would ever make me resort to zapping her. I'd rather keep her on a leash at all times.

My outrage boiled over. Shelley accused Isis of "still" having aggression issues? She didn't have any aggression issues at all before this class! What started as lashing out at Genny had developed into leash aggression on our walks, made worse, it seemed, by the pinch collar they told me to use. All this started at Firgrove. Maybe it wasn't fair of me to expect Shelley and Walter to prevent Isis from ever lunging at Genny, but once the behavior started, how come they weren't able to help me stop it? I certainly wasn't going to listen to this new advice to get a shock collar.

Besides, Isis wasn't an aggressive dog, not like that pit bull that attacked Lexis during tune-up class.

When I got home, I looked at our test results. We'd lost points for forging, lagging, and crowding. Looked to me like Walter had been unnecessarily harsh in his scoring. One point off for sniffing. I remembered that one, but for the life of me, I couldn't think of any time that she'd "crowded." I didn't even know what that was. She'd lost points for the drop on recall, which I guessed was reasonable, but nine points from off-lead heel, and six points from on-lead? Even if she executed the long sit and down perfectly, she still would have scored only 169 points. We needed 170 to pass. I felt so discouraged. Isis was smarter than all of those dogs, so why couldn't she pass the stupid test?

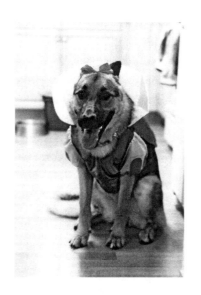

Chapter 4: New House Rules

At our house, Halloween came in a close second to Christmas. Rob and I shared a penchant for dressing up as comic book superheroes. More than once, he grew full mutton-chop sideburns to play Wolverine, and my red costume as ninja assassin Elektra earned rave reviews. Isis's first Halloween with us fell on a Wednesday when Rob had to teach until eight p.m. and then work the next morning at eight a.m., so he didn't plan to do anything costume-wise. Happily, I had a new dress-up partner.

Finding German shepherd-sized costumes wasn't easy, but through the magic of the Internet, I located a Snow White costume for Isis. I would be the Wicked Queen. I figured Rob could wear a flannel shirt, carry an ax, and call himself the Huntsman if he decided to go somewhere with us. The day Isis's costume arrived, I about died with joy when I slipped the blue frock with puffed sleeves and white collar over her head.

If Disney had made Snow White a dog, they could have modeled her after Isis.

I let her run across the house to find Rob.

Daddy, see my new dress? Mom says I'm a princess.

Rob fawned over her and she beamed back as I took her photo.

Some people, like my brother, have very strong feelings against dressing dogs in costumes. Andy even hated it when my mother's dog groomer put a ribbon on Barney's collar after his weekly bath. I loved putting reindeer antlers on Barney each year, but Andy always confiscated them within minutes. He would have argued that Barney didn't enjoy wearing the costume. But to see Isis's bright eyes and happy smile, anyone could tell how pleased with herself she was.

I knew the costume itself meant nothing to her, but she was beyond thrilled to make me and Rob very, very happy.

Unfortunately, we weren't invited to any dog-friendly Halloween events, so the entirety of our celebration consisted of walking around the neighborhood and taking pictures. I wore my purple-and-black velvet Wicked Queen dress, high-collared cape and plastic black tiara, and held a shiny red apple in front of Isis's face. As Rob snapped the camera shutter, Isis opened her mouth and brought her huge white teeth down on the apple.

Even though dog toys already littered our floors, I couldn't resist buying Isis a Halloween present: an elongated plush squeaky with a dog's head and a black outfit painted with the bones of a skeleton. As she squeaked her heart out,

I congratulated myself for having a dog who knew the difference between toy and non-toy. She never accidentally tore apart a shoe or a book, for example.

By the time we went to bed that night, Isis had torn the ear off the skeleton dog. I figured she was working on its torso when, from my sleeping state, I heard the sound of fabric ripping. The tearing sound grew ever more enthusiastic and woke me all the way up.

Looking in the direction of the sound, I saw Isis with a chunk of blue carpet in her mouth.

"Bad dog!" I never called her a bad dog, and even then, with the evidence before me, I couldn't back up the condemnation with much anger. She looked up at me, mouth open in a smile, eyes shining, looking adorably pleased with herself.

Did you say something?

"Isis, you're killing me."

I got up, flipped on the light, and assessed the damage. She had torn an eight-inch hole all the way through the padding to hardwood floor underneath. My mouth gaped. Hardwood floor? All the bedrooms in our house had the same worn ice-blue carpet. The bit of hardwood I could see through the carpet hole was a revelation.

I couldn't explain the cause of Isis's new destructive behavior, so I focused instead on preempting future damage by removing the temptation entirely.

"We're tearing that carpet out," I told Rob, who had slept through the tearing and scolding.

"All right," he mumbled.

"As soon as possible. I can't stand to look at that hole." My fantasy was that Rob would get up immediately and start work on the carpet removal, but since it was the middle of the night, I refrained from requesting as much. Before I turned off my light, I wondered how we would get the carpet out from underneath the furniture. From my side of the bed, I peered down at the mess of dust and dog fur conglomerated behind the enormous nightstand, coating the pens and dental-floss containers that had fallen back there.

Isis hopped up on the bed beside me and I snuggled back under the covers with visions of sleek hardwood floors dancing in my head.

The next day after work, I asked, "Should we cut out the carpet in strips? Or try to roll it up and move the furniture to a bare spot before tearing the rest out?"

"I don't know," Rob said. "I'll see if Matt can come over on Sunday. He's good with stuff like that." Matt was a high school buddy of Rob's who likely would be very helpful, but not until Sunday? It was only Thursday.

"I think we should get started on it tonight." I went in the bedroom and tried to do it myself. Rob did not join me. I called out, "Do we have something that will cut through this?"

"No," he said.

Dammit, why wasn't he helping? Surely we had something that would work. I retrieved a pair of scissors from the kitchen to widen the hole a bit, just to see if the floor underneath was viable. What were we going to do if it was damaged or moldy? The padding underneath smelled bad, but I hoped that once we got the carpet out, the smell would go with it. When my hand cramped from trying to cut through both layers with the scissors, I tried to tear it with my hands. No luck.

"What are you doing?" Finally, Rob had come to help. I threw my arms down at my sides and let out a dramatic sigh.

"It can wait until tomorrow, honey," he said, rubbing my back. Wrong approach. I didn't want my back rubbed, I wanted my problem fixed. But I let it go for the evening, having grown to accept this trait of Rob's. He operated on his own timetable, but he always did get stuff done. When I came home on Friday, there were huge strips of carpet and padding piled up outside our front door. Isis was in the backyard, and Matt was in our bedroom with Rob. They'd made great progress.

The hardwood underneath was an attractive dark brown, but apparently, someone had painted the ceiling without bothering to throw down a drop cloth. White paint splattered the entire floor.

"Do you think we're going to have to sand that down?" I asked. "Or will we be able to get it off with turpentine or something?"

"We'll have to see." Rob was using a small pry bar to loosen the strips of wood nailed down around the perimeter of the room. I smiled, cheered considerably. Evidently, removing the carpet was more strenuous than I anticipated. I was relieved that Rob and Matt were doing the heavy lifting.

Once the carpet was out, Rob's mom helped me scrape off the paint. With a little elbow grease and a little Murphy's Oil, the hardwood cleaned up pretty darn good. Probably it was the house's original floor, making it more than thirty years old, but it still looked better than the carpet, even before Isis tore the hole.

While I wound up feeling grateful to Isis for the accidental bedroom remodel, the random act of destruction troubled me. Early on, when she was teething, she sometimes idly gnawed on the corners of our nightstands or dresser, and we'd tried bitter-tasting sprays designed to deter chewing. Even more effective, at Walter's suggestion, was unscented roll-on deodorant. The peculiar taste and texture of the powdery white coating kept Isis from doing serious damage to our wooden furniture.

This carpet incident was the first time she ruined something beyond repair.

***

If we'd briefly entertained the idea of leaving Isis out of the crate now that she was a year old, she convinced us otherwise by eating the carpet. Not that she minded the crate; she went in happily enough and didn't screech anymore when I left her there. She tugged my heartstrings when I let her out, though, by leaning her long body forward so that her back legs were straight behind her and her belly almost touched the floor. The inspiration for yoga's upward dog, no doubt. Then she reached her front paws forward, with her hips high in the air (downward dog), luxuriating in the stretch.

Her crate was plenty spacious, but when she stretched like that, I felt guilty for leaving her caged up all day.

With the autumnal time change, it was dark by the time Rob and I got home from work. Gone were the lazy days we'd sit for hours in the backyard tiring her out with the soccer ball. At best, we squeezed in twenty minutes of backyard playtime plus one morning walk a day.

I would have fantasized about quitting my job to be a full-time stay-at-home dog mom, except that I had Rob's parents going above and beyond the normal duties of dog grandparents. Once Isis was old enough to last eight hours without having to pee, I told Jerry and Alice they didn't absolutely have to come over every day to let her out. They did anyway.

Alice called Isis "The Little Girl." Jerry stayed at our house when we went out of town because he didn't think the baby should have to sleep alone. Isis was equally crazy about them. As soon as she saw Grandma or Grandpa, she raced to the back door. If a soccer ball had been left inside, she'd pick it up and wait by the door with the ball in her mouth.

During Alice's midday visits, she taught Isis a variation of her usual game of jumping six feet in the air to catch the ball. A twenty-foot alder tree trunk had fallen amid the blackberry bushes that lined the creek along the north end of our property, and short-yet-powerful Alice lugged the trunk out into the yard for Isis to use as a hurdle. Holding the soccer ball in her hand, she asked Isis to run in a loop at least three times, jumping over the fallen tree trunk. Isis wore a muddy groove in the grass, circling and jumping. After three loops, or five, or ten, Alice lobbed the soccer ball and Isis scrambled across the yard.

Having retrieved it, she trotted back to Grandma and walked a circle around her—a victory lap—before setting the ball down at Alice's feet.

Alice called me at work one afternoon to give me an update after leaving our house, greeting me with a crisp, "Hi. It's me."

My breath always caught in my throat, bracing myself for terrible news: Isis had escaped the yard and been hit by a car. A gunman had broken into the house and shot her in her crate. Whether it was cynicism, pessimism, or paranoia, I couldn't help myself. By always expecting the worst, I sort of felt like I had protected myself from something terrible actually happening.

"Hi." I waited for Alice to speak again.

"Isis was so funny today." Amusement crept into her voice. "She caught a rabbit."

"She caught a rabbit? Oh my god. Did she kill it?"

"No. I said, 'Isis, put the rabbit down.' She just looked at me and then she dropped it."

"Was it hurt?"

"I don't think so. It ran off into the bushes."

Like any dog, Isis loved chasing bunnies in the backyard. She bounded into the junipers after them, but never caught up because the bunnies had a head start. I thought perhaps Alice exaggerated, because I had a hard time picturing Isis actually catching a rabbit, let alone dropping it unharmed.

But at least I could breathe easy knowing that she was safe while I was at work.

The allure of bunnies was one of the reasons I never let Isis off leash on the trails near our house. I loved living in a dog-friendly town, but couldn't understand how some owners trusted their dogs not to chase rabbits on the trails. Or run into traffic.

Considering our history, I developed an active dislike for dog owners who let their dogs off leash. Once, a woman distracted by her cell phone allowed her dog to careen toward Isis and me. I stuck my leg between my barking dog and the other, and Isis's teeth made contact with my leg. The other dog trotted obediently back to the woman when she bothered to call it. Isis had not torn my jeans, but my leg ached the rest of the walk. I iced it as soon as I got home, and a huge bruise bloomed anyway. I didn't count the injury as a dog bite, even though Isis's teeth were the weapons. Rather, I felt like my leg got in the way of her barking jaw.

Never in a million years would Isis bite me.

Leash aggression definitely seemed to be the root cause, and soon after, Isis started targeting people too. Bicycles and joggers became as threatening to her as fellow canines. Without a bark or growl to warn me, she'd lunge silently for passing cyclists, then look over her shoulder at them as I urged her to keep walking forward.

Even slow-moving pedestrians prompted an alert sort of excitement. I knew I wasn't supposed to, but I choked up on her leash whenever I saw someone headed for us. What was I supposed to do, let her get close enough to bite them? I tried to keep walking calmly, giving the other person as wide a berth as possible. Often Isis turned her head as they passed, rearing up on her hind legs, but not necessarily barking at them. I'd throw a "Sorry" over my shoulder, not looking back. I didn't want to know to what degree the sudden, intrusive movement of my terrifying dog had caused someone's heart to skip a beat.

Isis's outbursts soon escalated to include snarling and barking. Based on Walter's teachings, I tried jerking the hell out of her pinch collar and screaming "Out!" It didn't make any sense, since I understood on some level that this method exacerbated the very problem I was trying to solve. Choking and screaming at Isis only agitated her further, of course. When in life has screaming and yelling stopped someone else from screaming and yelling?

But I didn't know what else to do.

In my online search for a solution I hadn't gotten from Firgrove, I discovered a class affiliated with a pet store in Seattle, an hour-and-a-half drive away. The description sounded perfect:

> *This class is designed to help dogs that are overly assertive when they encounter other dogs. This class is not for dogs who have harmed another dog or person. It is specifically for dogs that need practice interacting with other dogs appropriately and for owners who need to learn how to manage their dogs'*

challenging behaviors, including leash aggression, lunging, excessive barking, and growling. We work in a highly structured setting with multiple experienced instructors.

"Maybe I'm crazy," I told Rob. "There's probably a similar class between here and there, but what the hell? It's on Sundays at five o'clock, and it's near Half Price Books, wanna come?"

I meant, of course, come with me to the class, and go to Half Price Books after, but Rob wanted to go to the bookstore instead of the class. He would have gone with me if I'd insisted, but I didn't see the point, since he'd lost interest in Firgrove so quickly. I didn't need the added stress of worrying whether Rob was having a good time; I'd have my hands full with Isis.

If this class turned out to be awesome, Rob could always come along next time.

I dropped him off and drove to the pet store, surprised to see a CLOSED sign on the door. Isis and I waited in the car, thinking the teacher would arrive to open the door any minute. A couple walked by with a black Lab and Isis went predictably nuts, alternating between barking aggressively and sounding desperately worried. I tuned her out and flipped through the paperwork for the class, wishing I'd printed out the part that included details about where to park and precisely where the classes were held. I called the number on my registration form and got the voicemail because, of course, it was after hours on a Sunday.

A few minutes later, a gray-haired woman with a small white dog approached the pet store and waved to an employee who had appeared inside. I rolled down my window to listen. The young female employee opened the door and said, "Sorry, we're closed."

"I'm here for a class?"

"They usually enter in the back," the employee said, in quite an unhelpful tone. They had classes there all the time; wasn't she used to people coming to the door looking for them?

I waited until the woman and her dog rounded the corner, then let Isis out of the car. She immediately strained against her leash to get at yet another dog passing by. The instructions for this class were to have Isis wear a flat collar, not a harness or a prong collar, so Isis was especially hard to steer.

"Thanks for demonstrating just how desperately we need this class." I maneuvered Isis around the building. "I can't even get you from the car to the classroom without incident."

The pet store had a small gravel parking lot in back and a chain-link fence that blocked access to the door. Lights were on inside the building, but I saw no discernible entrance. The woman with the white dog stood in a cluster with a few other students, their little dogs yipping their heads off, obviously too close to each other. I kept Isis far enough away that she didn't bark and lunge at the other dogs, even when a woman about my age arrived with a dark German shepherd.

Finally, another student discovered an opening in the chain-link barricade and led the way to the classroom where two female trainers waited for us with canvas pouches of treats pinned to their pants. Some of the other students wore similar pouches. I carried an unopened bag of dried salmon treats called Yummy Chummies, and made a mental note to get my own treat pouch.

The blonde trainer greeted me and Isis. "What a pretty girl! I just love sheppies."

She directed me to sit in one of the chairs that had been arranged about five feet apart in a circle. My fellow classmates were trying to distract their dogs from all the other dogs by waving treats in their faces. Isis shot darting glances across the room, flattening her ears against her head, but didn't bark at anyone.

"Good girl," I murmured, opening up the Yummy Chummies. This must be what they meant by positive reinforcement training, I thought as I hand-fed her the treats.

The blonde, Tracey, and her sidekick, Lorna, introduced themselves. Tracey had five incorrigible Australian shepherds, and Lorna bred giant Schnauzers.

Next, each of the seven student dog owners went around the room and explained our various situations. A couple of the little dogs tended to fear and/or chase big dogs, and wouldn't you know it, the other German shepherd had a real taste for small white dogs. I didn't know what Isis's preference was, but that didn't matter. I signed up for this class to practice being around other dogs in a controlled environment, allowing us to hone our coping mechanisms. Until now, our walks had been a crapshoot. I preferred not to encounter any dogs at all, but if we happened upon one, I carried the eternal hope that I could properly use the situation as a teaching moment. I never once succeeded. Isis always wound up snarling and lunging, and I always wished I'd done something differently.

Tracey explained that all our dogs' problems began at home. "Does this sound familiar to anyone? Your dog free-feeds, meaning he eats whenever he wants. The bowl is always full."

Nope.

"He can go outside whenever he wants, through a doggie door…"

Not at our house.

"There are toys all over the place. He decides when to play, with what, and gets your attention with a nudge or a bark or a whine."

Uh-oh.

"Maybe your dog nudges you with his nose. 'Hey, I'm here. Look how cute I am.' And you play with him."

Busted.

Isis loved to drop a squeaky toy or ball next to me when I lay on the couch. She'd set it down, then back up a few steps, asking sweetly with her eyes: *Wanna play?* Her expression made me melt and I'd throw the toy across the room for her to bring back again and again, never tiring of the game. I didn't always give in to her demands, though. Like when I was asleep, for example. Sometimes I'd wake up to find her squeaky lotus flower toy tucked in my arms, pretty sure I hadn't cuddled up with it when I went to bed.

I'd heard warnings against giving a dog attention whenever she asked for it, but didn't see the connection to dog-on-dog aggression. Our situation wasn't like Tracey described. Isis didn't think she was the boss of the house; she knew I was boss. She did, however, consider Rob a littermate. Not that our habits were so firmly entrenched that we were unwilling to change, I reminded myself.

We were there to learn.

Tracey handed out a worksheet detailing several house rules she expected us to implement for the duration of the course. Some of the rules were things I already did, or would be easy enough to start doing, like getting Isis to sit before feeding her. Make her work for it. I'd heard that before, and since she knew how to sit, that wouldn't be too much of a stretch. Next, "roadwork" the dog four times a week. Take her for walks. Great. We already were walking at least that often.

We also were supposed to have the dogs lie in a long down-stay for thirty minutes once a day.

Isis wasn't quite up to that length of time, but working toward that would be fun.

Another doable one, but not as fun-sounding, was to give her only one toy. We decide when she plays with it and we take it away whenever we want. I wondered what she was supposed to do the rest of the time without any toys to play with. Chew the carpet?

The worst mandate, though, was this: We weren't supposed to let our dogs on the couch or the bed. At all. I was willing to do anything to improve Isis's behavior, but I couldn't see Rob going along with that part. Our initial plan when we got her was to keep her off the furniture, but after about a week, Rob scooped our two-month-old dog into his arms and lay down with her, singing, "Whee! Isis is on the bed!"

On the drive home that night, I told Rob the new rules and was astonished that he expressed a willingness to go along with them. As I expected, the most confusing part to Isis was the suddenly off-limits human bed. I moved the dog bed from her crate to our bedroom, and she was extremely good about lying down there when I told her to. Her eyes looked sad though, like she couldn't figure out why she wasn't allowed on the real bed. In the middle of the night, I woke to the warm, wet sensation of Isis pressing her nose to my hand. She usually did this at least once a night.

I liked to think of it as her checking on me. *Oh, you're awake, good. Now take me outside.*

I was supposed to ignore her, but a half-second later, I had to get up to pee anyway. "You wanna go outside?" I made her sit, let her out for a minute, and then we went back to the bedroom. As was her habit, she beat me there, jumped on the bed, and lay down on my pillow.

Rob moaned "Uh-uh" in his sleep. Man, he was really going along with this.

I had to pull Isis off the bed several times, but she eventually did stay on the floor.

The next morning when I left for work, I wanted to modify the toy part of the plan. I couldn't leave her in her crate with only one toy. And what about her deflated soccer balls in the backyard? Should I put away all but one? I decided that the balls didn't count, because she couldn't get those whenever she wanted, only when Alice came over.

What stupid rules. Then I remembered how Isis stole my pillow every night and pulled ahead of me on walks. Maybe she did think she was the boss. I intended to obey these new house rules for the duration of the six-week class, but saw it as a very bad sign that on the second day, I already was trying to find ways to cheat.

Rob got home before me that night and called me on my cell phone. "What am I supposed to do with her dinner?"

"Make her sit first."

When I walked in the door, Isis ran around me in circles. I touched her head lightly. Was I allowed to do that? I felt strange, unsure of how to interact with my dog. Rob boasted that she had stayed in a down for several minutes until he called her, and he'd made her get off the couch when she jumped on it.

Good boy, Rob.

What next? I consulted Tracey's instructions, highlighted and posted on the refrigerator. We were supposed to run through Isis's obedience skills really fast twice a day and praise her without touching her. I called Isis to me and she came, sitting right in front of me, so close I had to fight to resist petting her head as I cheered. "Good girl!" I told her to "Finish," and she didn't. If she'd been wearing her training collar, the correction, per Walter's lesson plan, would have been to guide her around to my left side.

I grabbed her flat collar and she turned her head, wrapping her vampire teeth around my wrist.

"Hey! Don't ever use teeth on me!" Even though she barely put any pressure on my wrist, I was alarmed. Was Tracey's strategy creating new problems where there weren't any?

I put Isis in a down-stay and turned on the TV. What was that thing about her toys? Could I leave one on the floor for her to play with? If she brought it to me, was I supposed to toss it to her, or take it away? I couldn't remember. Later, I dozed off in front of the TV, ignoring her pleas to be let out into the backyard, thinking: *That's right, this is tough love.*

At bedtime, I went through the confusing new routine of ordering Isis off our bed and onto hers. I let her out at two a.m. as usual, and pushed her off my pillow again when we came back in the bedroom. In the night, I felt her jump onto the foot of the bed, but wasn't ready to wake all the way up to force her off again. She tested my limits by creeping her way to my pillow and stretching her belly across my face. I guided her off the bed and put her in a down-stay on her own bed, and didn't hear from her again until my alarm went off. Isis slept at our feet on the bed, moaning in her sleep like a walrus.

"Well, look who's here," Rob murmured, seeing Isis through half-asleep eyes.

Isis wiggled up, just a little bit, and rested her head on my leg. I stroked her warm head. This was not a dog demanding attention. She had waited patiently until I woke up. Nor was she demanding to be fed.

Rob petted her belly. Enjoying the rubdown, Isis moved up higher and licked my face. Not that I would ever intentionally kiss my dog on the mouth, but the warm wetness of her velvety tongue felt so sweet. What was the harm in keeping morning snuggling as part of our new routine?

When I got home that night, Rob was watching a *Seinfeld* rerun in bed, with Isis sitting at his feet.

"Isis! Off the bed," I ordered.

"She's not allowed to be on the bed at all?" Rob asked.

"Well," I hedged. Hadn't I just amended the rule this morning? "She's not supposed to, but I don't mind if she gets up here in the night, as long as she stays at the foot of the bed."

"That's really confusing," he said. "How is she supposed to know all that?"

"Oh, I don't know," I said, irritated. "Just work with me on this."

"But I like visiting with her." Rob's voice carried a slight whine. Why did he have to be such a softie? He weakened my resolve and I blamed the new trainers. I sat down on the bed and when Isis jumped up again, I let her.

"Those rules are for bad dogs," I told her. "We have a good dog."

Isis agreed with me by smiling open-mouthed, her tongue protruding just slightly over her bottom teeth. Why was I bothering with these ridiculous rules that had nothing do with us? Isis was the sweetest, most loving girl, and kicking her off the bed was not going to improve her behavior on walks.

I'd all but abandoned the new house rules within the week and was late to the second class in Seattle. I hit traffic and when I realized I was going to be about twenty minutes late to the hour-long class, I thought of turning around and going home, but that seemed foolish. When Isis and I got there, everyone was still sitting in the circle of chairs.

What we'd missed was the recap of how their weeks had gone.

"How was your week?" Tracey asked me.

I conceded that we had a hard time keeping Isis off the bed.

"One of my Aussies was used to being on all the furniture," she said. "I didn't think anything of it, until he started ignoring me in agility class. Once you start taking privileges away, it makes a huge difference in the relationship."

I nodded, but her words only justified the decision I'd already made not to follow her rules. My relationship with Isis was perfect. What I wanted to change was her relationship to other dogs.

Isis seemed to be doing very well in the class environment, though. A few times, she locked eyes with the dark German shepherd, and the fur on both of their shoulders went up. She didn't bark at the other dog, and when I turned her attention away, she calmed down. I was proud of her for not snarling at her classmates, though we hadn't yet gotten to the dog-on-dog lessons. All we did in that second class was put our dogs in sits and downs and feed them tons of treats while Tracey and Lorna approached and petted them. At least I was satisfied with my treat pouch. Rather than buy a new one designed for dog training, I repurposed one of Rob's old leather fanny packs.

Toward the end of class, Tracey addressed the issue of dogs pulling on their leashes. I sat straighter in my chair, eager to hear her technique, the answer to my prayers. Some great strategy Walter and the Dog Whisperer and the entire Internet had been keeping from me.

Turned out, her strategy was to give the dog a treat every two steps to get her to stay right beside me. Swell. I'd tried this before. It worked about as long as there was nothing else on the street for Isis to look at. A bird flying by was enough to distract her from the treat in my hand.

When it was our turn, I practiced walking across the room, shoveling salmon treats in Isis's mouth, then asked, "When would you do this?" The two trainers looked at each other and back to me blankly. I hadn't meant to sound bitchy or disbelieving. "I mean, you couldn't do this on, like, a twenty-minute walk."

"You're trying to teach a new behavior," Tracey said. "So, yes, if you took her on a twenty-minute walk like this, you'd have her walking beside you on a loose lead."

Right. Just as long as I kept feeding her treats.

"Keep working on the house rules," Tracey said, addressing the whole class. "I know it's hard, but you're trying to change the whole dynamic of your relationship with your dog."

As far as I was concerned, Tracey's method had changed Isis for the worse. She used to gobble up her kibble as soon as I put down the bowl. But the past week, after being asked to sit for her morning meal, she didn't take a bite. Instead, she nervously followed me around the house because she wanted more Morning Snuggle Time. Nowhere did the description of the class mention changing my relationship with my dog or starving her for affection. I signed up to "practice interacting with other dogs appropriately." When were we going to do that?

Tracey turned to a young couple with a Springer spaniel/pointer mix. "You've already noticed a big change, haven't you?"

They nodded.

My inner journalist kicked in. "What do you think made the biggest difference?"

"Oh, just showing her that all good things come from me," the woman said. "Like her toys and her food."

That was no help. Isis already knew that. I remained unconvinced and was sorry I'd made the drive. Isis didn't mind, though. She hopped happily in the car. *That was fun. What's next?* Between the dog school and the freeway, she kept stepping on my lap with her front paws, trying to look out my window at Seattle by night. Maybe a more responsible dog mom would crate her in the car, or get a dog seatbelt harness, but then I'd miss out on the coziness when Isis settled down on the passenger seat with her chin resting on my right thigh, sleeping so soundly she snored.

The next day I tried luring Isis down the driveway with treats. In class, she took treats without her teeth touching my fingers at all, but in real life, she was so eager to get to the wild salmon treats, she nipped my fingers hard. As soon as we got to the sidewalk, a bicycle went by and I lost her attention. Isis pulled ahead of me and didn't even come back for the treat. I kept walking, feeling mad, hot, and frustrated. Another bicycle rounded the corner. Treats at the ready, I tried to distract Isis, but she'd already zeroed in on the bike, staring at it with her mouth closed tight. Using a page from the Dog Whisperer's playbook, I tried to urge her forward by bumping her with my leg. She lost control and barked viciously at the passing cyclist, catching my thigh in the crossfire. Mid-bark, her jaw clamped hard on my leg.

"What the hell? Isis!"

Isis kept barking at the bicycle, even after it headed away from us.

"Isis! Calm down. It's fine. Shhh."

I limped home, grateful not to see any more bicycles but completely discouraged by Isis's escalating aggression. She, of course, was quite satisfied with herself for protecting me from that person on wheels. I'd had such high hopes that Tracey's class would cure Isis of this excessive barking on walks. Not such a wild fantasy, since that's what they literally advertised. But treat luring didn't work, the house rules were stupid, and not even the Dog Whisperer's move prevented Isis's most recent outburst.

Clearly this class had been a waste of $175, but I figured I might as well keep going, if for no other reason than to give Isis practice being in the same room with other dogs.

The next Sunday, we practiced approaching the other dogs. Tracey set up a couple of chairs as a barrier and we walked toward each other, pouring treats down our dogs' throats so they didn't bark at each other.

Isis did well, didn't snarl once, but she had horrible diarrhea the next day from being force-fed an entire bag of treats. I didn't bother returning for the next three classes. Tracey didn't have any answers that I hadn't already seen in the dog books, and her method didn't work in the real world anyway.

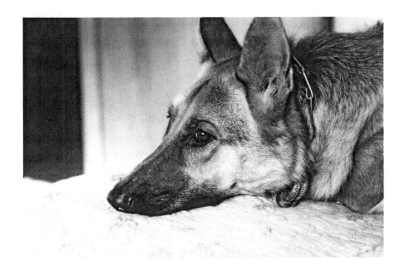

Chapter 5: Out of the Crate

Early the following spring, Rob and I craved a little adventure, so we planned a three-week trip to India and Nepal. We hated to leave Isis that long, but Jerry stayed at our house while we circled Mount Everest by plane, watched water buffalo bathe in the Ganges River, and photographed Buddhist monks with their camera phones in front of the Bodhi tree.

I printed out a color picture of Isis romping in our backyard, and pasted it to the front cover of our itinerary. Whenever I felt lonesome for her, I gazed at the image and pictured her racing circles around the fallen tree in our yard with Grandma, knowing that's what they were doing every day. Alice e-mailed me about their days together, telling me Isis had a bath one day after getting muddy, and the next day that they were expecting snow.

Meanwhile, Rob was complaining about the heat as our legs stuck to the plastic seats on a sweltering boat ride from Mumbai to Elephanta Island.

"How long is this boat ride?"

"An hour," I said.

"And what will we see on this island?"

I referred to our tour book. "A bunch of Hindu and Buddhist temples carved inside caves. Why? Did you have something better to do today? Would you rather be watching the BBC in our air-conditioned hotel room?"

Rob laughed. "Good point."

Once on the island, we had to climb about a million stairs past endless souvenir stands to get to the caves, but the ancient carvings were impressive enough to be worth it. Mercifully, the caves were cooler than the boat. Rob took pictures of me posing in front of the carvings with one leg up like the Hindu god Shiva dancing in a ring of fire.

On the boat ride back, I wondered aloud, "What do you think Isis is doing right now?"

Rob smiled. "She's lying at the top of her little hill, rolling her soccer ball to my mom."

"And then racing down to grab it away when your mom takes too long to throw it."

"My mom doesn't take too long. She tries to kick it high over Isis's head, but Isis jumps straight up to catch it."

That night, we took refuge from the heat by seeing an English-language Indian film. After we bought our tickets, we sat on the front steps of the theater, watching a yellow short-haired dog play with a section of black rubber hose. The dog had pointy ears, like Isis, but that's where the resemblance ended. The street dogs of India seemed to be of a common breed, resembling street dogs I'd seen in Mexico and Thailand.

This must be what dogs would look like if allowed to breed freely. As the dog lolled to his back, hose in mouth, I saw clearly that he had not been neutered. He wore a red collar, though, so he was somebody's dog, or had been at some point. Scars lined his rib cage and he was smaller than Isis, scrawny, but not emaciated. He stood and shook his head from side to side, relishing the rubber hose flopping against his face. We'd seen lots of street dogs on our trip, most of them with bugs crawling around their eyes. This was the first dog I wanted to play with. He lay down and watched us, before rolling to his side and pawing his precious hose.

The hose was to that dog what a soccer ball was to Isis.

"That is the happiest dog in India," I told Rob.

I placated my need to play with him by taking his photo and counting the days until I would see the happiest dog in Bellingham. According to Alice, Isis was counting down until we came home, too. Every day Alice made an "X" on the kitchen wall calendar, marking the days we'd been gone. She e-mailed us that once when she forgot, Isis sat beside the wall looking pointedly at the calendar to remind her.

I hoped that Rob's folks would bring Isis with them when they picked us up at the airport, but they did not. Rob had started to feel feverish and nauseous on our flight from Delhi, and I was practically sleepwalking myself. When we arrived home, Jerry went inside the house ahead of us to let Isis out of her crate and into the backyard.

We all expected some huge emotional reunion, but Isis was busily running around with her soccer ball and didn't even notice me or Rob when we stepped onto the back patio. Alice said, "Look who's back!" and Isis ran down the hill to circle us both, rubbing against our legs like a cat, then raced back up the hill.

"Isis! Is that all we get? We missed you so much," I said.

She ran back down to us and dropped the ball. *I missed you, too. You were gone a really, really long time. Do you want to throw my ball to me?*

"Let's go inside. We're exhausted."

Isis walked beside me as I went in the house. Rob immediately collapsed into bed and Jerry and Alice went home, so I flopped down on the loveseat and Isis hopped up beside me, lying across my feet. I snuggled into her warm golden fur. "I'm sorry we were gone so long, Smiley Bird."

Her understated welcome in the backyard didn't offend me. I knew Isis had a blast at home with Alice while Rob and I were on our adventure. My bond with Isis was enduring and strong. We were connected even when I was a world away. She knew I'd be back, and I knew she'd be waiting for me.

Rob, it turned out, was violently ill with campylobacter. Apparently, the foodborne illness is commonly transmitted via undercooked poultry, but I suspected unclean glassware at a restaurant near the Taj Mahal. He stayed in bed for the better part of a week, and during that time, Isis roamed the house unsupervised while I was at work, with Rob flat on his back in bed, in no shape to keep a careful eye on her. She took up residence on a taupe couch in our library, one of our nicest pieces of furniture. My grandmother died a few months before Rob and I got our house, so we inherited the couch, the loveseat, three lamps, end tables, and a coffee table, along with the bedroom dresser and nightstands. Out of her crate, Isis spent most of her time on that couch.

Since Isis didn't get into any trouble that week, we started leaving her alone loose in the house. The first time, she ran to the library windows and watched us walk down the front steps, yelping, *Wait! You left me out! I'm supposed to go in the metal box.*

For the next week, she still dutifully trotted into her crate when she could tell I was about to leave for work. "No, Isis, you don't have to go in your crate." I remembered a time when she wouldn't go in there unless I lured her with a treat or used bodily force. Enormously proud of her, I wondered why we crated her so long. She hadn't destroyed anything of ours in a long time, not since the bedroom carpet incident.

Still, I felt guilty that I wasn't doing enough to challenge her mind. Forced to entertain herself, she often spun circles in front of the couch, chased her tail until she caught it, then collapsed on the floor, twisting her head under her hind leg and making strange raspy noises.

"Easy there, T-Rex," I said. "Don't you ever make normal dog noises?"

She froze, head still tucked under her leg, then unwound and looked at me, closing her mouth, changing her expression from smiley to worried.

"No, you're fine. Keep doing what you're doing."

Her spinning momentum broken, Isis turned her attention to nibbling her right foreleg.

Walking her was still a pain in the ass, and the fenced-in dog park no longer met our needs. Isis didn't particularly like the dogs there, so instead of playing with them, she wound up sniffing the dirt. I didn't care for their people anyway. They looked rather tough: lots of shaved heads, scary tattoos, and strange piercings. I'd heard good things about another park. Although not fully fenced, this other park on the south side of town was bounded on all sides by shrubs and a hill. Since Isis hadn't bolted from me embarrassingly in several months, I didn't think she was likely to repeat her ferry-terminal antics.

She never ran away from me at the fenced dog park, anyway. Always followed me right to the gate. Probably afraid I was going to leave her there with those weird people and their dogs.

We tested out the new park on a Saturday afternoon in July when Rob had to work. Because it was the first sunny day in weeks, I expected the park to be teeming with dogs, but Isis and I were the only ones there. A gravel path led from the parking area through a cluster of shrubs that opened into a huge inviting field, brown with dried grass. I sat down on a wooden bench in the middle of the play area, watching Isis run around by herself and wishing I'd brought a ball. Rob would have brought a soccer ball. He would have packed a whole bag with treats and toys, poop bags, and antibacterial wipes.

I, on the other hand, had counted on other dogs entertaining Isis.

Later I discovered a definite schedule to this park. Large dog packs could be found weeknights between the close of the workday and sunset. The people were more social than the weirdos at the other park, making small talk about dog breeds and training. I scoped them for potential friends, but never exchanged names with anyone, satisfied just to interact with other humans sharing a common interest. The dogs were well-mannered and Isis enjoyed chasing and being chased. In addition to the large field, there were short trails where I could take Isis off leash and she greeted other dogs without snarling or lunging. When it was time to go, she obediently followed me back up the trail to a sign warning that dogs beyond that point must be leashed.

Isis made friends with a small, manic boxer who usually raced onto the field well ahead of his owners, a couple a few years older than me. The boxer would jump up on me, quivering with excitement. This dog needed to run off some energy, and Isis was happy to help. He'd engage her with a pounce and they'd go off running. Trailing slightly behind, she turned her head and put her teeth on his haunch, herding him. I could tell it was a natural way for a German shepherd to behave, and watched the boxer's owners to make sure they didn't think her overly aggressive. The boxer certainly didn't seem to mind.

We went to this park a few nights a week all summer. I stayed until the very last dog left, as long as there was a sliver of light to see my black-and-blonde beauty frolicking with her friends. But as with all the things that started out so well, giving me hope that this activity would solve all Isis's problems, giving her enough exercise that I didn't have to walk her, and making new friends for us both, the good times didn't last.

Late in the summer, Isis and I emerged from the cluster of shrubs to see that the only other dog at the park was a black miniature pinscher resting in the shade beneath its owner, who apparently was napping on the bench. Isis, already off-leash, raced over to sniff the min-pin, who sniffed back, then mouthed off at Isis with a series of shrill yips.

Wow, what's his problem? Isis chased the min-pin around the bench, giving him a menacing piece of her mind. "Grrrrrrrowl. Woof woof woof woof!"

The woman stood and whacked Isis on the back with a tennis-ball launcher. "Get away from my dog!"

I grabbed Isis and reattached her leash as the woman snapped, "Yeah, you better keep him leashed."

Isis and I slunk off the field toward a trail that ended where the railroad tracks ran along Bellingham Bay. My initial embarrassment over Isis's outburst gave way to anger. I seethed with the unfairness of the situation. Even though the min-pin was one-tenth of Isis's size, approximately the size of a loaf of bread, clearly it had instigated the skirmish. Just because Isis was a big scary German shepherd, she automatically was judged the bad guy. No one but me considered the likelihood that Isis was afraid of that yipping min-pin. Unfortunately, this wasn't the first time Isis got snarly with a little dog, but they always started it! Isis didn't run after little dogs minding their own business, just the ones who sniped at her first, and she never actually hurt any of them.

Small-dog owners never monitored dog-park behavior as carefully as I did.

Isis's image wasn't helped by her tough-looking prong collar. We'd given up Firgrove's training philosophy in general, but I found the collar to be the best way to control her. A bright blue knotted rope about two inches long hung from the collar, a remnant of our off-leash class in which we used the short rope to deliver a correction (or pull her off a min-pin, as the case may be).

After the min-pin was gone, we returned to the field to play with the normal-sized dogs. A familiar old German lady named Ilka showed up with her squat beagle, Greta. Isis had met the woman and her dog a number of times, but had shown little interest in either. Ilka asked me about the training collar, and as I explained its purpose, Greta grabbed the blue rope in her teeth. Isis reprised her earlier performance, growling and snarling as Greta screamed like she was being eaten. Both Ilka and I intervened and I kicked myself for leaving the collar on. By tugging the blue rope, Greta constricted the prongs around Isis's neck, delivering a correction designed to mimic a dog's bite. Of course Isis fought back.

Ilka scooped up Greta and I apologized profusely.

"Oh no, no, it's not your fault," she said in her thick German accent. "My dog started it."

Yes. Yes, she did, and I was delighted that at least one other person in the dog park was willing to take responsibility for her dog's actions.

From then on, I avoided the park when there weren't big dogs for Isis to play with. I parked atop a hill that afforded a view of the playfield, getting back in the car and going home a few times when I saw yippy dogs playing down there. My theory was that little dogs freaked Isis out by walking underneath her belly. When she could no longer see them, she snarled and snapped at them out of confusion and fear.

One Friday evening, Rob and I picked up Mediterranean take-out and planned to have a picnic at the dog park while watching Isis play. As soon as we set foot on the field, Isis inexplicably got into it with someone her own size, a white dog with unusual black and brown spots. We scolded her with a bunch of sharp "Heys" and urged Isis away from the dog.

I widened my eyes at Rob: *What was that about?*

I still intended to sit down and eat, but Rob stiffened and said, "Let's keep moving."

We walked to a wooden bench opposite a lagoon that had been restored for salmon habitat and was fenced off from dog use. Separated from the other dogs, Isis idly sniffed some plants and found a nice place to pee. I was disappointed. Playing with other dogs was the whole point.

As we watched the sun set over the bay and ate our gyros, my familiar defensiveness rose up. Isis's behavior was perfectly normal. Dogs snarl at each other all the time. What was the big deal?

"We could have stayed in the other area," I said. "Something about that one dog must have set her off, but she was fine. She plays with those other dogs all the time."

"I wasn't digging it," Rob said.

"What exactly didn't you dig? That she got all snarly?"

"All those people giving us the stink-eye."

"I don't think they were giving us the stink-eye. I know those people. They love Isis."

I'd been justifying Isis's bouts of aggression for nearly a year, but Rob rarely had been witness to them. When I came home from the park and described incidents like the one with the min-pin whose owner battered Isis with a ball launcher, he was sympathetic that I'd had a hard time. Then he looked at our lovely little girl, who had never once snarled at either of us, and waved off the whole incident, implying that perhaps I was overreacting, because there was nothing wrong with Isis.

Except here we were; he'd seen it too, and there was no explanation.

We'd broken the first rule of dog-park manners: dog-aggressive dogs not allowed.

The next time I saw Ilka at the park, I watched Isis carefully to make sure she didn't have a problem with Greta. Out of nowhere, in the middle of polite conversation, Ilka told me in her thick accent, "When dogs are a problem, they can't come back. We can't have that."

Did she mean Isis? Was she talking about the time Isis snarled at her dog, or had people been comparing notes about the other scuffles Isis had been in? I had thought Ilka was on my side, but suddenly I felt like an outcast.

On a Sunday afternoon in October, only one other dog was there, a boxer we didn't know. Isis body-checked and herded him, as she had dozens of times with dozens of other dogs. The couple that accompanied the boxer left abruptly, and I went home feeling like an uncool kid who'd cleared a lunch table with my presence. Isis played perfectly appropriately, so why did they take their dog away?

Maybe their departure had nothing at all to do with Isis. Maybe I was just in a socially insecure mood, but I never took Isis back to that dog park.

The time change made it too dark after work anyway. So we were back to the schedule of waking up early and trying to walk before work, timing our departure not to coincide with the cyclists commuting to work. I motivated myself by laying out my clothes before bed and throwing them on as soon as I woke, instead of showering first. Isis figured out that when my alarm went off at seven a.m., a walk was imminent, and she helped urge me awake by resting her head on the bed.

Don't even think about hitting snooze, Momma.

Isis's leash manners improved that fall, thanks to months of regular walks (and I lost five pounds). She stopped chafing my hands with her leash-pulling, and she only lunged and barked at some of the passing bicycles. I mentally graded her each morning, giving her a B+ most of the time, with a few C's when she had an outburst.

To earn an A, she'd have to pass another dog on a leash without barking.

Most dogs on their own property were no problem. A few barked at us from behind gates without provoking the slightest concern from Isis. One dog drove her wild every time: a golden retriever frequently loose behind a three-foot picket fence in her front yard. The golden barked and ran toward us, and Isis went berserk. Usually, the gray-dreadlocked homeowner heard the kerfuffle and opened the front door, calling his dog inside and allowing us to walk by. I resented this dog and its owner. How unfair to put a sentinel in our path, preventing us from passing.

I tried crossing the street and walking on the opposite sidewalk, nudging Isis with my leg, like the Dog Whisperer advised, to get her to keep moving.

Once, as cars passed by on their way to work, Isis lunged hard enough that her leash slipped out of my hand and she darted through traffic to the fence. She met her nemesis nose to nose through the pickets, barking wildly. Dreadlock Guy didn't come to my rescue that time, so I dragged Isis barking and lunging back in the direction of home.

Lesson learned: If the golden was out, turn around and go home.

I found alternate routes to give us a satisfyingly long enough walk without taking us past Isis's nemesis. I cut through a community garden across the street from our house to get to the wooded creekside trail. One morning, we reached the trail just as a man jogged by with a black Labrador on a leash. We'd seen the pair once before when they came around a blind curve on the trail, startling us off the path. An unfazed Isis earned her first A that day for not uttering the slightest snarl or lunging, even though the other dog passed within a few feet of us.

This time, however, the dog ran perpendicular to us, giving Isis enough time to assess the threat. She erupted with barks and strained against her leash to get to the dog, jerking my arm with enough force to challenge the connectivity of my joints. My shoulder followed and my feet slipped in the wet grass as I stumbled trying to hold onto the leash.

I fell to my butt and slid twenty feet in a patch of mud until Isis reached the Lab and chomped down on its haunch.

I scrambled to my feet and yanked her leash, pulling her back to me, and looked at the jogger with astonished eyes.

"Oh my god, I'm so sorry." Such a familiar refrain, and yet Isis always caught me off-guard. Barking and lunging I was used to, but pulling me off my feet? That was a new one.

The man glared at me with contempt and moved along, without accepting my apology or responding at all. Isis hadn't sunk in her teeth enough to draw blood; his dog was fine. I sat back down in the mud and pulled my cell phone out of my jacket pocket. Rob hadn't left for work yet.

"Isis just dragged me through the mud to get to another dog and bite it."

"Are you guys okay?"

I said that we both were. I wished he could come pick me up, although that was impractical, since we were well off the road. I could do nothing but stand up and keep walking, feeling the mud seep through the back of my jeans and trying to map out future morning walk routes to avoid both the golden and the jogging Labrador.

Our one remaining option was the trail to the high school where Isis played her first and only league soccer match. During the school's Christmas vacation, we never passed anyone on the narrow rocky uphill path. I figured that once school started again, kids would be walking in the same direction as we were, limiting the potential for head-on encounters. This route served us well until February, when I saw a curly-haired girl coming toward us. Most likely a college student, since she was heading away from the high school. We were on a part of the trail with trees to one side and a steep downhill slope on the other. No room to swing wide around the girl.

I smiled and tried to relax my shoulders as we passed, but Isis silently lunged and made contact with the girl's elbow.

"Oh my god, I'm so, so, sorry." I was certain that Isis hadn't really bitten the girl, but gave her a good scare. "Did she get your skin or just your coat?"

"I think she got my skin." The girl slipped her arm out of her coat to check. She was breathless and her face was frozen into a look of shock as she rubbed her arm, which didn't look red to me. How hard could Isis have nipped her? Not as hard as she'd nailed my legs those couple of times I got in the way of her barking, I hoped.

"I'm so sorry," I said again, feeling like the world's biggest jerk. Isis sat calmly at my feet.

"Has she had her shots?"

"Yes, yes, of course."

The girl went on her way, and I imagined her arriving to her next class saying, "Holy shit, you guys. I was just attacked by a huge, scary dog." Probably a fellow classmate or teacher would ask if she got my number or called the police, but I hadn't even given her my name. She couldn't press charges if she didn't know who I was.

Shame and guilt weighed on me. What kind of person lets her German shepherd get close enough to nip someone? What kind of German shepherd grabs a stranger's arm with no warning at all, for no reason? I was desperate to understand why Isis lunged for that girl. Was she just too close? Isis was so unpredictable; she only barked and lunged some of the time.

Just before we reached the trail that morning, we'd passed pretty close to a guy on the sidewalk helping a girl park a car. Isis barely noticed them.

Although I couldn't explain it, I couldn't deny it either. Walking Isis had become dangerous. I was at a loss, because according to the Dog Whisperer, walking was the solution to all dog-behavior problems. Episode after episode of his television show depicted people who neglected to walk dogs that barked or chewed or begged at the dining room table. The Dog Whisperer asked of each family, "How often do you walk your dog?" Not: "Do you walk your dog?" How often. Some people sheepishly admitted, "Not enough." Others seemed astonished to learn that dog walking was a requirement.

Watching his show gratified me when I saw dogs with way more serious issues than Isis. Dogs who couldn't pass any dogs or people at all without barking. The solution, the Dog Whisperer insisted, was walking more often. As long as the person gave off calm, assertive energy, the dog's behavior would improve.

Well, Isis's behavior had not improved; her aggressive outbursts had escalated.

"What are we supposed to do?" I asked Rob after work that night. "Stop walking her altogether?"

"Yeah, I'd say hold off on walks for a while," he said. "If this keeps up, we could get hit with medical bills, or a fine, or worse."

Rob sat in a green recliner in the TV room, and I was on the couch. Isis lay on the floor between us, pulling squeaky red, yellow, and blue rings off a blue plush bone.

"I just wish I knew what she was thinking," I said. "The girl didn't do anything threatening. Isis showed no sign that anything was wrong, and then, chomp!"

Sliding off the recliner, Rob crawled across the area rug to Isis and rubbed her belly. "You were just trying to protect your momma, weren't you?"

The hairs on the back of my neck stood up. "Oh my god, you're right," I said. "She never does this kind of stuff when I'm not around." Not that she had much opportunity. I could count on one hand the number of times Rob had walked Isis without me.

Still, how could I have been so stupid? Isis's parents were bred to be police dogs. She must have reached an age where her protective instincts had kicked in, but no one had shown her what to do with them. We had failed to help Isis realize her true potential. Sure, Walter and Shelley knew German shepherds, and Tracey knew how to train misbehavior out of naughty dogs, but Isis needed something special. She needed a trainer experienced with protection dogs.

I searched online and pinned my hopes on a local trainer named Ken, who coincidentally had trained with Quin's dad in Southern California. His website convinced me that Ken could teach us the secret to training the perfect companion/protection dog. One who barks at prowlers, not invited guests, and bites serial killers, not innocent passersby. I hoped to enroll in a group class with other dogs, but Ken suggested we meet first for a free consultation.

Rob and I dressed Isis in the pinch collar and drove to Ken's farm-like property about fifteen miles north of Bellingham. I parked beside a shed and wasn't sure what to do next. Should we bring Isis out of the car? What if she barked and lunged at Ken upon first sight?

Leaving her in the car, we found Ken and made our introductions.

"Let me get the little monster." I felt disloyal as soon as the words were out of my mouth. Isis was no monster. I only called her one out of my own embarrassment over her aggression issues. At least Ken could consider himself warned if Isis snarled at him. I might as well have said, "Here she is, my beautiful, sweet angel," because she hopped out of the car with a smile on her face and greeted Ken like a perfectly friendly dog.

In spite of the incidents that led us there, I still didn't characterize Isis as "aggressive" or "vicious." I reserved those words for dogs with malice aforethought. Instead, I explained to Ken that Isis had become increasingly "protective," so we wanted to channel that in a productive manner. He worked us through a few exercises, which flooded Isis with anxiety. She closed her mouth, widened her eyes, and looked furtively around the football-sized grassy field. Ken asked me to hold onto Isis while Rob walked across the field and out of sight.

Isis called after him in a high-pitched, desperate whine, pulling to the end of her leash and looking back at me, screeching, *Daddy's leaving. We have to go with him!*

"She's very attached to Rob, I see," Ken said.

I just smiled. Yes, she was crazy about Rob, but I had a feeling her attachment to me was the problem.

For the most part, Ken's advice sounded awfully familiar: We needed to be consistent. Work on her sits, downs, and stays, since she knew those commands, but obeyed them selectively. He offered one fresh suggestion: practice rapid-fire sits, downs, and stays on our walks. These were more stimulating than doing laps around our yard with a ball in her mouth. He added that extended down-stays (as instructed by Tracey) were as unstimulating as sitting in her crate all day.

Most significantly, Ken took two links out of Isis's pinch collar. I'd wondered whether it was too loose because I'd seen pictures of short-haired dogs like Dobermans and boxers with pinch collars sitting much higher on their necks. I had experimented with taking a link out, but it looked so uncomfortable. With two prongs removed, the collar fit very snugly even before Ken pulled the leash for a correction. As the expert, he insisted it fit properly, then maneuvered Isis around for forty-five minutes.

She showed no sign of physical distress and seemed happy enough, obeying him perfectly.

At the end of the consultation, Ken's assessment was, "She's a really nice dog. You don't have any real behavior problems."

Rob and I went home much reassured that there was nothing wrong with our dog, and we were perfectly capable parents. If Isis were truly an aggressive dog, Ken would have been able to tell. And since he didn't give us any kind of sales pitch for his group protection classes, I felt no compulsion to pay more money and have to drive to another out-of-town class.

★★★

Convinced that Isis's reactions to the black Lab and the college girl were freak occurrences, I kept walking her for the next several months, following Ken's suggestions the best I could, as much as I could. On our walks, I never let her get close enough to bite anyone, and we stayed off the wooded trails, walking only on the wide sidewalks where we could see oncoming bicycles, joggers and dogs in plenty of time to cross the street, turn around, or brace myself for the unavoidable barkfest.

That summer, I missed taking Isis to the dog park, because I really did think she played well with most dogs. But it simply wasn't worth the risk of her getting into fights with the handful she didn't like. Rob and I made it up to her by lounging in the backyard for hours on summer evenings, throwing her the ball over and over again.

I liked to read in the sunshine. All of my books wound up smeared with mud where Isis wiped her ball across my lap, urging me to throw it one more time. Sometimes I let the ball fall to the grass and read a minute or two longer, while Isis lay down and waited, looking at me with eager eyes until I paid attention to her again.

And maybe I played with her in the mornings longer than I should, leaving late for work, but I knew I'd never miss that lost ten minutes at my desk, and that extra ten minutes of soccer meant the world to Isis.

Every day when we came home, we'd see her sleeping on the couch in the library. I suspected she waited there for us the entire time we were out, alternating between sleeping and staring out the window at the driveway and street. I got a webcam so I could find out for sure. Rob teased that I wasn't going to get any work done, that I was going to stare at my computer screen all day watching Isis. The first day the camera was up and running, I logged on as soon as I got to the office. There she was, lying on the couch, just like I thought she would be, her pointed head resting on the arm of the couch, facing the window.

I really am going to watch her lie still like this for hours, aren't I? Wait! She just moved her head. I giggled to myself, delighted with the new setup, relieved of my guilt over leaving her home alone. No longer did I have to feel lonely all by myself in the office. Now I could watch her, be with her, anytime I wanted. Eyes glued to the computer screen, I didn't want to miss it when she stood on the couch and barked at a jogger passing by on the street.

Very quickly, I checked both my work and my personal e-mail accounts and jotted a couple of notes to my mother and Rob, singing the praises of my cool new petcam, before clicking back on the image of my library with its sage green walls and mahogany bookcases. Isis had moved to the other end of my grandmother's couch and looked more alert. She pressed her nose into the stuffed armrest and pulled out a puff of white fluff. Then another.

Small white feathers hung in the air as she moved faster and more enthusiastically, eviscerating the armrest.

Ack, oh my god. I had to make her stop. We still had an actual answering machine, not voicemail, so I dialed the home number. "No! Isis! Hey! Stop!" I croaked through the phone, still staring at her image on my computer, not seeing any sign that she heard my voice over the answering machine speaker in the kitchen. I grabbed my car keys and got in the car, driving the half-hour home. Of course when I got there, Isis was no longer in the process of devouring the couch. She greeted me at the door.

Hello. You're back early.

I dragged her by the scruff and pointed at the carnage, screaming myself hoarse with "Bad Dogs." I put her outside while I cleaned up the feathers and fluff. She had torn a huge swath of upholstery off the armrest. Released from its confines, the stuffing expanded to fill an entire garbage bag. The couch was irreparably damaged.

What was I supposed to do now, crate her again? The crate wasn't even still in the house; we stashed it in the garage since she wasn't using it anymore. The library was in an open room with no door, so I had no way to shut her out. What could I do to deter her from resuming her couch meal as soon as I left? I grabbed a sheet from the linen closet, one she'd already torn, and covered the couch.

I opened the sliding glass door and let Isis tiptoe past me with her head low, looking up at me with remorseful eyes. Scolding accomplished: She knew she'd been a bad girl and I felt like shit. I'd never screamed at her like that before, and

I had no way to know whether she understood what she'd done wrong or if she'd do it again. I very briefly considered staying home, but wound up getting back in my car and returning to work. Isis didn't watch me leave from her usual spot by the window and I didn't see her on the petcam the rest of the day.

I must have scared her away from the couch with all the yelling.

She'd been doing so well in the house and I'd walked her that very morning. Why had she just out of nowhere, after all those months, turned on her favorite couch? I obsessed over her motivation until I remembered all the times she pulled the stuffing out of the dog bed in her crate. She chewed up and destroyed every stuffed bed, pillow, and blanket we put in there with her. This was no different. So she wasn't in a crate anymore; she still was spending her entire day lying in one place waiting for us to return.

We'd never trained her not to chew the bedding in her crate, so we shouldn't have been surprised she chewed "her bed" outside the crate.

Just like when Isis interrupted a soccer game by stealing the ball, chewing up the couch was a completely predictable thing for a dog to do. I had always pictured her absentmindedly picking at the blankets in her crate out of boredom, but that's not how she looked on the petcam. She worked at that couch with such intent, like it was her job.

9 a.m. Stare out the window.

9:30 Liberate the contents of my armrest.

... 5 p.m. Joyfully greet Daddy at the door.

Chapter 6: Bring Your Daughter to Work Day

Alice called one December morning to tell me she wouldn't be able to come by to see Isis that day. Was that all right?

Of course it was. Isis and I had just finished a splendid morning walk, and she was two years old. She could survive eight hours by herself in the house. Or, maybe I could take her with me. She hadn't accompanied me to the office in a while, but it was Friday, after all. Fridays were always slow.

Often I was the only one there. Typically, I sat at my desk, writing e-mails, drafting stories, and communicating with my colleagues in the other satellite offices via online chat. If the phone didn't ring, the only time I used my voice was to order lunch.

Gone was the paranoia I felt when Isis was a puppy that I might appear unprofessional by bringing my dog to work. Lots of people in the Pacific Northwest had dogs with them at work, especially those of us with outdoorsy jobs.

The day before, a couple of biologists brought their dogs along on a salmon spawning survey with me. The German shorthaired pointer and Labrador were very friendly, ignoring their masters' requests to give up their seats on the boat to me. I didn't care. I had a blast. The weather gods smiled on me; I'd scheduled the outing on the last sunny day of the year. The dogs posed as charmingly as the salmon carcasses and eagles I photographed, leading me to fantasize about taking Isis on an outing like that someday. Bringing her to the office could be the first step.

Since we'd already been for a walk, she might be tired enough to lie quietly at my feet and not bark at the people passing by my window. And at least I'd have someone to talk to.

When we pulled into the strip mall parking lot, I groaned when I saw the Honda hybrid belonging to my co-worker Al, with whom I rarely interacted. On days when just the two of us were there, sometimes the only words I threw his way were, "I'm grabbing lunch," and "I'm heading out. Have a nice evening." I'd call these social niceties over my shoulder as I pushed open the glass door, not even looking back.

Since I wasn't completely inconsiderate, I left Isis in the car so I could alert him she was with me. I found Al in the conference room plugging in a space heater and starting the coffee maker. Oh, no. A meeting. Our office housed video-conference equipment so associates in the region could participate in meetings without having to drive two hours south to Olympia.

But not usually on Fridays.

Flustered, I blurted, "Hey, I brought Isis today. I didn't realize we had a meeting."

Al expressed no emotion either way about Isis being there. I contemplated getting right back in my car and going home. All I had to do that day was edit the quarterly newsletter, and I could do that from home. Except I also had a lunch date. In my effort to expand my social circle, I'd made plans to have lunch with Dawn, a copy editor at the local newspaper where I used to work.

I rushed to the front desk to see what the meeting was for and figure out who was likely to show up. I was friendly with a few of the biologists; they might even like to meet Isis. If we were lucky, the less friendly types would park behind the building and stay back in the conference room all day. They wouldn't even know Isis was there unless she barked.

I brought her inside. She obediently turned left at the first opportunity and went inside my office where I unhooked her green leash and closed the door. Isis sniffed the water-stained purply gray carpet, perhaps detecting a whiff of her own scent from when she knocked over her plastic water container there as a puppy. She circled and settled down while I sat at my desk with my back facing the window to the parking lot. A couple of people passed our closed door, walking the length of the office on their way to the video-conference room.

Isis raised an unconcerned eyebrow. *Just let me know if you need anything.*

I relaxed a bit myself and became absorbed in proofreading the sixteen-page newsletter I helped design four times a year. We were in the final review stages for the winter issue and I had just a few tweaks to make here and there. I got busy adjusting column widths, enlarging photos, and correcting the grammatical errors that waited until the last second to catch my attention. My desk was strewn with printed-out pages of the magazine graffitied with black ink noting my edits.

Isis shook me out of my workflow by sounding her fierce German shepherd alert, standing and barking at the door. Al had passed on his way outside for a smoke.

"Relax, Isis," I said when she repeated her routine upon his return. Al shouldn't have triggered this protective response. He wasn't a stranger—she'd jumped on him when she was a puppy. Two years later, I still didn't know Al well enough to determine whether he thought she was adorable or irritating. Either way, her raucous barking behind the closed door embarrassed me.

After the threat passed, she slipped under my desk and lay across my shoes.

"Good girl. We don't want to be disruptive. You just lie here and keep my feet warm for a little while longer and then I'll take you for a walkie walk."

Mid-morning, I clicked the pinch collar around Isis's neck and took her outside for a few minutes. When we came back inside, I kept her leash on and left the door open. She lay down beside my desk and I set my foot down on top of her leash in case she tried to go anywhere. A male voice carried down the hall, the terse "Mmms," "Yeahs" and "Uh-huhs" of a business cell phone call. I murmured, "Relax, just relax" to Isis, who didn't even open her eyes as a handsome dark-haired biologist named Ryan walked past us on his way out the front door. *Wow, she's super-relaxed.* Isis didn't even notice when Ryan walked back through the office, nor did he stop to say hello. I figured about ten other people were participating in the meeting, but no one else ventured as far as my office.

After making the last edit, I saved the files to a flash drive. A huge snowstorm was on the way and my work was done, so I planned to go straight home after lunch. Isis waited in the car at the teriyaki restaurant while Dawn and I caught up on each other's lives since we'd worked together. As smart and funny as Dawn was, I wished I'd made an effort sooner to hang out with her. Her eyes shone as she told me she'd recently gotten engaged and planned to move to California with her husband-to-be. I was thrilled for her, and disappointed for myself. I already had plenty of long-distance friends. I needed like-minded people to have lunch with on weekdays.

Lunch finished, Dawn walked with me to my car to meet Isis. I had a moment of trepidation as we approached the car. Would Isis bark at the stranger or do anything scary? No, she just pushed her nose into the slit I'd left open in the window, welcoming me back with a desperate look in her eyes.

You abandoned me! I was so lonesome.

My boss had left a couple of messages on my cell phone with questions about the newsletter, so I drove back to the office and brought Isis inside while I made his last-minute edits. Again she slept at my feet, wearing her prong collar and trailing the green leash. While saving the finished document, I glanced away from my screen to see a friendly biologist named Frank strolling toward the front door.

As his eyes met mine, Isis awoke and sprang to her feet, barking.

"Isis! Hey! No!" I shouted, scrambling for her leash. I was too late; Isis was beyond my reach. She snarled and barked ferociously, backing Frank into the corner beside the front door. Her powerful jaws gnashed several times against his pant leg. "Isis! No!"

In a panic, I leapt toward them and grabbed for her leash. I yanked her off Frank, which seemed to switch off the "attack" button. The rabid animal was gone and Isis was herself again, responsive enough to move easily with me away from Frank. Al peered out of his office, having heard the ruckus, but not witnessed the attack. Surely, he and Frank expected me to scream "Bad dog" and jerk the shit out of Isis's collar, but I'd missed my opportunity to reprimand her properly. At this point, she'd think I was punishing her for stopping the attack on Frank.

She looked up at me, bright-eyed and panting. *Hey, Mom, what's up?*

Isis, what did you do?

Stunned into paralysis, I stood gaping in the middle of the room, blood pounding in my ears. "Oh my god, Frank. I'm so sorry. Did she get you?"

"Yeah, she did." Frank was pale beneath his curly dark hair and goatee. "I don't understand. I'm usually very good with dogs." He rubbed his legs.

"I'm so sorry," I said again. "Can I get you some ice?"

"No, no, it's fine." His pants weren't torn, but I knew his legs had to hurt where she'd bitten him. Frank was quite a good-natured guy, but he couldn't possibly be "fine" after being attacked by my dog.

"Hold on, let me put her in the car," I said, grabbing the keys from my desk and guiding Isis out the front door.

We're in big fucking trouble, Isis.

She walked beside me and hopped in the car cheerfully, as though she hadn't just done the single worst thing of her life.

I would have screamed at her if that could have made everything all right, but that wouldn't take back what had happened. She moved into my seat behind the wheel, showing no sign that she knew she did anything wrong.

"I can't believe you," I muttered before slamming the car door and going back inside.

I pushed through the closed kitchen door to get an ice pack and found Frank with his jeans pulled down to his knees, examining two huge bruises on his thighs. "Oh! Sorry!" I started to shut the door. What was he doing? The men's room was right next to the kitchen. He couldn't have gone in there to pull down his pants?

"No, it's okay, come in," Frank said and showed me the damage. Isis hadn't broken the skin, not really. Maybe there were a few places her teeth made contact that tore the tiniest bit of skin, but there was no blood. Still, Isis was from a line of dogs bred for their ability to "bite and hold" criminals. The times she accidentally nailed my leg when I got in the way of her snarling at something else, it hurt like a bitch and left formidable bruises. And that was when my leg wasn't her intended target.

"Oh, Frank, I'm so sorry. She's never done that. I never would have brought her here if I'd known that could happen."

"Believe me, Kari. No one could be more understanding than me. No one."

Ryan peeked his head around the door to the kitchen and recoiled upon seeing Frank's briefs. "Whoa! That's more of you than I needed to see, Frank! What happened?"

We told him, and Ryan suggested he go to the doctor. Frank shrugged it off. "I live on a farm. I'm fine." I offered the ice pack again, but he declined and returned to the meeting.

My hands shook as I shut down my computer. I got in the car with Isis, who moved to the passenger seat and watched out the window as we drove home. I couldn't look at her. How could she do this to me? My heart ached with regrets. Why hadn't I just left her in the car while I made the last-minute changes? Why hadn't I tethered her leash to the desk? She probably was strong enough to move the enormous thing, but its heavy metal drawers at least would have slowed her down. If only I'd gone home right after lunch. Or shut my office door. She'd lulled me into negligence by being so calm earlier when Ryan walked by on his cell phone.

"You have no idea how lucky you are that Frank was so understanding." But was he? He could still report us to animal control or complain to the main office. I could get fired. Or sued. My company could get sued. Isis could get taken away. Although no one had ever told me so officially, we weren't really supposed to have dogs in the office. What would I say to explain myself? I ran through imaginary monologues in my head to convince them to let me keep my job after I'd broken the rules and brought a vicious dog to the office.

At home, I waited for Rob to return so he could share in my horror and fear. Like me, his primary concern was that Isis could get taken away, although we agreed that Frank was unlikely to report us. Despite being undone with shame and betrayal, I found it hard to stay mad at her. She snuggled up against me on the couch like nothing had changed. The snowstorm arrived as forecast, but I didn't feel like romping in the fresh powder with her. She had violated my trust.

All that night and the next day, I couldn't think of anything but what she had done.

"Do you think I should call Frank at home to see how he's doing?" I asked Rob on Saturday afternoon. "I'm afraid of what he's going to say."

"Do it. You'll probably feel better after you talk to him."

I shut myself in the guest bedroom so Frank wouldn't hear Isis if she barked. When he came to the phone, I apologized for what felt like the hundredth time. "How are you doing?"

"I'm a little sore, but I'll be fine," Frank said. "Actually, I was going to call you. My wife has a reactive dog and she works with a really good trainer."

Reactive. I knew Isis was "leash-reactive," and considered the word interchangeable with "aggressive." Isis was leash-reactive. Isis was leash-aggressive. Just on a leash. Not all the time.

I started to say, "Oh, Isis isn't reactive," but I was past the point of denying it. I let him give me the trainer's name and phone number.

"Linda is very good, but you need to listen to her very carefully. Really listen to her." Frank ended the conversation by saying, "She's a good pup. Don't give up on her."

His words lifted the shroud of anxiety off my shoulders and I almost cried with relief. As if I would ever give up on Isis. She was our precious little girl, not some "reactive" dog we would give away because she bit someone once.

I looked up Linda the trainer online. She used clickers and positive reinforcement. Her other clients' heartfelt testimonials encouraged me to fill out a contact form explaining what had happened. I described the bite in exhaustive detail, hoping the experienced dog trainer could discern from my words what the cause had been. It happened so fast. Isis was in the exact same position when Frank passed as she had been with Ryan. What was the difference? Well, Ryan completely ignored me, for one. She reacted so quickly to Frank's presence; did she have time to sense his intent? I remembered Frank's eyes meeting mine, and having a moment of recognition before Isis went crazy. I think I was starting to say "Hello," but she was up and moving before I breathed the first syllable.

Had Frank started to move toward my office door? Had Isis perceived that as a threat?

In a weird way, I felt lucky that Isis bit Frank of all people. I doubted Ryan would have been as kind, and Al was someone I had to see all the time. Not only did Frank not hate me, he didn't even hate Isis. And he had pointed us in the direction of a trainer who might be able to help where others had failed. Dare I get my hopes up again? Could something good come of what felt like the worst day in my life?

For sure, I could never take Isis back to work with me, but did this make her unsafe to take anywhere? We had planned to bring her with us to Rob's parents' house the next day for a holiday party. I suggested to him that we reconsider.

"We're not leaving her at home." Rob didn't have a single doubt in his mind. I reminded myself that he wasn't there when she bit Frank. He didn't see what she was capable of. But I let myself be convinced.

Our friends braved the icy roads to join us at Rob's parents' house, where Isis surprised me by behaving like a completely friendly dog. About a dozen people she'd never met clustered in the living room. She greeted them and let them pet her. She didn't even bark when the doorbell rang, like she did at home, probably because she didn't feel an obsessive need to protect Alice and Jerry's house.

Rob's eyes told me: *See, she's fine. Everything is going to be fine. The bite was a one-time thing and nothing like that will ever happen again.*

Chapter 7: Positive Reinforcement

Linda, the trainer that Frank recommended, finally got back to me after Christmas. Close to giving up hope of hearing from her, I was on the verge of signing up for the Dog Whisperer's expensive online class, *Mastering the Walk*, when she called. I rehashed the entire bite story on the phone, and she sent me a lengthy questionnaire and dog evaluation form that she would use to create a customized learning plan for Isis.

For the questionnaire, I described every instance I could remember when Isis had acted out. As I wrote, I considered the training philosophy that dogs feed off our energy. I confessed that I tended to tense up when a bicycle approached us on our walks, and maybe that prompted Isis to react. But I was completely relaxed right before she bit Frank. Same with the time she pulled me off my feet to get to the jogging Labrador. My guard was down both times. In fact, I felt like those situations were more serious because I wasn't braced to hold onto her, which allowed her to get to her target.

Filling out the forms was cathartic, giving me an outlet for all my frustration and confusion from the past two years. Finally, someone authoritative would hear me out and explain to me what was wrong with my dog. Linda wouldn't just offer me the same old prescription I got from Tracey and Ken and the trainers on TV. She wasn't going to assure me blindly, like Rob and Alice did, that Isis was perfect and I was overreacting.

Linda's questionnaire required some soul-searching:

Q. *List your priorities. What would make life with your dog easier? What can you tolerate? What can't you tolerate?*

A. *Life would be easier if I didn't have to worry so much when taking her out in public. I would like to walk her without her lunging and barking at bicycles. I certainly want to prevent her from biting people. I would like to take her to the dog park. I would like to have visitors over without her barking at them when they arrive.*

After pages of describing Isis's flaws, I smiled at the final question.

Q. *Last but not least, what is wonderful about your dog?*

I loved that question! I imagined other dog owners going through this application process, fed up, ready to rehome their dog, thinking they had the worst dog in the world. Here was Linda reminding those people to stop and remember why they had a dog in the first place. Not that I needed that reminder.

A. *Pretty much everything. I asked Rob, and he said, "Her smile." It's true, she is a very happy, friendly dog. Very smart, affectionate, and sweet. I love playing with her and walking her (when she's not barking and lunging at things, or pulling on the leash). I love when she rests her head in my lap. I love watching her chew on her toys and race around the backyard and chase soccer balls. Before she started getting into trouble at the dog park, I loved watching her play with other dogs.*

Linda's schedule was close to full. She lived a couple of hours away on Whidbey Island, but had a lot of clients in Bellingham and traveled up once a week. We scheduled our consultation for a Monday in mid-January, which I had off for Martin Luther King Jr. Day.

While waiting for Linda to arrive, I fretted about how Isis would behave. Two months ago, I wouldn't have worried at all, but after she bit Frank, I didn't know what Isis was capable of. Linda had told me to keep Isis contained for the first part of our consultation, so we could talk. Since Isis didn't use her crate anymore, the best option was the backyard. At times, Isis could be perfectly happy alone in the backyard, oblivious even to a knock on the front door. I put her outside with her pinch collar on, knowing that Linda, a practitioner of positive-only training, would frown at the gear. The collar made me feel more secure. I wanted the option of grabbing Isis by the little blue cord that still dangled from it.

I threw the ball a few times, then went inside where I could keep one eye on Isis in the backyard and the other out the front window. Isis chirped and threw herself at the back door a few times. No chance of Linda getting inside without Isis knowing it; she practically had her ear pressed against the glass.

Linda's green truck pulled into the driveway, and I was so eager to get started fixing Isis that I had to refrain from throwing open the door and calling out, "Thank god, you're here!" I waited an excruciating few minutes for her to open the car door, stand, and run a lint roller over her fleece vest. A middle-aged woman, Linda's wispy light brown hair bounced over her shoulders as she made her way up the stone steps to my door. I led her into the library and invited her to sit on my grandmother's couch.

Isis yelped from the back door.

"I hope she'll calm down in a few minutes," I said, trying to concentrate on what Linda was saying.

"What I do isn't obedience training," she explained. "It's behavior modification. There's no magic bullet. In my experience, most reactive dogs were not properly socialized during their first four months and they'll be playing catch-up the rest of their lives. It can take anywhere from fifteen to thirty weeks or more to modify a reactive dog's behavior. A lot depends on your commitment and how much time you're willing to devote to the process."

"I'm willing to do whatever it takes."

"Great. The first thing you need to do is take control of your home."

Oh, no. More house rules. We hadn't been able to implement those before, but things were different now. We couldn't risk blowing off Isis's training (or behavior modification, or whatever it was) and having her bite someone else. To underscore the importance of this work, Isis ramped up her backdoor aria, her yelps growing more intense and morphing into an unrelenting stream of high-pitched barks.

"You must be worth listening to," Linda continued, ignoring Isis's pleas. "The goal is willing, reliable, trustworthy voice control. We want to strive for zero reactivity. If Isis has one reaction, she's likely to have another, so if you can't walk her around the neighborhood without having a reaction, that means you don't walk her around the neighborhood. You have to stop before you can go."

What??!! All this time, I had been walking and walking Isis. Every time anything went wrong, I blamed myself for not walking her enough. Walk, walk, walk. If there's one thing I learned from the Dog Whisperer, that was it. ("Don't get me started on the Dog Whisperer," was Linda's take on the celebrity dog trainer.)

Furthermore, Linda said, Isis needed to have at least one hour of relaxation a day in a totally boring room with no visual or outside noise stimulation. "If she is alone during the day, she should be in an area that is fully relaxing. Put soothing music on a timer for her to listen to when you're gone."

"Usually, she hangs out in here and looks out the window," I said. "I thought that would be better for her than being in the crate with nothing to look at. She doesn't usually get into any trouble, but one time she tore up the armrest on that couch."

Without needing to inspect beneath the sheet masking the couch's defect, Linda said, "That's in direct correlation to visual anxiety. She saw something out that window, probably another dog, and redirected her anger at the couch. When her anxiety increases, her brain gets a chemical bath of adrenaline, norepinephrine, cortisol, and other nasty stimulating chemicals."

Strike two. Two things I thought were good for Isis were root causes of her aggression. Here I thought Isis loved looking out the window, but really I had increased her need to be vigilant, protecting the house from all the dangers passing on the street.

"German shepherds don't need any special training to protect their owners," Linda said. "If you're in danger, she'll know what to do. What you need to focus on is keeping her safe, because her need to keep you safe is fueling her anxiety, which fuels her reactivity."

Completely my fault. Every time I walked out the front door, I said, "Isis, guard the house." We used to say that ironically to my mother's little Lhasa apso, because of course, there wasn't much Barney the blind lapdog could do to deter burglars. Isis, on the other hand, heeded my request.

Out back, Isis had slowed her barks to one every four seconds.

"I wanted to wait until she stopped barking completely, but maybe that's not going to happen," Linda said. "Why don't you introduce me to her now?"

"Okay. I'm not sure what she's going to do. We haven't had any strangers over since the bite, but she's usually fine when she meets people in the backyard."

"I'll follow your lead."

As we walked to the back door, I wondered if Linda had ever been bitten during a first consultation. "I'll throw her ball to her," I said, thinking if Isis had a soccer ball in her mouth, she couldn't bite.

Isis looked at me eagerly through the glass, letting out a few halfhearted but not particularly threatening barks in

Linda's direction. I slid the door open a sliver and grabbed the half-deflated soccer ball, tossing it up the hill. Isis scampered after it and I turned to Linda. "I think it's okay, come on out."

We stepped onto the back patio. Isis raced over and circled us, dropping the ball at Linda's feet. *That's my ball. Wanna throw it?*

"For me?" Linda picked up the ball and threw it up the hill, Isis close behind.

"I think we're good." I relaxed for the first time since Linda arrived. We walked to the edge of the back patio, looking up at Isis crouched next to the junipers partway up the hill. Eyes bright, Isis used her nose to roll the ball down to our feet.

As I watched Linda throw the ball for Isis, part of me expected her, like Ken, to announce, "There's nothing wrong with this dog!"

Instead, Linda said, "Her body language shows a lot of stress and anxiety."

Isis looked pretty carefree to me, romping in her backyard, her favorite place in the world. What Linda saw was a dog who couldn't sit still or make eye contact with either of us as she darted around after her ball and spun in circles chasing her tail.

We brought Isis inside and Linda handed me a two-inch-long oblong red plastic clicker with a yellow button. "Clickers are tools that focus on what the dog does right, instead of punishing them for what they do wrong. You get better communication and a better relationship with your dog."

Linda clicked, then handed Isis a treat. "First, we need to prime the clicker." Like Pavlov's dogs before her, Isis caught on very quickly that the click meant something good was coming next. "Now, you can start clicking for the action you want, and give the reward when she's in the position you want." Linda asked Isis to sit, and clicked as soon as she started to lower her butt. When Isis had completed the move, Linda handed her a treat. "I'm reinforcing the position of sit by giving her the treat now."

I practiced a few times, thrilled by how much Isis enjoyed the game. After each click and treat, she looked up at me eagerly.

What's next, Mom?

"Clicker training creates an attentive dog who loves to go to work. I've been truly amazed at the results I've seen with clicker training and don't understand why any dog trainers would still use choke collars or negative reinforcement."

I looked guiltily at Isis's pinch collar.

Linda pulled a small digital camera out of her pocket and took a picture of Isis, then scrolled through the photos on the back of her camera. "I have a client with a Doberman mix who had a very serious scuffle with the family's other dog. His arm was so mutilated, he needed thirty stitches."

"The dog did?"

"No, the owner." Linda showed me the tiny camera screen lit up with the dog's face. Of course I wanted to know all the gory details, but thought it kind of inappropriate for Linda to share them with me. I certainly didn't want her telling anyone else the story of the stupid owner who let her dog attack a man at the office.

So I changed the subject. "What's the next step?"

Linda said she'd write up a behavior modification plan and e-mail it to me, along with instructions on the gear we should use. "I write behavior modification plans based on a dog's specific triggers, and we re-evaluate after every three sessions. With Isis, I'm going to recommend fifteen sessions to start, but you should know, she might need more than that. All of this will take consistency, persistence, patience, and commitment. The magic bullet is commitment."

Magic bullet? That was the second time she used that term. I hadn't asked for one, and didn't expect there to be one, but I was pretty sure she started out our meeting by saying there was no magic bullet. Regardless, commitment to Isis was something I had an abundance of.

I remembered Frank's words, "Don't give up on her."

No chance of that.

I thanked Linda and walked her to the door, filled with hope and eager to get started with our personalized lesson plan. In the meantime, Linda gave us some things to work on at home. The most important new routine was going to be extremely difficult to enforce, I already knew. Whenever we "reunited" with Isis, whether we were coming home after being gone for hours, or simply entering one room from another, we were to greet her calmly, then go completely passive. Basically ignoring her.

No eye contact, no talking, no petting.

"You are speaking dog here," Linda had explained. "Leaders come and go as they wish and don't make a big deal about it."

Based on this communication from me, Isis should learn to lie down and completely relax for five whole minutes. If she got up after four minutes, we had to reset the clock. After five minutes, we could call her to us and load on the affection. This finishing move would allow us to practice her recall, make her eager for interaction with us, and establish trust and bonding.

Naturally, our old routine involved lavishing affection and attention as soon as we laid eyes on Isis. I would have ruled out this Five-Minute Rule immediately were it not for three things. One, Frank had said, "Make sure you really listen to Linda." Two, I had read in other dog-behavior books that it was a mistake to fawn over puppies too much because it made them think they were the center of the universe. Truthfully, Isis was the center of our universe, but recent events had me doubting that was for the best. Three, Linda said that this technique would show Isis she could defer to my guidance and relax, because she was not the head of the household. This third point made some sense, and didn't seem arbitrary like Tracey's "no dog on the furniture" rule.

According to Linda, Isis's need to protect me caused her a great deal of anxiety. If the Five-Minute Rule was the first step to alleviating some of that anxiety, I was willing to give it a try.

Rob actually had an easier time than I did "going passive" with Isis. Usually, the first thing he did when he got home from work was check his personal e-mail. He could sit at his computer until Isis settled down on the floor beside him for five straight minutes. Some self-control was required when Isis tucked her head under his right arm while he worked the computer mouse. *Pay attention to me.* Her head popped up next to him, pressing her back against his arm, lifting it off the mouse. *Pay attention to me!* Rob found this slightly irritating, but she got what she wanted; he paid attention to her.

When I came home from work, I typically tended to a variety of things around the house. The first order was to let Isis outside. Then I fed her and maybe loaded the dishwasher or folded laundry. Isis was not likely to lie down and relax while I was moving around the house, so I had to find something to do that involved sitting still. I sat in front of the TV and waited for her to lie down. She wandered into Rob's computer room. I heard him talking to her.

"Rob! We're supposed to be ignoring her!"

Isis trotted back into the TV room and sat near my feet, whimpering nervously. "Hrmm hrmm." *I'm not sure what I'm supposed to be doing right now.*

My dog-speak wasn't translating.

Something outside demanded her attention. She barked out the front window, then ran into the library and pressed her nose into the blinds, which I had lowered after Linda's visit. The threat passed. Isis ran back into the TV room and looked at me. Then she chased her tail, spinning, spinning, trying to find the answer to what I was asking her to do. She sat for a few seconds, chewing voraciously at her leg before getting up again.

Linda insisted that I was not to ask Isis to lie down. Isis had to figure it out for herself.

"It could take a while the first couple of times you do this," she said.

Isis had not lain down for one second, let alone five minutes, by the time we had to leave for Rob's martial arts class. Even if she had, we'd have to start over when we got home anyway. Familiar angst tightened in the back of my neck. Once again, a trainer gave us simple enough instructions that we could not carry out.

What was I supposed to do if she never lay down? Never pay attention to her again?

★★★

Isis and I met Linda for our first official session in the parking lot of a community football stadium called Civic Field. A few scattered cars were parked in the lot, and I easily spotted Linda's green truck. She climbed out to greet me, wearing her same uniform of light blue jeans, fleece vest, and running shoes. She smiled as I brought Isis out of my car wearing a pink harness that fastened in the back, which we'd been instructed to acquire.

"How pretty Isis looks in her new harness," she said.

Linda demonstrated how to connect my leash with "two points of contact," meaning it had latches at both ends. She fastened one clasp to the loop on Isis's back, then fed the leash through the front of the harness, across Isis's chest, and fastened the other end near Isis's left shoulder, like a horse on a bridle.

"This is called a balance lead," she said. "You hold the leash with both hands. Your right hand, in front, lets her know when to turn."

Linda created an obstacle course across several empty parking spaces, with a couple of planks—which she called a cavaletti—a row of orange cones, and a couple of hula hoops. Using the balance lead, I guided Isis over the cavaletti. She was supposed to step over each plank, but since neither of us had ever done such a thing, she bumped her feet into them and was generally unfocused, veering off to the side.

Thanks, I think I'll walk around this thing.

We nailed the cones, though, weaving around them. Then we approached the hoops and I asked her to sit dead center in each. Bullseye. At least we learned something at Firgrove.

These exercises fell under the heading, *Preparing to learn.* The real lesson hadn't yet begun. I was eager to get to the meat of Linda's training: the scenarios.

"Nobody else does this," Linda had told me. Each of our fifteen sessions would include real-life scenarios that Isis found challenging, and we would train her to respond to them calmly. From bicycles, to other dogs, to strange men in my office, Isis was going to practice not reacting to the things that set her off.

First up: Dog. Linda brought out Dakota, her dark brown Belgian Malinois, about Isis's size, and stood thirty feet away. At Linda's instruction, I asked Isis to sit, let her look at Dakota for two seconds, then held a treat under her nose before taking a step backward. By following my hand with the treat, Isis turned her back to the other dog, which earned her the reward of eating the treat.

We repeated this move for less than a minute until Isis turned her head to me before I presented the treat.

"That's a jackpot!" Linda called from across the asphalt. "Say 'Jackpot' and give her five or six treats in a row."

"What a good girl!" I shoveled treats in her mouth, thrilled to see the training take effect so quickly. While Isis's back was turned, Linda moved Dakota closer. At the end of five minutes, Linda and Dakota had gotten as close as twenty feet away, and I had nearly depleted the stash of treats.

While Linda put Dakota back in the truck, I went to my car to refill my fanny pack. I walked Isis back to Linda and noticed a group of people coming across the parking lot. I jerked my head in their direction to alert Linda.

"This is an opportunity to practice a real-life situation," she said. "Use the same classical conditioning techniques you used with Dakota."

I asked Isis to sit, but she ignored me, continuing to stand between me and the approaching group. She similarly ignored the treat I held under her nose, locking the strangers in her gaze until they passed.

"She wouldn't take the treat," I said, mildly discouraged.

"Yes, she was feeling a lot of stress, but the good news is, she did not bark, aggress, or react. She did really well today.

We have to be careful not to do too much too soon, but she learns fast and you're a wonderful handler. She's already looking to you for guidance. Based on your level of commitment, she's going to advance quickly."

Isis and I went home worn out from the two-hour session, but I was buoyed by Linda's faith. She could see how hard I'd been working, and how much Isis's well-being meant to me. The lesson plans and homework assignments were overwhelming, but I just had to take it one step at a time.

An important theme had emerged: Set Isis up for success. I realized that one of the ways I had failed Isis in the past was expecting her to overcome challenges before she was ready. We needed to start small, not try to walk past a moving bicycle twenty feet away when she hadn't mastered passing a bicycle at fifty feet.

My first mission was to find a brand of treats I could buy in bulk, since we'd be going through a lot of them. I'd sneered at Seattle trainer Tracey for telling me I had to treat Isis for every two steps she walked beside me. Bad enough we went through two or three expensive bags of treats in one class, but for Isis to have terrible diarrhea afterward seemed horribly wasteful.

Linda explained that the treats were meant to reward a specific behavior. She also validated my theory that once Isis was barking and lunging at something, it was too late to "distract" her with a cookie. Still, I ran through the treats just as quickly with Linda because I had to stay ahead of the reaction. During our exercises with Dakota, I fed Isis treat after treat after treat to reward her for not barking. All the while I feared that if I slowed down the dispersal, Isis would use the opportunity to react.

I liked the dried salmon treats I'd used during Tracey's class, but they were pricey and perhaps too rich for Isis's system. We needed a milder treat that didn't upset her stomach. I discovered that Isis adored the small, round, not-too-expensive Charlee Bears, which resembled oyster crackers. They left crumbs in my fanny pack, but were otherwise user-friendly.

Another good buy, if I bought the biggest bag, was a brand called Train-Me. These treats, about the size of a pencil eraser, were softer than the Charlee Bears and tantalized me with their aroma. I gave up eating meat almost ten years earlier, but I loved sticking my nose in a freshly opened bag of bacon-flavored Train-Mes.

Sometimes I splurged for freeze-dried beef liver, because Linda stressed the importance of using high-value treats. The dried liver didn't have as appetizing a smell to me, but the sponge-like consistency made them easy to handle.

Linda also insisted that I rule out a medical cause for aggression—a thyroid problem, in particular—so I took Isis to the vet clinic. I unhooked her leash in the exam room and let her trot around, sniffing the corners. Isis had never shown any fear of any of the vets there. Last time we were there, she barked and lunged at a dog in the waiting room, but as long as I made sure there were no other patients in our way, we were fine.

The door opened a sliver and Dr. Hall, an older male vet we hadn't seen before, poked his head through the crack. "Let's see what we have here. Oh! You look perfectly friendly."

Of course she was perfectly friendly. What reason did he have to think otherwise? I hadn't said anything about the reason for our visit when I scheduled the appointment.

"Her chart warned that she's an aggressive dog," he added, coming all the way into the room.

One of the receptionists must have observed Isis in the waiting room last time and put a scarlet letter in her permanent record. Since our secret was out, I explained that yes, we had some issues with aggression and I wanted her thyroid tested. He asked me what other symptoms she'd shown of hypothyroidism, and I felt a little stupid because she didn't have any other symptoms. Dr. Hall took a blood sample and found her thyroid levels to be in the normal range, which was partly a relief and partly a disappointment, because if there had been a medical cause, there might have been an easier cure.

★★★

Linda e-mailed me six pages of exercises to work on before our next meeting. I was supposed to take Isis to low-distraction environments and practice getting her to make eye contact with me, stay close on a loose leash, come racing toward me every time I said her name, and look to me every time she saw something that made her nervous.

I attached the red clicker to a lanyard around my neck and took Isis back to Civic Field on Wednesday after work while Rob was teaching his class. It was dark already when we got there, but stadium lights brightened the parking lot. Isis was amped up, as if we were in a completely unfamiliar place, even though she'd been there a few days earlier. I let her out of the car with one end of the leash attached to her pink harness. She darted to the end of it, moving erratically and sniffing the ground.

I tried to get her to sit next to me and "prepare to learn." Nearly all the exercises were supposed to begin with Isis in a sit position, but I couldn't get her there, so I skipped to an exercise that at least let her move around. I clipped one end of her leash to my belt and started walking. Every time she was near my left side, I clicked and treated. If she forged ahead, I stopped and went the other direction. I knew this dance from my Firgrove days. We were aiming for a solid heel, which Isis had yet to master. In this low-distraction parking lot, she was right there beside me, her entire focus on the treats in my hand.

Interesting. Tracey's treat method hadn't gotten Isis to walk beside me properly. What was different now?

The clicker.

Isis had learned that the sound of the clicker meant a treat was forthcoming. When I started to walk, she followed dutifully. I clicked as soon as she reached my side, which made her pause long enough to take a treat from my hand and process that the click marked the place where she was supposed to be. Major progress. Without the clicker, she might take the treat on her way past me to charge ahead, but I had no way to communicate that I would prefer for her to walk beside me instead.

This clicker business was genius!

I was fastening the second point of contact to the side of her harness when I heard shouts and the grinding of wheels on asphalt. Three teenagers on skateboards looped around the empty parking spaces. I thought they probably were headed to the skate park across the street and tried to gauge what route they'd take, so I could move Isis far enough away to keep her from reacting. But the guys weren't traveling in a straight line, and the skate park did not turn out to be their intended destination. I steadied myself for a real-life scenario. First, I needed Isis to look at the skateboarders, then I'd lure her to look away with a treat. Except Isis hadn't yet noticed the skateboarders were there. She looked everywhere else. As soon as she homed in on them, I planned to let her look for two seconds, then hold out a treat. But the teens' movements were unpredictable, and by the time she saw them, they were too close.

She didn't bark and lunge, but I could tell she was stressed and she wouldn't take the treat or look back at me.

I decided to quit before she really freaked out, so we got back in the car and watched the skateboarders for a few minutes while I tried to determine whether there was anything we could accomplish with those guys monopolizing the lot. How frustrating. The skateboarders were either too close or too far away. How were we going to make any progress when we couldn't control the outside stimuli? I drove home, trying to figure out how Isis and I were going to get our homework done. I considered trying to coordinate with a friend who could ride by on a bicycle or skateboard, and wondered where we could go to be sure no other bikes or skateboards would get in our way.

In any case, Civic Field was too distracting, so maybe we should start someplace more familiar. Like our driveway. I wouldn't even have to call a friend, I realized. Bicycles whizzed by our house every morning.

I woke up early the next day, eager to use those cyclists to our advantage instead of having them derail our morning walks. I harnessed Isis before taking her out front, awaiting the opportunity for her to look calmly at a bicycle and then back at me.

Isis was as unfocused in our own driveway as she had been the night before. Maybe she was confused by the new gear. Maybe I was confused about how to use it. She wouldn't sit next to me or lie down, so I guessed it was just as well that not a single bicycle passed by while we were out there.

Linda's take was that Isis had not been in a "learning state" either time, and that I shouldn't even attempt training without Isis first being able to focus on me. I also should always end on success.

"She must process success. If she processes anything else, that's what she absorbs and the behaviors you don't want will continue. Do something simple that she can accomplish successfully, end there, and then try again later."

Something simple, like sitting? What was I supposed to do if she was so stressed she couldn't even do that?

Then there was the Five-Minute Rule. After several excruciating days of my avoiding eye contact and refusing to pet her, Isis figured out that I was not going to pay attention to her if she smiled eagerly or rested her adorable head on my lap.

Resigned to entertaining herself, she picked up Squirrel Dude, a six-inch-long purple rubber squirrel with triangular stoppers around a hole at his base. When Rob and I left each day, we filled Squirrel Dude with kibble. The rubber stoppers held in the food, giving Isis a little challenge. Stuffing toys with food was a recommended way to keep dogs busy when left alone. In the wild, wolves spent most of their time looking for and eating their food. But since domestic dogs tended to scarf entire bowls of dry food before their owners finished a morning cup of coffee, they had a lot more time on their hands, which was what the experts said led to separation anxiety and torn-up furniture.

Isis had Squirrel Dude figured out. She picked him up in her mouth, then hurled him on the floor with enough force to dislodge several pellets of kibble. Again and again, she bounced Squirrel Dude off the floor. Whenever we cleaned under the couches or behind endtables, we'd find, along with grotesque balls of fur, rogue kibble that had rolled out of her reach following Squirrel Dude's tumble.

Squirrel Dude depleted, Isis gave in and lay down, which was what the Five-Minute Rule required of her, except by then, I'd lost confidence in the spirit of the assignment. Her smile was gone, leaving behind a worried face, not exactly relaxed. At the five-minute mark, I called her to me and lavished praise on her. She scrambled to her feet and wiggled under my touch.

Oh, thank goodness, I thought I had turned invisible. Did I do something wrong?

"You're a good girl, Isis, such a good girl. I missed you so much while I was out."

Isis basked in my attention, flattening her ears to her head as I kissed her temples. She still looked uneasy, as if at any moment, I might withdraw my affection again. Would Linda consider this a success? I didn't feel victorious; Isis was acting needier than ever. This exercise was supposed to get Isis to respect my authority, but I'd rather my dog know how much she was loved.

At least we could move forward to the fun part of Linda's regimen: interactive playtime. I had collected all the toys in the house, sweeping my arm under couches and dressers to recover long-forgotten chew toys coated in Isis hair. I threw these, along with some low-budget toys she'd never used, into a square footstool with a lid. The Five-Minute Rule observed, I picked up the toy box and dumped out the menagerie of stuffed animals, rubber squeakies, rope tugs, and balls on the living room floor. "Toy Time! It's Toy Time, Isis!"

Hearing my giddy announcement, a grinning Rob joined us from the computer room. Technically, according to Linda's rules, Rob had just crossed a threshold, so he was supposed to go passive until Isis lay down for five minutes to earn his attention. But there was no going back. Toy Time had commenced and Rob wanted in.

Isis's longtime favorite toys included a stuffed tree trunk with five squirrels inside; an especially durable ring with a pink and purple leopard pattern, which we called the donut; and a plush blue fish stuffed with squeaky eggs. The point of Toy Time was to give Isis fifteen minutes of playtime where she chose whichever toys she wanted. To our surprise, she singled out a white plastic squeak toy about eight inches long, in the general shape of a dog bone labeled with the words Milk-Bone in raised black letters. Isis held the Milk-Bone in her mouth while she investigated a hard orange ball, rolling it with her front paw. I hurled the Frisbee-sized donut across the living room, bouncing it off the dark brown folding doors of the linen closet before it hit the wood laminate floor.

"Isis! Get the donut, get the donut," Rob said as Isis scrambled across the room, her nails clicking on the floor. She skidded to a stop by the donut and weighed her options. Dropping the Milk-Bone, she picked up the donut so it hung over her lower canines like a pink Christmas wreath. Then she set down the donut and picked it up again, along with the Milk-Bone, and brought them both back to us, where we heaped praise upon her for her retrieving and carrying prowess.

Rob grabbed the hollow Milk-Bone from her and sat cross-legged on the area rug to play keep-away, passing the toy from hand to hand behind his back and under his legs, making Isis run circles around him. He gave her clues with a squeak here and there until she darted her pointy nose under his knee and snatched her prize out of his hand.

"Yay! You did it! Isis got the Milk-Bone! Yay, Isis!" We cheered her on and she beamed back at us.

When our fifteen minutes were up, I sing-songed, "It's over! Toy Time is over!" We put the toys away, leaving out just two for her to enjoy until next playtime.

At each consecutive Toy Time session, Isis zeroed in on the Milk-Bone and we marveled at her affection for it, with so many higher-quality toys to choose from. We had learned early on not to spend too much money because the life span was short for a dog toy in a German shepherd's mouth. Never in a million years would we have picked out a plain squeaky bone thinking it would be her favorite. We tried to rotate the toys we left out between Toy Times, but the Milk-Bone was so obviously the one she loved the most. We confiscated it when we watched TV, because we couldn't hear over the squeak-squeak-squeaking.

The incessant serenade paused when she accidentally dislodged the noisemaking apparatus. I happened to have a spare, because the toy had come as part of a doggie gift set Quin gave to both Isis and my mother's dog for Christmas. My mom's shih tzu, Millie (adopted after Barney died), didn't play with toys, so Mom gave me hers. I retrieved the Milk-Bone from Millie's gift set in the garage, thinking Isis would reject the first toy for a functioning one. Instead, Isis held both toys in her mouth, one in the traditional way a dog holds a bone, the other sticking out like a white plastic bone-shaped cigar. She looked at us, brown eyes expectant, wanting to play with us, but not willing to part with the toys. She squeezed her mountain range of white teeth around the silent toy, releasing quiet puffs of air until she manipulated the squeaker back into place, giving the toy voice a while longer.

★★★

I appreciated the real-life nature of Linda's training method. Classes like the one in Seattle were useless because it didn't matter whether Isis could behave in a controlled environment unless she could transfer what she learned to our walks through the neighborhood. Linda called that "generalizing." Isis couldn't yet generalize that if leashed dogs were safe to be around in a classroom, they also were safe to encounter on a walk.

"Getting her to generalize requires going to new places and having a long history of keeping her safe and non-reactive," Linda said. "If she doesn't see you as her anchor in a scary environment, she will lose focus and not pay attention."

That much was clear at the beginning of our second session. We met at the local cemetery, which I thought was an odd choice, but apparently Linda worked with dogs there a lot. Unlike the asphalt of the Civic Field parking lot, the cemetery lawn was rife with alluring smells. Isis pressed her snout to the ground and snuffled voraciously, ignoring my request to sit. Before we could begin our lesson, Isis had to greet Linda properly because a solid meet-and-greet would set her up for all future interaction with humans. I was supposed to have her sit beside me, about five feet away from Linda. When Isis was calm and put her attention on me, I'd say, "Go say hello," and walk with her to Linda, who would put out a flat hand for her to touch, or if Isis was really lucky, give her a treat.

Since Isis was too distracted to perform a proper meet-and-greet, Linda said, "Let's let her be a dog for a few minutes, since this is a new environment."

While Isis familiarized herself with the grass and dirt and everything else she could find within an inch of the ground, I noticed that a popular hiking trail ran behind the cemetery. Her survey complete, Isis remembered I was on the other end of her leash and greeted Linda like a lady.

"Make sure whenever you are practicing that Isis is ready to meet someone," Linda said. "Otherwise, you could be setting her up for failure."

We moved on to obstacle work. Linda had set up cones and Hula Hoops near some trees just outside a black fence that cordoned off a Jewish cemetery from the rest of the graves. Isis and I hadn't entirely found our groove yet, and we knocked over a couple of orange cones the first few times. Isis again became completely fascinated with individual blades of grass beneath her feet.

"Guess she wasn't done being a dog," I said.

"No, this is something different," Linda said. "Sniffing is a stress signal. By turning away from you and sniffing, she's letting us know she's not comfortable. You need to learn to read these signals before she has a reaction."

Her authoritative tone made me feel a little stupid. There was so much to keep track of. If sometimes Isis sniffed because she's a dog, and sometimes it was a stress signal, how was I supposed to know the difference? Some stress signals were obvious, like baring teeth and raising the fur between the shoulders, but Linda told me about others I hadn't been aware of, like a full body shake, lip licking, and yawning. And apparently, sniffing.

I redirected Isis to our next task: a complicated configuration where I had to lead her from a center cone around four others laid out in the shape of a square. We executed this one more deftly than the straight weave.

"Well done! That one is harder to master," Linda said. "I'm impressed with your ability to work as a team."

I stroked Isis's head and she smiled, our confidence boosted at having completed an advanced task. Then, Isis closed her mouth, alert to something in the distance. A loose golden retriever ran beside a man on a bicycle.

My eyes widened, panicked. *What do we do? What if the dog runs up to us?*

Linda saw the approaching threat and opened the black gate to a grassy area beside the Jewish cemetery. "Let's move behind the fence. Click and treat her for looking calmly."

I led Isis behind the gate, not bothering to ask her to sit. No time for that. She looked at the loose dog and I clicked, causing her to whip her head toward me to take the piece of freeze-dried liver, her teeth scraping across my finger. She looked back toward the pair rounding the path just on the other side of the fence, as I reached into my fanny pack for another treat and clicked again. Isis looked back to me and practically took my finger along with the treat. By the time the man and dog were out of sight, my index finger was bleeding. I wiped the cut with my thumb, hoping Linda wouldn't notice. Taking a treat hard was another stress signal.

Bloody finger or not, I was thrilled with our success. Isis had not barked at the cyclist and dog, her two biggest challenges. Job well done.

★★★

The best way to control Isis's head, and therefore her attention, Linda said, was with a head halter. The Halti brand had a strap that stretched over the nose, supposedly having a calming effect, and the leash attached under the chin. I couldn't just shove a Halti on Isis's face and expect her to like it, though. I had to get her used to it by holding out a treat and having her put her nose through the loop to get the reward. Once Isis was comfortably sticking her nose in, I could clasp it and leave it on for ten seconds while giving her treats. Then twenty seconds. Thirty. Up to ten minutes before she was ready to train with it.

Isis adapted to the Halti fairly quickly. Since I couldn't safely walk her around the whole neighborhood, I drove her to the small park-and-ride at the end of the block, where we'd be less likely to be ambushed by a bicycle or another dog. We walked laps around the parking lot, and with one end of her leash clipped to the Halti and the other connected to her pink harness between her shoulders, Isis stuck right beside me.

Tra la. Lovely day for a walk.

"Seriously, Isis? This is all it took? We could have been using this all along instead of that awful pinch collar?"

I couldn't believe it. For two years, I'd searched desperately for a solution to the leash-pulling. Nothing worked, and I felt like a complete failure at dog training because I thought I'd tried everything. Sure, I'd seen these head halters before, but never dreamed one would make such a drastic improvement. Isis had to bite someone in order for us to find a trainer who gave me the answer.

I asked Isis to sit, then swapped out her Halti for a twenty-foot lead to practice her emergency recall. I let her wander out to the end of the leash before calling her back to me. She was sniffing overgrown weeds at the edge of the small patch of asphalt when I saw a bicycle round the corner. Isis saw it too. I remembered Linda's instructions to deal with oncoming distractions: run backward and give Isis a cue that meant something fun was going to happen.

"Isis! Party time!" I trotted backward, still facing the bicycle, and Isis bounded to me with an open-mouthed smile, completely unconcerned about the bike.

"Yes! That's my girl!" I rewarded Isis with a jackpot of several treats.

What a miracle this positive reinforcement was. I thought back to our miserable experiences at Firgrove, all those frustrating and confusing training sessions. Thanks to Linda, Isis was making progress, finally.

I actually looked forward to our lessons because Linda provided structure as well as mental and physical stimulation for Isis. The work left me feeling proud and encouraged. After each session, Isis smiled and panted on the drive home and slept the rest of the day, alleviating my guilt over not being able to walk her, or take her to the park, or even play with her very long because it was so damn cold and dark in our backyard.

Our next training session was held at the home base of Linda's operation, the Island County Fairgrounds. I took a day off work to drive the two and a half hours there. The grassy fields and stables were otherwise empty, and we worked inside a plain-looking 4-H building with linoleum floors. Linda wanted to reenact the scene in which Isis bit Frank, so I sat at a table as though it were my desk and had Isis lie beside me. Isis was not fooled in the slightest. Not only did she already know Linda, but she also already knew Linda was in the building. Perhaps the idea was for me to practice what I'd do the next time someone walked by while Isis was sleeping under my desk. For this simulation, Isis lay happily at my feet, gently taking treats from my hand like she didn't have a care in the world.

"This is just one piece," Linda said. "We will replicate the incident more and make it more challenging for her. Prevention and management are going to be the key to keeping her successful."

Right. If I bring her to the office, I'll be sure to close the door and tie her to the desk.

We moved on to a dog scenario. After three sessions, Isis showed fewer stress signals as Dakota moved closer, so Linda decided she was ready to meet her other Belgian Malinois, Duke. She instructed me to stand in the middle of the room with Isis. After Linda brought Duke in, I'd have Isis perform simple tasks like sit, down, and touching the palm of my hand when I said, "Touch." This would show Isis that she was capable of functioning in the presence of another dog. While Linda got Duke from the car, I warmed up by asking Isis to sit and touch.

After nosing my hand and swallowing the reward, Isis stood up.

"Isis, sit."

Still standing slightly in front of me, she whimpered a few times before letting out a worried high-pitched bark. The two of us were alone. Her shrieks escalated in volume and echoed off the 4-H room's walls as I tried to keep my own body relaxed. When Isis reacted, I was supposed to go completely passive until she calmed down, but she wasn't calming down. She pointed her nose to the ceiling, sounding her desperate, terrified alarm.

I took deep breaths and braced myself for Duke's entrance.

When the door opened, Linda was alone. "That was enough of a scenario, so I put Duke back in the truck."

"What happened?" I asked. "She couldn't see him, how did she know he was coming?"

"She heard him. We were about ten feet from the door when she started barking. That wasn't just an alert that someone was coming. That was a very intense reaction and shows a lot of insecurity."

My ears still rang from the barking. Disappointed for the scenario to end so soon, I felt like Isis and I had failed. Last time, she'd been calm when she could see Dakota twenty feet away, so I couldn't wrap my head around the severity of her reaction to a dog outside that she couldn't even see. From the tenor of her voice, I could tell how afraid she'd been, and a new understanding of Isis started to take shape.

A barking and lunging dog strikes most people as vicious or mean, and a dog who bites is considered aggressive. But on this day, Isis had shown me how deeply her aggression was rooted in fear.

"A fearful reaction like that can turn quickly into anger," Linda said.

"What am I supposed to do when that happens?"

"Our goal is to keep her below threshold. Once she's having a reaction, she's in hindbrain and all you can do is stay neutral. In this case, we had to remove the stimulus." Hindbrain referred to Isis's state of mind when she was mid-reaction, overstimulated, and operating on instinct. In hindbrain, she was too far gone to listen to me, or even remember that I was there.

"We'll try it again sometime," Linda continued. "Let's move on to something else so we can end on success." She pulled out a plush red squeaky ball. "This is a present for Isis."

Linda set out two identical cups and placed a treat under one of them while Isis watched. Then she put the red squeaky ball on top of one of the cups. Isis was supposed to figure out that the treats were under the cup with the red squeaky ball on top. She nailed it every time. Mental enrichment games like this were more stimulating to a dog than heavy exercise, Linda said.

I wondered who measured that and how, but was happy to have something else to do to entertain Isis inside.

If Linda wasn't discouraged about Isis's reaction to Duke, then I wouldn't be either. Maybe Isis wasn't cured yet, but at least I'd found a specialist who could help get her there.

Chapter 8: Meet and Greet

When we bought our house a few months before Isis came into our lives, we planned to construct a steel building in our backyard for Rob's martial arts club, where he could cultivate training partners and make use of the vast array of martial arts and fitness equipment he'd acquired over the years. As is the case with most home-improvement projects, the process took much longer than anticipated. We finally broke ground when Isis was about two years old. She handled the disruption better than I expected. I imagined having to stay home with her every day to keep her from standing at the back door and barking nonstop at the construction workers, but she got used to them. She barked when they first arrived for the day, then settled down once she saw what they were up to.

Even though the site preparation completely altered the landscape of her backyard paradise, she was happy as long as she had a soccer ball. We tore out a cluster of juniper bushes at the base of the yard, and chopped down some of the alders that buffered us from the adjacent freeway. Because of the slope of the yard, we had to bring in heavy equipment to dig up the earth at the top and fill in dirt at the bottom. The junipers and lawn were replaced with three levels of dirt bound by large stone retaining walls resembling a castle. To get the machinery in, we tore down the fence between our yard and the house next door, the one rented by college students. The fence hadn't been completely enclosed anyway; it ran the length of our yard nearly to the back corner of our house, leaving about a five-foot gap.

Despite her checkered past at the dog park, Isis had a friendly history with the dogs that lived next door. Our first neighbor dogs were a pair of mastiffs who poked their noses through rotten fence boards and sometimes wandered around to our side of the fence. The summer before the fence came down, Rob and I left Isis out back sometimes while we exercised in the garage with the door open. Between workout sets, I'd peek out the laundry room window to see Isis lying happily in the sunshine. Pretty soon, Isis discovered she could walk around the creek side of the house and find us in the garage. Once, she trotted into the garage with a golden retriever, the neighbor dog at the time, in tow.

Chloe, these are my parents.

"Isis, you have a friend over?" Laughing, I led the buff-colored dog to the house next door, where her owner was quite surprised to learn that our dogs had a playdate.

During the major earthmoving, orange-and-black mesh barriers were staked around the construction site, not that they kept Isis out. Rob liked to punt the soccer ball for Isis to leap over the barrier, skidding across the exposed dirt. One afternoon after the fence was gone, Rob took a break from playing with Isis to check on something inside. Left unsupervised, Isis leapt the barrier to visit Chloe, who was hanging out with her people in the yard next door.

"Isis!" Rob called her when he came back outside, but she did not return, so he climbed over the mounds of earth to get her.

As he told me the story later, Rob's dark eyes were disappointed and he sounded frustrated. Maybe even angry, like Isis had done something deliberately bad. Since I wasn't there to read Isis's body language, I don't know what exactly happened, but when he reached for her collar to lead her away, she got snarly with Chloe, who ran in the house. Isis tried to go inside after her, which I think is what embarrassed Rob the most. At least no one got hurt.

The setback ended a long streak of exemplary behavior on Isis's part. Since her freakout at the fairgrounds with Duke, she'd had negligible outbursts during our training sessions and I'd managed to protect her from all scary things on our walks. Mindful of the bright side of every mishap, I decided maybe this was a good thing to happen on Rob's watch. Surely this had taught him to be more vigilant.

But it broke my heart whenever I thought he was mad at Isis.

"She snarls when she's afraid, she's not trying to be bad or mean to the other dog," I said. "This is why we're doing all this training, to teach her that we will keep her safe no matter what. It's not her job to keep us safe."

I left unspoken the fact that he had failed to keep her safe by leaving her alone out back.

★★★

One evening, Rob asked his friend Paul to come over and help with his computer. Whenever people came over, I was overwhelmed with anxiety about what Isis would do. She barked like crazy when they came to the front door, and if I tried to hold her back, she barked and lunged more fiercely, like a fighting dog desperate to get to its opponent. Classic barrier frustration, Linda explained. I remembered the term from when I first started researching leash aggression. Arousal in dogs can spiral out of control when there's a barrier between them and the thing that's arousing them. From the dog's point of view, a leash is a barrier.

Since Linda hadn't yet trained us how to welcome visitors into our home, I decided to try a meet-and-greet with Paul in the driveway. I took Isis out front to practice our eye contact drill. When she looked at me, I clicked and handed her a treat. I varied the length of time she needed to hold my gaze. Five seconds. Click. Treat. Seven seconds. Click. Treat. Three seconds. Click. Treat.

Paul's enormous SUV arrived. I expected him to park near the tree at the bottom of our driveway, like everyone else always did, but he pulled all the way up, right between Rob's car and mine. I backed Isis up near the garage door, but the strange car was too close.

Isis rumbled and barked, lunging toward Paul, a fairly big guy, as he exited the vehicle. I mentally aborted the meet-and-greet plan, but Paul smiled and moved toward us. Rob opened the front door. I waved Paul away as nonchalantly as I could while maintaining a grip on my ferocious dog. "Just go on inside."

I stayed with Isis in the driveway, expecting her to calm down, but she didn't. She let out several high-pitched, stressed barks. *Did you see that guy? What's he doing in there with Dad?*

Frustrated and embarrassed, all I could do was hustle Isis through the house and unleash her in the backyard, where she completely forgot about the danger inside and turned her attention to the soccer ball. A few minutes later, Rob and Paul stepped onto the back patio where Isis barely registered the presence of a guest.

"Guess we should stick to the plan of having her greet all visitors out back," I said to Rob before the men returned inside.

The backyard hadn't been my first choice that evening, because recent rains left it slick with mud. By the time Isis was ready to come in, her legs and the entire underside of her belly were coated in muck. We went directly into the bathroom where she hopped dutifully into the tub. Isis had grown to love baths, and seemed to know when she needed one. She didn't automatically jump in the tub every time we came in from the yard, just when she was particularly dirty.

I tried to rinse her belly, but she twisted and squirmed in a frenetic effort to eat the water spraying out of the handheld showerhead. I cleaned best as I could, accidentally dousing myself as well, and then wondered what would happen when I let her out of the bathroom.

This is the sort of thing that owners of normal dogs don't think twice about. Before Isis bit Frank, I wouldn't have either. Isis was so friendly most of the time, and Paul wasn't a stranger. But what if she forgot he was there? What if he walked by at the exact moment I opened the bathroom door, and she attacked him?

I toweled her off and held her collar lightly as I slowly opened the bathroom door. The door to the computer room was closed, but I didn't want to risk having Paul come out and surprise Isis. I opened the door and led her into the room where she could see Paul sitting beside Rob. She sniffed Paul cheerfully, then followed me into the TV room where I sat anxiously until Paul left, and I knew for sure we were safe.

About a week later, Rob invited our friend Manis to come see the impressive progress on the studio. The blue steel building loomed over our house from its pedestal atop castle walls. At 2,100 square feet, Rob's exercise room was larger than our house. The concrete floor was bare and much work remained on the electrical and water connections, but completion was in sight and Rob was eager to show the building off.

Isis had met Manis, a six-foot-plus Haitian-American, many times, and usually wound up licking his ears at some point during each visit, but she barked ferociously at him when he came to the door, just like she did with everyone else except Rob's parents. Because the meet-and-greet with Paul had been such a failure, I took Isis out back and played with her until Manis arrived. Rob and Manis passed uneventfully by us on their way up the stone steps to the building. Isis and I went inside, and when Rob and Manis came back in the house, Isis blinked at him, but looked otherwise unconcerned.

"Now we basically ignore her until she lies down quietly for five minutes," I said.

The three of us sat in front of the TV and within ten minutes, Isis settled down on the rug, squeaking away on her Milk-Bone toy. I called her to me and lavished attention on her, holding out my hand and asking her to touch. I clicked as soon as her nose touched my palm, and gave her a treat.

Rob held out his hand. "Isis, touch!" I clicked when she touched Rob's palm.

"Here, Manis," I said. "Hold your palm out flat." I pointed to Manis's hand and said, "Isis, touch!"

Isis looked at me askance. *Wait. Whose hand do you want me to touch?*

I nodded again toward Manis's hand and she tentatively jutted her head forward to nudge him with her nose. Click. "Good girl! Isis, you are so smart." Rob and I cheered and Isis basked in our praise. We took turns letting Isis touch our palms, laughing and cheering her on.

"Man, I want to get a dog," Manis said.

My heart soared. Nothing could have gratified me more than to have someone acknowledge how wonderful Isis was. Linda's training hadn't changed our relationship with Isis, but instead made it possible for her to have relationships with other people. After her aggression escalated, I worried our friends might witness an outburst and be terrified of her. I wouldn't blame them. To see Isis bare her teeth and lunge was to fear her. Even if they weren't afraid of her, they might judge us for not being able to control her.

But here was Manis, who several times had been on the other end of Isis's fearsome bark. He didn't think she was crazy or vicious. He envied us for having her. That kind of feedback was the inspiration I needed to keep going.

★★★

From the time I left Los Angeles several years earlier, my mother visited me two or three times a year, staying with me wherever I lived, in whatever city. Chicago, Washington, D.C., Prague, Olympia, and now Bellingham. Our household dynamic shifted very slightly, as is natural, once I started living with Rob, but he and I made a point to buy a house with a guest room for my mother. She drove to Bellingham with a van full of my things in time for moving day. For his part, Rob was always perfectly easygoing about my mother's visits.

The family addition that really complicated things was Isis.

My mother had made clear that she was afraid of large dogs, German shepherds in particular, since the day we brought Isis home. I had a hard time taking this phobia seriously when Isis weighed twelve pounds, but by the time she was two years old and biting people, I was more understanding. I didn't tell Mom that Isis bit Frank, at great effort considering I always told her everything. I almost let it slip a few times, but she'd never feel safe with Isis if she knew. I made sure Rob and Alice never brought it up in Mom's presence either, not that it was a frequent topic of conversation.

During Mom's first visit after we'd started training with Linda, I was eager to show off our new techniques. We'd finally learned how to keep Isis from rushing the front door. When the doorbell rang, she still barked, but was learning to go to her bed and wait patiently for the guest to enter. We practiced this a lot with Rob's parents, which was excruciating for her. She had a special melancholy cry when she had to wait to greet Alice.

Grandma is right over there. Why can't I say hello? She might leave if I don't let her know right this second how happy I am to see her.

Isis struggled to contain herself and had to be asked to go to her bed multiple times before I allowed her to say hello to Grandma. We kept a cookie jar of bone-shaped biscuits on the bookcase by the front door. I used these to reward Isis for staying on her bed, and Grandma (or whoever was visiting) rewarded her for saying hello nicely.

I explained this procedure to my mother on the way home from the airport, then asked her to wait outside the front door while I got Isis to lie on her bed

"Good girl, Isis. Stay."

I opened the front door, handed Mom a biscuit, and showed her where to stand next to the bookcase. Mom stepped tentatively inside and stood on her mark, shifting from one foot to the other. Breaking a biscuit in half, I walked over to Isis and handed her a piece. "Good girl, Isis. Okay, Mom, now hold your hand out flat with the cookie. Isis … say hello!"

Isis scrambled over to my mother and eagerly took the biscuit from her hand. *I remember you. You sleep in that room next to the library.*

My mother squealed. "Oooh, I felt her teeth."

Isis circled Mom and trotted back to me, where I gave her the other half of the biscuit.

"She used her teeth, really? Did it seem like she took the treat hard?"

"No, it wasn't like she bit me." Mom wiped her hand on her pant leg. "But I didn't like having those huge teeth against my hand."

Damn, I'd planned to do this exercise every time Mom entered the house. Revising my strategy, I showed Mom where we kept the biscuits and encouraged her to carry a few at all times. Anytime Isis was near her, she could ask Isis to sit or lie down, and throw a cookie. Since Isis was a pro at catching, this would be a fun game for everyone.

Unfortunately, it resulted in Isis lurking and staring at Mom in hopes another cookie would rain from the sky, making Mom nervous. I was disheartened. Not only did I have to create an environment where Isis felt safe around my mother, I had the added pressure of making sure Mom felt safe from Isis.

The next day, I watched a news program with Isis at my feet while Mom took a shower. When Mom crossed from the guest bathroom through the library to her room, I praised Isis for her complete relaxation. She was lying down with her chin outstretched and her eyes open. A few minutes later, Isis's ear twitched at the creak of my mother's bedroom door opening.

As Mom moved back through the library, she started to ask me a question from across the house. At the sound of Mom's voice, Isis was on her feet and bolting toward her, barking. My heart stopped as the memory of Isis attacking Frank melded in my mind with an image of her biting my mother.

"Isis! No!" I raced after her.

My mother froze and Isis must have reconsidered her attack because by the time I reached them, she was sniffing Mom's pant legs.

"She didn't bite you, did she?"

"No," Mom said in a very calm, low voice. "It felt like she put a paw on my leg, but I'm not hurt."

Knowing all too well what the worst-case scenario might have been, I nearly fainted from the closeness of that call. My nearly sixty-five-year-old mother would not have been as understanding as Frank if Isis had bitten her.

I tried to steady my heart and figure out what the hell just happened. Based on my training with Linda, my response to the incident should have been to "go passive," but I wasn't going to let Mom think I let Isis get away with charging houseguests. I called Isis a bad dog and put her out back.

Totally rattled, I returned to Mom. "Are you all right?"

For someone with a lifelong fear of being attacked by a German shepherd, my mother was amazingly unruffled, while I was on the verge of falling apart. But then, my mother didn't know Isis's bite history.

After we all had a chance to get our heart rates down, I let Isis back inside and asked Mom to give her another cookie. "Go say hi!" Isis did. I hoped that meant we were all friends again.

I sat down at my laptop on the kitchen table to e-mail Linda while the details were fresh in my mind. Mom sat beside me and Isis poked her nose in her lap. *Hey, do you have any more of those bone-shaped cookies?* I stood and moved between my mother and my dog. Linda called this "splitting." I had to do it a few times until Isis lost interest and went in the other room.

As I returned to the table, the gentle strains of dulcimer music tinkled from the library. At Linda's suggestion, I had set a timer in the room where Isis hung out the most. Every day at noon, the CD player clicked on, playing meditation music I bought in Thailand. Isis never mentioned whether she found the music of Chamras Saewataporn soothing or not, but whenever I was home to hear it, the eleven-minute opening song, *Journey on the Earth*, floated in my heart, reminding me of the first time I heard it playing from a CD stand in a Bangkok skytrain terminal. I tried to let the sweeping, dreamlike tones wash over me and take me back to an easier time. Hearing the music made me long to curl up and take a nap with Isis on her favorite couch.

I was completely mystified about what prompted Isis to behave aggressively toward Mom, but Linda thought it was "crystal clear." Isis's ear twitch was a sign of what she was about to do. An eyebrow raise was another common signal, she said, especially in herding dogs. How stupid had I been? When I saw Isis's ear twitch, I actually thought, *Oh good, she hears that noise and she's not troubled by it.*

I hadn't made the connection how similar the scenario was to that day at my office. Isis was lying down. I was sitting. Someone approached.

Unfortunately, recognizing a pattern didn't give me any insight to prevent Isis from ever doing it again. I asked Linda how to handle the rest of Mom's visit.

"Think about why Isis likes your mother-in-law and see if you can give your mom a few tips in that regard," she said. "Maybe have her toss a ball for Isis."

First of all, Isis didn't "like" Alice. She adored her! And why? Because Alice doted on her like a human grandchild. My mother would never feel that way about Isis. She couldn't even bear to hand-feed her treats. But throwing a ball? She probably could manage that. Everyone loved playing soccer with Isis.

I invited Mom to sit beside me in the beige plastic Adirondack chairs in the backyard. Isis dropped her half-flat mud- and slobber-coated soccer ball at our feet.

"Kick it," I said.

Isis zeroed in on the ball and Mom's foot, clad in a black ballet flat. I mentally willed my dog not to lunge for the ball before Mom kicked. Mom swung her foot against the ball, which didn't travel far—its deflatedness hampered its aerodynamics—but Isis snapped at it, catching it with supernatural speed, before dropping it again at our feet.

"Wow, Isis, you're fast," Mom said.

"That's nothing." I picked up the ball and flipped it high in the air. Isis leapt vertically and caught it before twisting backwards. "If we throw it just right, we can get her to back-flip." I gave a few more throws to demonstrate.

Mom smiled and clapped. The beauty of Isis's love of soccer was twofold. One was her extraordinary athleticism, the way she leapt to catch the ball at its apex, apparently unaware that it would come down to her level on its own. The way she seemed to have springs in her legs, jumping and flipping and spinning before each landing. And two, her absolute joy while playing. The devotion she felt toward the ball translated directly to the person playing with her. She lay down on the grass, tongue hanging out and eyes shining as she gazed at Mom.

If you kick me that ball, I'll be your best friend.

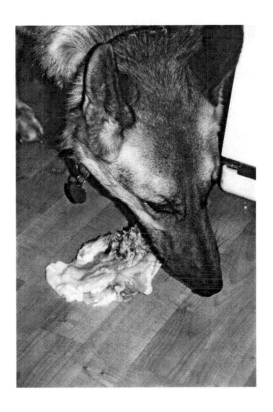

Chapter 9: Raw Meat and Root Canals

In the late spring, the weather was dry and warm enough to train outside at the Island County Fairgrounds. We practiced scenarios with Linda's dogs and a "stranger," played by one of Linda's other students who dropped by to help with Isis's training. Also, an actual strange man rode by unexpectedly on a bike, and I managed to keep Isis successful the whole time. Even a pack of bunnies bouncing around on the grass didn't derail her.

"You are becoming a true team leader and Isis is keeping her focus on you," Linda said. "Keep up the good work."

Linda and I both beamed at the end of the session, and so did Isis. *That's right, my mom and I are a great team. We did an awesome job today.*

As I drove the winding highway home, Isis sat on the passenger seat and I stroked her chest. She panted and smiled, revealing her lower teeth. I had noticed for a while that her canines—the tallest fang-like teeth—had lost some of their sharpness. At a stoplight, I looked more closely and saw that the lower left fang was completely squared on top, as though the pointy part had been sliced off. The whole tooth was a pinkish gray and a ring had appeared in the center, like the rings used to count the age of a downed tree. Her three other canines had a similar appearance, but only the one had changed color.

I took her to the vet, where she was perfectly well behaved (after I made sure there were no other animals in the waiting room). We saw Dr. Wendy, who confirmed that this tooth was either dead or dying, and might need a root canal because extraction was not the best solution. As big as Isis's canines were, a lot of tooth remained under the gum surface, like an iceberg. Dr. Wendy had extracted a canine the day before, and described it as an extremely involved and difficult procedure. She didn't perform root canals, anyway, and referred me to a veterinary specialist just north of Seattle.

"We're very lucky," Dr. Wendy said. "There are only a few board-certified veterinary dentists in the country and two of them are a married couple in Shoreline."

Lucky me, my two-year-old dog needed a root canal.

"How does this kind of thing happen?" I asked.

Dr. Wendy asked if Isis chewed on rocks.

"Not that I know of."

"Tennis balls? Dogs can wear their teeth down by chewing on tennis balls, because the surface is really quite rough."

"No, she hasn't chewed on tennis balls since she was a baby. Soccer balls, though, she loves soccer balls."

"That's probably it," Dr. Wendy said.

I didn't see how. Isis didn't chew on the balls for hours at a time, just carried them around in her mouth when she was outside.

I never heard of a dog's teeth eroding like that, and so young! Naturally the Internet was full of such stories and warnings of the hazards of leaving a dying tooth untreated. A dog root canal was likely to be an expensive endeavor. But what was I going to do, not get Isis the best dental care? She would need those teeth for many years to come.

I wanted to schedule the procedure as soon as possible. First Isis had to have a consultation with the Shoreline vet dentist, and the first opening was a week away. At least Isis didn't show any signs of discomfort from the worn-down tooth, but surely this signified a deeper problem. Could it be a nutritional deficiency? A lack of calcium? We'd always fed Isis the expensive dry food from the pet store. Nothing you could get at the regular grocery store. For a while, we fed her a chicken-and-rice blend until she lost interest and started leaving the bowl untouched. We switched to a herring-flavored kibble, which she seemed to enjoy, but maybe this dental problem was a sign we should feed her something else entirely.

Linda mentioned at least once every time I saw her that she fed her dogs a diet of raw meat. Although she'd never flat-out said I should do the same, I could tell she was a big believer in the health benefits. In her earliest correspondence, she suggested that Isis's behavioral problems could be nutritionally based, stopping short of telling me not to feed her kibble. She must have been waiting for just the right moment to go into full proselytizing mode, a time when I faced something serious enough to consider feeding my dog whole raw chickens. And tripe. Organs.

All I had to do was ask, "Do you think there's something wrong with Isis's nutrition that would result in her teeth eroding like this?" And Linda e-mailed me a long list of the vitamins a dog needs and how best to feed them. I knew Linda well enough by this point to have expected nothing less.

I'd been a vegetarian for nearly ten years and never dreamed of feeding raw meat to my dog. But my research (and Linda's) told me that raw-fed dogs shed less, had better-smelling breath, smaller poops, and shinier coats. Some people credited raw diets with curing all kinds of ailments, including allergies and itchy skin. Isis did seem to chew on her legs an awful lot. Could that be the cause of her eroded teeth? Friction of her fur against her teeth? The benefits of raw feeding started to outweigh my squeamishness.

Linda assured me, "Everyone is squeamish at first, but once you make the transition and feed your carnivore the way she should be fed, you will never turn back."

She had a point. I didn't eat meat because I felt bad for the animals, but the most animal-friendly thing I could do for my own critter was to feed her a diet as close to nature as possible. That's how I rationalized it, anyway.

Chicken was the generally agreed-upon choice of starter meat, because it was comparatively mild to the dog's stomach and easy to acquire. Linda's instructions for raw feeding were as overwhelming as her training homework assignments. So much to keep track of. She suggested a prey model, based on the idea that dogs in the wild (i.e. wolves) eat whole animals, so we want to feed our dogs the equivalent of Franken-prey: eighty percent meat, ten percent bones, ten percent organs.

No need to worry about all that at first, just hand the dog a chicken drumstick and see what she does.

Isis took the drumstick from my hand and worked the meatiest part between her jaws, the bone sticking out of her mouth. Within the first minute or so, she crunched through the bone, breaking down the structure of the drumstick so the whole thing fit in her mouth. Crunch. Crunch.

"Isn't that going to hurt her teeth?" Rob asked.

"It's not supposed to."

"I thought chicken bones were bad for dogs."

"Cooked chicken bones can splinter, causing them to choke, but raw bones are quite soft."

Isis swallowed the ball of raw chicken and bone and looked at me eagerly. *More please?*

"Sorry, Smiley Bird, we're supposed to ease into it a little at a time. Don't want to upset your tummy."

Isis loved the raw chicken, which gave us vicarious pleasure. She no longer left a single morsel of her food uneaten, and started waking me up earlier and earlier, standing beside the bed expressing a new vocabulary that cracked us up each morning.

"Arrrawwr Rooowwwwwrrrrooo." *Chicken! It's time for chicken! I want chicken. Chickennnnnnn.*

"Listen to that," I said. "That's her voice."

Rob and I lay in bed, listening to the musicality of our dog's plea. More than a whimper or a whine, her sound had tonal quality different from the growls and barks that seemed to originate in her chest.

"It is her voice," Rob agreed. "Those are words."

After a short time on the raw diet, Isis's coat looked shinier, and I knew we'd made the right decision for her health. Feeding a raw-meat diet was somewhat controversial; plenty of veterinarians still advised against it because of bacteria like salmonella. I sided with the raw enthusiasts who said dogs weren't susceptible to the foodborne illnesses people get. After all, humans are the only species in nature that eat cooked meat. Every other carnivore eats a raw diet.

Now that I'd given the matter some thought, I could not believe that a processed kibble diet was healthier for dogs than eating whole meat, organs, and bones, as their ancestors did.

★★★

The only advantage to not being able to have Isis's dental work done right away was that I had time to buy a pet medical insurance policy. I considered pet insurance when Isis was a puppy, but the premiums seemed expensive and she'd hardly been to the vet since her spay operation. Now, with the prospect of expensive procedures in the future, I revisited the concept. Maybe a thirty-dollar-per-month insurance policy would reimburse me enough to be a worthwhile expense. Might as well try it and see.

Board-certified veterinary dentist Dr. Bowman thought Isis probably needed a root canal, but wouldn't know for sure until she X-rayed her mouth. I offered my theory about poor nutrition being a cause, but the dentist didn't buy it. Actually, she had no interest in diagnosing the cause, just treating the existing condition. She also was suspicious of an upper canine and a worn-down lower front tooth. That lower tooth concerned me a year earlier, but Dr. Wendy had told me not to

worry about it. I hadn't made the connection between the
worn-down tooth and Isis's eroded canines until Dr. Bowman
said the lower incisor probably should be extracted.

Extracted? Leaving a gap in Isis's beautiful smile?

I hoped that wouldn't be necessary. I'd already decided
that extracting any of her canines was not an option. If necessary, we would have them capped. Unfortunately, I'd learned
that dog dentists didn't cap teeth with the same tooth-colored
material used on human teeth. If we wanted to restore Isis's
canines to their former pointed glory, we'd have to cap them
in silver. I couldn't decide which would cheapen Isis's beauty
more: worn-down canines or a shiny grill. Rob voted in favor
of the gangsta-rap metal caps, but he wasn't taking the cost
into consideration. One root canal cost more than a thousand
dollars. If, on top of that, we capped that canine, we'd have to
cap the other three to match.

In all likelihood, a root canal would suffice, but first, Isis
had to be anesthetized and X-rayed. Assuming endodontics
were necessary, Dr. Bowman would perform the work right
away. Isis had general anesthesia once before, when she was
spayed. Anesthesia was no big deal, I tried to convince myself,
but I was terrified of something going wrong. I pictured Isis
lying unconscious on an operating table with tubes coming
out of her mouth. Could vet anesthesiologists be as conscientious as people doctors?

On the day of the surgery, we had to check in by seven
thirty, which meant leaving the house at six a.m. I checked
Isis in at the front desk where Camille, a young blonde in
pale green scrubs, went over the estimated cost of the procedure. At minimum, the X-rays and dental cleaning would
cost about $800. (Were there people who paid $800 for yearly
dental cleanings for their dogs?) On the high end, a root canal

could cost $1,400. I signed the estimate, and Camille told me to expect Dr. Bowman to call in an hour or so, after she had a look at the X-rays.

As Camille led Isis away, my dog turned back to look at me, eyes round and ears flat against her head. *Wait, where am I going? Mom?*

I had to turn away before my heart shattered. At the sound of Isis's high-pitched whine, I rushed to the exit. *She'll be fine. She'll be fine. Dogs have dental work every day.* If dogs were dying right and left during routine procedures, I would have heard something about it. I would have found cautionary tales when I Internet-searched terms like: *Dog deaths under anesthesia* and *Dr. Bowman complaints lawsuits.*

I contemplated hanging out in the waiting room, but since Isis would be in surgery for hours, it made more sense for me to go to work. My chest felt empty and I chewed my lower lip during the hour-long drive to my office.

My poor little girl. She thinks I abandoned her.

I held my phone on my lap, even though it was still too soon for Dr. Bowman to call. At the office, I carried my phone with me to the bathroom to make sure I didn't miss the call. I didn't get any work done, just stared at my phone until finally it rang.

"Isis is doing great," were Dr. Bowman's first words. That was nice, very reassuring of her to address my fear that Isis might have dropped dead on the table. Dr. Bowman continued: As she expected, the lower incisor needed to be pulled. Rob wasn't going to be happy; our child was going to have a gap in her teeth. That wasn't even the worst news. Not only did Isis's lower left canine need a root canal, so did the upper right canine.

"Can you go ahead and do both of them today?"

"No, there's not enough time today."

Maybe I shouldn't have scheduled Isis's appointment for a Friday, when the office closed at two.

Dr. Bowman said they'd call when Isis was out of surgery, around noon. I was already in my car headed there when I received the call. "I'll be there in half an hour," I told the male tech on the other end of the line.

"Oh, all right." The tech sounded surprised. "Well, she's still recovering from the anesthesia, but she might be ready to go by then."

Dr. Bowman apparently left immediately following the procedure; I never even saw her. When I got there, Camille handed me copies of the X-rays and diagrams of the procedures Isis had undergone. Then she revealed the adjusted bill. Isis had needed more X-rays than anticipated and they'd used more anesthesia, driving the price above the high estimate by a few hundred dollars. I scanned the itemized expenses, stunned by the cost of a single root canal, knowing I would have to pay the same for a second one. I understood that anesthesia and fluids had a set cost. Nursing care cost $15. Root canal instruments cost $37, but *Root canal canine tooth* cost $460. Was that just the labor? Dr. Bowman could charge whatever she wanted for that.

My stomach clenched as I handed over my credit card.

Isis had not come fully out of her anesthetic haze, but they deemed her ready to go. Camille led her staggering out of the back room with a bandage around one of her front legs where they had shaved her for the IV. She didn't bound toward me, in fact, she didn't even realize I was there until she was just a few feet away, and then she wagged her tail.

You came back. Thank goodness.

The gap in her lower teeth was slightly bloody, but didn't detract from her smile. She didn't look like a hillbilly after all, more like a little girl awaiting her first visit from the tooth fairy. Her canine looked the same, but X-rays taken during the procedure showed that the infected root canal had been filled. Dr. Bowman also had painted a seal on top of each canine to slow further erosion, and a tech had trimmed Isis's nails while she was under.

The pedicure, at least, was free of charge.

Isis peed at length on the lawn outside the dental office before I helped her into the car. She curled up on the passenger seat and I stroked her, overjoyed to have survived such a trying experience. I contrasted the bliss of having Isis by my side with the terrified emptiness I felt that morning.

See, it all turned out fine. I was silly to be so worried.

Alice called before I even reached the freeway. "How's the little girl?"

"She's wonderful. I have her with me now." I was grateful that Alice shared my anxiety and relief. After we hung up, I called Rob at work to tell him Isis's smile was still beautiful.

Isis hadn't been back to my office since the day she bit Frank, but on this Friday, I really was alone in the office. Plus, Isis was so loopy from the anesthesia, she lacked the agility to attack any intruders. As added protection, though, I locked the front door. She slept quietly on the floor while I went through the motions of working the rest of the day.

Before leaving for home, we went on a short stroll, Isis still wobbly on her feet. As we headed back to my car in the strip mall parking lot, a truck pulled into a driveway in front of us, blocking our path.

A man rolled down the window. "Is she fixed?"

"What?"

"Is she fixed? I'm looking for a mate for my male." A large German shepherd head poked out the window over the man's shoulder.

"Oh, yes, sorry. She is fixed."

The man thanked me before backing out and driving away. I laughed. "Isis, that was the equivalent of a stranger calling out, 'Nice ass!' as you walked down the street."

Isis staggered along beside me like an oblivious drunken co-ed.

Of course, the strange man and his dog hadn't been close enough to see the gap in Isis's teeth, but I took great satisfaction that even with a bandage around her leg and an unsteady gait, people in passing cars could appreciate her exquisite beauty.

That night, I told Rob that Isis was scheduled for another root canal in about a month.

"Why couldn't they just do them both today?"

"That's what I said! Apparently Dr. Bowman didn't have time because she works a half-day on Fridays."

When I complained to my parents about the cost, my father told me I was under no obligation to pay more than what was agreed or reasonable. Easy for him to say, but they had my dog! I wasn't going to haggle with them at the front desk over the price of anesthesia.

I diligently filled out the paperwork to file a claim with Isis's pet insurance company. They asked for her vet records from the last year, then rejected the claim, stating that Isis's dental problems were a pre-existing condition. Of course they were, but I'd hoped we could skate by on the fact that she hadn't yet been diagnosed as needing a root canal at the time I purchased her policy.

I wondered how much they would have reimbursed if I'd been paying $30 a month since Isis was born.

The insurance policy did cover $100 of routine yearly dental work, which conveniently was very close to the amount on the itemized receipt next to *Canine dental cleaning*, but it didn't account for the $200 of anesthesia, $50 for the IV, and $75 for X-rays. Guess that was the price I paid for going to one of the only board-certified veterinary dentists in the country.

About a week before Isis's second root canal, bolstered by my dad's advice, I worked up my nerve to call the clinic to try to negotiate a lower price. When Camille answered, I expressed my frustration that Dr. Bowman didn't do both root canals on the same day because she only worked a half-day.

"Oh, no," Camille said. "We wouldn't do two root canals on the same day anyway. The dogs can't be under anesthesia that long."

"Oh." That took the wind out of my sails. "I'm just really worried about the cost. Are any of the charges negotiable? Do you have a 'buy one, get one free' deal?"

"Well, some of the costs are fixed, but we might be able to knock something off the total amount."

"Oh, thank you, that would be wonderful." I was so grateful to save any money at all that I got off the phone in a hurry, not wanting to say anything to blow the deal.

As promised, the second root canal cost a mere $1,204, a whole $154 less than the estimate. By then, I'd already resigned myself to spending upwards of $3,000 on dental work for my dog that spring. The second time around, I let Isis fully recover from the drugs before I picked her up, and she nearly pulled Camille's arm out of its socket, straining against her leash to get back to me.

Chapter 10: Practice vs. Real Life

Isis's passion for her Milk-Bone toys did not fade after their squeakers were silenced for good. The rounded corners bore small tears in the plastic, which softened with use and accumulated a film of dirt around the eroding black letters. Still, every time we threw one, she slid across the room to retrieve it, even if she already had the other one in her mouth.

Our interactive playtime evolved into a game of solitaire in which Isis refused to drop the toys and instead carried them back to her bed. She lay down, sometimes holding one in her mouth. Sometimes just resting her head beside it. We started losing track of how long the toys were out, and Toy Time stretched far beyond fifteen minutes.

We got lazy; after dumping out the toys, we sat on the couch watching TV while she extracted the Milk-Bones. I tried removing them from the equation to see what else she'd play with. She sorted through the toys on the floor and peered inside the empty box.

I know they're here somewhere. Her eyes turned to me, frantic. *Mom, have you seen my squeaky bones?*

"Yes, Isis, I have them." I pulled the toys out from under the couch cushion where I'd stashed them. She snatched both from my hands, and I felt like a mean mommy for trying to deprive her of them. "Sorry, I didn't think you'd notice they were missing."

Rob and I still honored the spirit of Toy Time and the Five-Minute Rule, even if we weren't following the rules precisely. Rob never had been a fan of any militant house rules, and he wasn't a fan of Linda. That said a lot, since Rob got along with everyone. As a martial arts trainer, he noticed other teachers' styles, and found Linda to be more negative than encouraging. I disagreed with him on that point because she had plenty of times commended me and Isis for our hard work.

Still, he was right that she was bossy and opinionated. I heeded Frank's advice to "really listen to her," but she wasn't a great listener herself, and often launched into speeches that either she'd told me a dozen times, or seemed to directly contradict something she'd told me a dozen times.

"Licking her lips is a calming signal. She's calming herself down."

"Licking her lips is a stress signal. Any second she could explode into a reaction."

She frustrated me sometimes, but I endured it because I could measure Isis's improvement. While Isis had the occasional violent reaction during training scenarios with dogs, she excelled at the people work. We moved quickly from sitting quietly while a stranger-friend walked parallel twenty-five feet away, to properly executed meet-and-greets, where she either touched the stranger's hand with her nose, or took a treat from them.

Among Linda's volunteer "strangers" were fellow clients Sue and Mark, an older couple who lived near me with their reactive black Lab/pit bull mix, Rita. Linda encouraged us to get together between our sessions with her, so I met Sue and Mark each weekend at the cemetery. We parked at opposite ends of a grassy patch of graves and practiced meeting and greeting each other's dogs, while the other waited in the car.

These meet-and-greets alone weren't quite challenging enough, but neither dog was ready to do a scenario with the other. Just watching me greet Rita a hundred feet away was good practice for Isis. Plus, another loose dog usually turned up out of nowhere, or a pair of moms pushed their strollers too close to my car, so the excursions offered other opportunities for Isis not to react.

One Sunday, I looked across the graveyard to see a stranger walking his dog past my car, and my nervousness gave way to palpable joy because Isis looked calmly out the car window from the passersby to me with a smile on her face.

"Good girl, Isis!" I called to her, as Sue and Mark hustled Rita behind a tree to keep her from seeing the stranger and his dog.

Sue had short white hair and was easily rattled. Mark had a gray mustache and an easygoing demeanor, reminding me of Rob. Like most of the dog-owning couples I met in training, the woman was the primary handler, so whenever Mark held Rita's reins, Sue became very nervous that he might miss something in Rita's body language.

"Mark! Mark!" she screeched. "There's a jogger coming. Turn her this way! Mark!"

Their dynamic was a clear display of what not to do. Certainly I tended toward the uptight and anxious, especially where Isis was concerned, but at least I managed to keep my voice calmer than Sue's. Couldn't she tell that her tone was not helping? Maybe Rita was used to it. While Sue and Mark always seemed to be struggling with their dog, I never saw Rita have a violent reaction. A few times, when something set her off, she gave an eerily low bark, but nothing like Isis's frenetic bouts.

On weekend days when I wasn't meeting Sue and Mark, I brought Isis to the cemetery on my own, or to Civic Field, or one of the nearly empty university parking lots. Completely fixated on Isis's training, guilt overwhelmed me every time I drove by one of these places on my way somewhere else, thinking I should be working harder, training more often. I'd want to rush home right that second and harness Isis up.

Maybe if I worked with her twice as often, she'd progress twice as fast, but Linda always said not to rush things.

"Moving too quickly leads to regression. But without regress, there is no progress." Whatever that meant.

I couldn't deny the progress Isis had made with walks around the neighborhood. She still had occasional reactions when she saw bicycles, joggers, or other dogs, but not every time. The Halti/harness combination, along with the positive reinforcement of the clicker training, had turned her into a much more manageable dog. Only every so often, while sniffing a grassy patch, she threw herself on her side and wriggled, wiping her face against the grass.

Just a second, I think I can get this thing off.

Linda called this "fooling-around behavior," saying it was a stress signal, but I thought it was funny. Best I could tell, Isis had grown tired of having the Halti strap across her beak. My job was to keep her moving.

I urged her back to her feet. "Come on, Smiley Bird."

An area where I could step things up was practicing meet-and-greets with other people. Isis could pretty reliably wait on her bed to greet visitors to our home, and she consistently succeeded during the meet-and-greets I set up with Linda's other students.

That didn't necessarily mean she'd be able to sit calmly in a real-life situation with a stranger. Even with friends like Manis, whom Isis knew pretty well, I didn't trust that she wouldn't bark and lunge if he walked up to us on the street.

I was therefore self-conscious to recruit people to help me with our training, but by that summer, I had no excuse. Our backyard building was complete, and Rob moved his martial arts club there. In addition to being the culmination of Rob's life dream, this meant that three nights a week we had an assortment of people on our property.

After class one night, I asked a student named Ann if she had a few minutes to help me out. Of course she said yes. Who would mind saying hello to our lovely dog? Ann was in her mid-twenties and had been training with Rob for several months. She was committed to mixed martial arts training, so she seemed likely to respect my instructions regarding a dog-training exercise. She also socialized with us sometimes and had met Isis before. In fact, she'd been at the party at Rob's parents' house a few days after Isis bit Frank.

"Okay, we'll do this on the sidewalk in front of the house, so it's not on her turf." I handed Ann a bag of jerky treats. "Wait for me there. I'll bring Isis down and ask her to sit. You should just stand there. Don't lock eyes with her or anything, keep your body language relaxed. Then, when I say, toss some treats on the ground, so she approaches you to pick them up. Eventually, I'll tell her to say hello and she'll take the treat from your hand."

Ann nodded and headed for the curb. I suited Isis up in her pink harness, blue leash, and black Halti before walking her down the driveway. As I expected, Ann was precise in her actions, tossing the treats and waiting until Isis was ready to greet her. Isis also behaved predictably, although I realized with a deep exhalation that I'd been nervous.

I didn't talk to other people about Isis's problem behavior, so Ann didn't know we were practicing this greeting because Isis had once bitten a man.

None of our meet-and-greets had gone awry since the aborted attempt with Paul, which shouldn't even count, since Isis responded violently before the meet-and-greet even got started. So I shouldn't have been surprised that Isis took the treats from Ann sweetly, her face and body completely relaxed.

"Fantastic. That was perfect. Thanks so much." I turned to take Isis back up the driveway.

"No problem," Ann said. "Let me just get my stuff." She followed us up the driveway and walked alongside us for about four steps until Isis launched toward her, front legs off the ground, baring her teeth and snarling.

Ann's eyes were startled and she stepped about five feet farther out of Isis's reach. I struggled to get Isis to keep moving forward, but she was determined to get to Ann. I had been so explicit with Ann about the exercise, but neglected to tell her what to do afterward. Of course any reasonable person would think it appropriate to walk next to a dog who had just greeted her so pleasantly.

At that point, I should have said, "Freeze. Stand perfectly still until I can get Isis under control again." But I was using all my energy to hold onto Isis's leash and keep her from tearing Ann apart.

Finally I got Isis to the front porch and shouted over the barking, "Let me put her away." With a heavy heart, I shoved Isis in the front door.

Exercise failed.

"Sorry about that!" I tried to keep my voice bright as I returned to Ann on the driveway. "Thanks for helping."

"You're welcome," Ann said. "She really changed temperaments alarmingly quickly, didn't she?"

"Yeah, that's why we're doing all this training, to keep her from lunging and barking at people. She did so well on the sidewalk, I'm frustrated we didn't end on a good note. Did she totally scare you off of wanting to help ever again?"

"No, I'm definitely willing to help out. I have a long-standing fear of large dogs, so it's good for me too. You can train Isis to not freak out with humans, and train me not to freak out with dogs."

Wonderful. Ann had a longstanding fear that Isis no doubt just reinforced. I didn't ask her to help me again. Or any of our other friends. They all loved Isis when they met her in our backyard, so they expected her to be sweet and friendly under other circumstances.

But who could say whether the backyard was a hundred percent safe either? Once, our friend Owen came over on a Saturday morning and let himself through the back gate. Rob and I were inside while Isis was out back, closed in her dog run. We heard her "intruder bark," which had a lower pitch than the crazed, out-of-her-mind reaction bark. Full-blown reactions were hard to reverse without moving Isis far away from the thing she was reacting to.

When I poked my head out the back door, Isis was still barking at Owen as he tried to get her to sniff his hand through the chain link.

"Hey, Isis," he said. "You know me."

"Isis!" I said brightly, waving a cookie at her, and she trotted back inside the house. "Sorry, Owen."

Owen smiled like it was nothing, but I thought he'd narrowly avoided getting bitten. What if he'd been foolish enough to open the gate? What would Isis have done? I was ashamed of her alternate personality and wanted desperately for her to be the same loving dog all the time, not have a dangerous dark side I couldn't control.

I later learned that Owen grew up around German shepherds. He wasn't remotely bothered that Isis barked at him, nor was he afraid she would hurt him. Once I heard him tell her, "I could never be in a bad mood around you, Isis."

★★★

On a rare evening I got home before Rob, I stretched out on the gold-colored couch watching the news. When Rob pulled into the driveway, Isis scrambled to meet him at the front door, but as he came into the house, she raced back to where I sat on the couch.

"You're in her spot," Rob said. "It's a thing we do. Move over."

I scooted to the other end of the couch, allowing Isis to hop up beside me, propping her front paws on the armrest. Stroking her head, Rob kissed her and asked about her day while she squirmed with joy.

"We do this every day," Rob said. "We call it 'going to her spot.'"

I loved that Rob and Isis had a special ritual I didn't know anything about. My ritual with Isis happened every morning after Rob left for work, when I woke to find her lying at the foot of the bed. Seeing that I was awake, she climbed over me and plopped across my torso, looking into my face with her chin resting on my chest.

"Haaaawwwroooo."

"Yay, my Isis blanket." I stroked her head. "Sweet little girl, I love you more than you could ever know." With her hot breath against my neck, I inhaled her warm scent, reminiscent of fresh-baked biscuits. She smelled so good ever since we switched her diet.

After snuggling a while, we eventually dragged ourselves out of bed and shuffled into the kitchen where I pulled a quarter of a raw chicken out of the refrigerator and plopped it in her bowl.

Isis thrived on the raw diet, but since I didn't eat meat, and never cooked it for Rob, I'd had to ease into buying it. I graduated from bone-in chicken breasts and drumsticks to whole chickens I chopped up for her. Easy enough, but raw enthusiasts advised feeding a variety of meats. I added pork to the mix, buying fifteen-pound packages, cutting it into smaller servings and freezing it. We had Rob's uncle's old refrigerator up in the martial arts studio; I used its freezer side for Isis's meat.

Alice and Jerry picked up beef hearts and liver at the Navy Exchange, where they shopped once a week because Jerry was retired military. To introduce the new meat, I cut the beef hearts into small chunks. Isis was unsure about the texture at first, but grew to love everything I fed her.

I joined an e-mail list for a raw-feeding cooperative to get advice and group rates on dog food. The co-op offered a huge variety of unusual meats like pheasant, rabbit, llama, and elk. I thought I had been extravagant to pay thirty dollars for the large bag of "good" kibble, which lasted a month. Most of the meat from the co-op cost two or three dollars a pound, and Isis needed about two pounds of meat a day.

Other dog owners ordered things like whole sheep heads through the co-op, but I wasn't ready for that. My first order was "emu scrap" for just one dollar a pound. Unlike the more expensive emu "trim," the scrap consisted of necks, hearts, livers, and backs. When I picked up the forty-pound box of emu, it was not what I expected. All of the meat, organs, and bones were frozen together in a giant red block I had to defrost in the garage for several hours before I could separate the pieces.

As the block thawed, blood seeped through the cardboard box and onto the garage floor like something from a crime scene. My hands burned and shriveled from handling the frozen pieces. Small feathers clung to the red meat, which unlike chicken, had a distinct metallic smell. The emu necks, roughly the size of my forearm, were too big for the quart-sized bags I used to freeze pork, although the fist-sized hearts fit. The necks went into plastic grocery bags. After stashing the meat in the studio freezer, I warned Rob that if any of his students looked inside, they would think we stored dismembered body parts there.

For dinner that night, I put Isis in the backyard with an emu neck. She licked it a few times before wrapping her jaw around one end and gnawing for several minutes. Watching her eat raw animal parts entertained me more than feeding her kibble.

This extravagance fit with my image of myself as devoted dog owner. I hesitated to tell anyone I'd spent three thousand dollars on canine root canals, and I didn't even want to calculate how much I'd spent on "behavior modification," but I was proud to feed her a wholesome prey-model raw-meat diet. People might think I was crazy, but at least they didn't judge Isis for it.

★★★

My obsession with fixing Isis made it hard for me to hand the leash over to Rob. What if he made a mistake and Isis bit someone? What if she frustrated him so much that he lost affection for her? On the other hand, I needed his help when I went out of town. Isis couldn't go days without any training sessions. She might lose ground.

The summer before Isis turned three, I went to visit a friend for a few weeks, leaving behind explicit instructions on Isis's diet and the simplest possible training exercises Rob could practice with her. I didn't expect him to work with her as often as I did, but maybe he'd squeeze in a few sessions. I wasn't sure he knew how to put her Halti on, so I left the instruction manual in the folder with my typed directions.

Upon my return, I waited at the airport curb and smiled when I saw my bright blue Honda veering across the lanes toward me. There was only one reason Rob would drive my car instead of his. Isis stood on the passenger seat, pressing her nose against the glass, her worried brown eyes scanning the sidewalk.

When she saw me, she whimpered with gratitude, wriggled on the seat, and wagged her tail like crazy.

"Smiley Bird! I missed you so much." I shoved my bag behind my seat and grabbed Isis by her face, kissing the top of her beak. Guiding her to the backseat, I climbed in and kissed Rob. "I missed you too, Robbie."

Isis sat between our seats, resting her head on my shoulder as I recapped my trip for Rob. Then I asked, "Did you guys have a chance to do any training?"

"Yes we did. In fact, we had the best walk ever yesterday."

"Best walk ever? Wow."

"We walked to the end of the block around dusk. She tugged a little, but I used the Halti and just clicked constantly. Even before I started treating her, she was already walking next to me at a slower pace." Rob beamed, glancing from me to Isis. "I was so proud of her. She even heard two different dogs and didn't react at all. One little dog wouldn't stop barking, so I treated her for not barking back. Then, when we got to the parking lot, we played the eye contact game with intersection traffic over my shoulders. I think it was tough for her. She felt like she needed to look past me quite a bit, but she was able to hold eye contact for a few seconds at a time. It was fun. We crossed the street two different times to avoid people on the way back and she didn't bark once."

"It was fun? Did you say it was fun? Oh, Rob, you've made me the happiest dog mom in the world." I squeezed his arm as he drove, prouder of him than I was of Isis. Finally he could see that training her could be fun. Maybe not as much fun as dog jiu-jitsu, but still.

Rob's primary goal was to take Isis places. His confidence boosted by the best walk ever, he announced one August Sunday that we should take her for a walk around the lake. I was still in bed.

Groaning, I sat up. "I don't think she's ready for that. It will be really crowded."

"It will be fine. C'mon, get up."

I groaned again. My head was killing me. "I really don't feel well. Can we do this another time?"

"We don't need you," Rob said cheerfully. "Isis and I will go to the lake by ourselves."

"Fine, but make sure you take the clicker."

"Of course."

"And treats."

"Yes, yes."

"A poop bag, her harness, Halti, the leash with two points of contact." Had I left anything out?

"Yes, yes. I know."

"And if you see a bicycle or another dog, click right away and treat her so she turns her head away from the distraction. If you don't have time, move your body between her and the oncoming threat."

"I got it. She'll be fine."

I fell back asleep and didn't wake until they returned. "How did it go?"

Rob sighed. "Well, it was great at first. We walked to the dog water-play area and she splashed around. But then another dog went by and she pulled so hard on her leash that I could hardly even hold onto her."

Of course she did. That's what happens every time she sees a strange dog. Why didn't he listen? He described the rest of the outing, all very familiar to me. Barking and lunging at bicycles and joggers.

Isis hadn't done enough to discourage Rob, though, because a few weeks later, he told me he planned to hike with her to the bat caves. For years, the bat caves had been a symbol of my failure as an outdoorswoman. After Rob and I had been dating a few months, he suggested the hike, saying it would take about an hour, maybe two. The glacially carved mountain trail was steep, and it was raining the first time we attempted it. I never made it to the caves. While the canopy of evergreens kept us mostly dry at first, we had to cross several fast-running rocky streams. Terrified, I started to cry, refusing to cross one last ravine. I crouched down close to the earth and sobbed that I felt stuck, I didn't know how I was going to get off the mountain, and I didn't want to take one more step.

I tried to talk Rob out of taking Isis, saying that he and I should scope it out first to try to anticipate any problems. Then, maybe we could walk her there for five or ten minutes, and gradually build on positive experiences.

"It's risky because if she has a bad experience it sets her back," I said. "Remember how long it was before I wanted to go back after my bad experience? Oh that's right. I haven't been back."

Rob would not be deterred so I had no choice but to go with him. I couldn't let him take Isis up there without me. I reassured both of us that I could handle the hike this time. After all, I did a lot of hiking for my job. I was better equipped, not only emotionally, but with actual equipment. Like a backpack and sturdy hiking shoes.

The first part of the hike was a regular trail, although narrow and steep. Rob took off ahead of us and Isis and I kept losing sight of him. I didn't really mind, because Isis turned out to be a terrific hiking buddy after all. Thinking the Halti would be difficult to maneuver on uneven terrain, I attached her strong green leash to the pink harness. When Isis pulled ahead of me, it worked to my benefit to keep me moving uphill as the trail became steeper, rockier, and knotted with tree roots. I enjoyed the challenge of having to figure out where to place my feet. Isis cheered me along. All this was possible because no one was coming down the trail from the other direction, and no one passed us from behind.

My heart was weaker than my spirit, though, and I needed to take frequent breaks to allow my pulse to slow down.

Here and there, Rob stopped and waited for us to catch up, and I wondered if this was what he had in mind when he planned to hike with Isis, since he wasn't actually hiking anywhere near her.

About a mile in, we reached a lookout with a wooden bench where we could rest. The three of us sat, Rob and me on the bench, Isis on the ground beside us, and took in the hazy marine view. We sat a few feet from a drop-off where the Cascades Mountains met the sea. Framed by ferns and other shrubs along the hiking trail, Bellingham Bay stretched before us, dark blue water dotted with the San Juan Islands beyond, the turquoise sky capped with white clouds.

"Are we almost there?"

"We're about a third of the way there," Rob said.

We sipped water and offered some to Isis, who enjoyed the view with an open-mouthed smile.

Isis heard something before we did, and her mouth closed. Signal number one that she was about to react to something. An older gentleman came around the bend clicking his metal hiking poles, having caught up to us while we rested. Before my brain even processed his arrival, Isis was barking and lunging toward him. Fortunately, I still held her leash tightly and Rob grabbed her by the harness. We apologized over the sound of her rapid fire, fearsome alert. I moved her behind the bench, trying to get her to sit, but she was too far gone.

Her aggressive shouts rang in my ears and filled me with shame. Why did she always do this?

The man passed, but Isis and I both were too rattled to calm down. As usual, I tried to analyze what prompted the reaction. Maybe it was the sound of the hiking poles. Then another group of hikers passed, without poles, and she did it again. Could have been their backpacks or their hats, or maybe she was still too revved up from the hiking pole guy.

"We have to go back down," I said.

"She'll be fine," Rob said. "Let's keep going."

We barely returned to the trail when some hikers came toward us. More barking and lunging as I clutched Isis's leash and harness. Next thing I knew, her pink harness was empty in my hands. Somehow, Isis had twisted out of her gear, which I didn't even think was possible. Before she realized she was free, I grabbed her by the collar and fastened the harness around her again.

I looked to Rob desperately. "See?" This time he either agreed with me, or else he didn't want to argue about it, so we started down the mountain, with Isis barking and twisting out of her harness every time we saw another hiker. At least she never slipped all the way out of my grasp, but I was unraveling, wanting to crouch down against the earth and cry. All these people coming up the narrow steep trail. How were we going to get down? I couldn't tell if I was internalizing Isis's visible distress, or if she was feeding off my panic. She didn't freak out as much when I wasn't around, according to Rob and his mother. Either she felt more of a responsibility to protect me than Rob, or else my anxiety was the catalyst.

Regardless, there was no way I could get Isis down that mountain.

I handed Rob the leash and walked ahead of him. Every time I saw a group approaching. I called back to Rob to wait, and said to the hikers apologetically, "We have a dog with us. She's a little freaked out. Just to let you know." No one asked any questions and people with Dachshunds simply scooped up their little dogs.

Rob took Isis off the path to give the passing hikers plenty of room. While I waited, I clenched my eyes and braced myself for the barrage of barking. After each outburst, we continued our descent. Gradually, her rants lasted for shorter periods of time, then stopped altogether. Somehow, with Rob in control, people were passing without Isis feeling the need to react.

The hike down was worse than the hike up. Rob was doing the hard part, but I was alone with my thoughts. And of course, the whole theory behind Isis's training regimen was to prevent her from having any negative experiences, so this was a huge failure all around.

In a very small way, it was a victory too. Maybe Rob could have walked Isis all the way up to the bat caves by himself, without my nervous energy to set her off. But what if he couldn't, and I hadn't been there to be the lookout? Could he have gotten her down by himself?

In the end, we managed. The three of us managed. We made it back to the car, where Rob said, "That sucked."

And I managed not to say, "I told you it would suck." Because really, I had hoped that it wouldn't.

The truth was, Isis didn't share our dream of going out in the world. She'd just as happily spend hot days in our own backyard where we filled up a kiddie pool. She lay for hours in the water, her soccer ball bobbing beside her.

During my mother's visit later that summer, we land-scaped an unsightly dirt mound beside the martial arts studio. Because it was not prime planting time, we bought forsythia, wild rose, and wax myrtle on clearance. After planting, I pulled the hose from the side of the house up the hill to the studio. Isis raced after me and leapt up at the cascade of water as I tried to spray the plants. I held the hose over my head, trying to get the spray of water out of her reach, but she had springs in her hind legs.

Yay! Hose time!

The water pressure was stronger than I'd find pleasant in my own face, but Isis bounced up over and over, wagging her tail with each jump, snapping her jaw when she couldn't quite reach the spray, and swinging her head back and forth when she did. She paused between leaps, looking at me with her joyous tongue-hanging-out smile.

I could play this game forever.

Chapter 11: Reactive Dog Class

After Isis succeeded in tolerating Dakota at closer and closer distances on leash, it was time to advance to the next level: interacting with him. Because she at one time played happily with other dogs at the park, I thought probably if she met Dakota off leash, she'd be friendly.

Linda was more cautious. We tested Isis first with a fake dog.

When I arrived for a late afternoon training session in the Food Pavilion parking lot, Linda showed me a stuffed black dog a little smaller than Isis.

"This stuffed dog is in a very challenging stance," Linda said. "Lots of dogs feel threatened by it."

Yeah, right, I thought. *There's no way Isis would think this toy was a real dog. She's reactive, not stupid.*

Linda set the dog down on the asphalt between our two cars, while I geared Isis up and brought her out. With one look at the stuffed dog, the fur on Isis's shoulders spiked and her jaws sliced the air as she barked an assertive *Stay back!* to the inanimate object.

"Seriously, Isis? I had higher hopes for you than this." I moved Isis a little farther back so we were about thirty-five feet away, and clicked and treated her for looking calmly at the "dog." Slowly we worked our way closer, making our approach along an S-curve. ("Dogs never greet each other head on," Linda said.) Isis's mouth was open and she looked back to me easily, showing curiosity rather than hostility.

Linda wanted to make sure that Isis wouldn't tear the stuffed animal apart, but I had faith. I brought Isis close enough to sniff the toy. She nudged it, then whipped her head back to me.

Whoa. This butt smells weird.

"Good girl, Isis. Good hello. Come away," I chirped, rewarding her with several bacon-flavored morsels. We worked like this for a few more minutes, bringing Isis close enough to sniff, then moving her away.

Exercise completed, we moved on to some meet-and-greets with another Bellingham couple that trained with Linda. Meanwhile, lots of people passed by on their way to their cars, some of them pushing grocery carts. Isis handled each of these challenges with aplomb, as did I. A group of people walked parallel to the area where we were working, so I moved her into a corner of the lot, near some bushes. Hearing a rustling over my shoulder, I turned to see a bearded man in a bulky coat emerge from the shrubs carrying two plastic shopping bags.

"Party time!" I gave the cue I used when something threatening approached, when I wanted Isis to turn her attention on me as I moved her away. I trotted backward, guiding Isis to come along, facing me. She complied, and still managed to take treats from me, which was a sign I hadn't lost her attention. But then she glanced over her shoulder and saw the man walking behind my car.

Pushed over the edge into hindbrain, Isis's switch flipped to instinctive survival mode.

She erupted into a frenzy of barks. *Back away from our car or you'll regret it!*

The bearded man stopped, slowly turned to us, and leered at Isis. Well, maybe he just stared. Either way, making eye contact was not the appropriate move. Someone must teach somewhere that the way to fend off an attacking dog is to intimidate it by staring it in the eye. In my experience, challenging a German shepherd with direct eye contact is the last thing you want to do.

I took a deep breath and held onto her leash for dear life, because that was the only thing I could do until the man went on his way.

"Well, that was annoying," I said, when everything calmed down.

"You handled it well," Linda assured. "He was just one distraction too many. We learn from these things. She had a lot of successes today, and she's ready for more advanced work. I have a reactive-dog class starting in a few weeks that would be good for her."

A class! I was thrilled. After Firgrove and the class in Seattle, I thought I'd never have Isis in a class with other dogs again. Plus, a dog class might introduce me to some new human friends, fellow owners of anxious dogs.

Before Isis and I could make new friends, she had to prove she could play nicely with Dakota, Linda said. To earn this off-leash time, she had to walk a literal labyrinth. Next to the 4-H building at the fairgrounds, a low chain-link fence enclosed a grassy area where Linda laid out long Styrofoam noodles in a square, then divided the square into three lanes we had to walk through like a maze. We'd done this before. Walking through the labyrinth with me was supposed to boost Isis's focus, coordination, balance, and obedience. Like the cone work we did early on, the exercise also was meant to strengthen our bond, with Isis learning to read my body signals as I guided her. Sometimes when Linda set up the Styrofoam labyrinth, the wind rearranged its walls, but the weather was nice on this late summer day.

As a warm-up to Isis's date with Dakota, Linda and I walked the dogs through the labyrinth at the same time.

"Wonderful. She's very attentive to you," Linda said. "It really shows how much you've been working with her."

Next, Linda let Dakota run loose inside the fenced area, while Isis watched, on leash and wearing her Halti, from the other side of the chain link. I was supposed to click and treat her for looking calmly at Dakota, but at first, she didn't look at him at all. She suddenly became very interested in the grass at the base of the chain link.

"That sniffing is a displacement behavior that shows she's feeling a lot of stress," Linda called out. "When she displaces, she's in mild hindbrain where she can't listen to you or learn anything."

Linda's authoritative, almost haughty voice grated on my nerves. I felt like Isis was being unfairly criticized. Mild hindbrain was a huge leap forward from barking and lunging.

When Isis finished displacing, I brought her back in the fenced area where we practiced having her approach Dakota and lie down five feet away. First with her back to him. Then facing him. No problem whatsoever. Isis smiled at me with shining eyes. Linda and I very slowly reached down to our dogs and unclipped their leashes (and Halti, in Isis's case). The dogs remained lying down. Linda nodded at me and we both gave our dogs the signal.

"Isis, go play!"

Isis took a beat, still focused on me. *Wait, really? I can go see this guy?*

"Go play!" I said again.

Isis sprang to her feet and galloped over to Dakota, who gentlemanly allowed her to sniff his essential parts. Then they were off. Dakota was about the same size as Isis and similar looking, but with a brown face. Supposedly undersocialized as a puppy, Dakota was dog-reactive until Linda became a specialist and turned him into a teacher dog.

In the nine months I'd been working with Linda and Dakota, I never got much of a feel for his personality. In fact, I couldn't tell him apart from his brother, Duke, mostly because I always kept my attention on Isis. Dakota was a sweet dog, but didn't exude joy like Isis did. Then again, neither did he fire back at her any of the times she snarled and lunged at him during our exercises. Had to give him credit for that.

Isis reveled in the freedom to be with another dog. She frolicked and play-bowed, engaging him, tongue hanging out, happy. Dakota merely seemed to tolerate her, although according to Linda, he was modeling proper behavior. Isis raced from one end of the grass to the other, goading Dakota to chase her and looking as though she'd never felt so free.

After five minutes, Linda ended the exercise and asked me to call Isis. My girl ran to me without a second thought.

Catch ya later, Dakota. My mom needs me.

I was disappointed for playtime to end so soon. When we used to go to the dog park, we sometimes stayed more than an hour. Five minutes hardly felt long enough for Isis to get her ya-yas out. This was Isis's first interaction with another dog in a year. But I knew our goal was to end on success.

Isis had shown she could play with Dakota, and we could build on this so eventually she could have other doggie friends.

★★★

We were late to our first day of class. I knew exactly how long it should take because I'd been driving to the fairgrounds once a month for ten months, but I didn't realize I was supposed to arrive about twenty minutes early to set up our crate and get situated. For my one-on-ones, Linda didn't care if we started a few minutes late, and frequently was behind schedule herself. On our way to the first group class, Rob and I stopped to pick up food and got stuck behind a slow car on the winding highway, so we pulled into the fairgrounds fifteen minutes late.

Our fellow students were arranged in a circle outside, their dogs in covered crates. I rushed over to join them, leaving Isis in the car with Rob, who was polishing off his sandwich. Sitting down on a metal folding chair, I whispered, "Sorry."

Linda finished whatever it was she was explaining before saying to me pointedly, "We start class right at noon, so you need to get here on time."

"Sorry, I miscalculated." We were late, so what? Now that I knew it mattered, we'd make sure to be on time next week. Still, I didn't like starting off on the wrong foot, and was glad Rob was still in the car. Linda wouldn't have scored any points with him by snarling at me before we even got started.

Linda gave us a few minutes to lug over and unfold Isis's black metal crate. We draped a blue leopard-print fleece blanket over it and set out a water dish. Next was the moment of truth. I had to lead Isis through this group of strange people and dogs, although at least she wouldn't be able to see the dogs.

What if she freaked out?

She did not. Isis trotted happily beside me, noticing the people but untroubled by them. I guided her into her crate, sat beside Rob on the metal chair, and awaited further instructions.

"Let's begin with some Tellington Touch to get your dogs in a relaxed state," Linda said.

Linda was a big proponent of Tellington Touch, or TTouch, sort of like animal massage. Not only did the body-work promote relaxation, but practitioners also believed specific moves could speed healing and reduce behavioral problems. Linda had already taught me to do TTouch by pressing my hand against Isis's skin and rubbing in a circular motion one and a quarter times. So, if my fingers started at the six o'clock position on a clock, I'd go all the way around once and then up to nine o'clock before repositioning the hand and making another circle. I had no idea what this one-and-a-quarter thing was based on, or if it had any merit, but I was all for prescribed petting.

In class, we started with a flat hand down Isis's spine, all the way to the tail. Then we did zigzags down her side and made one-and-a-quarter circles on her back. Isis enjoyed the rubdown, shifting her weight to the side of one hip, which showed she was feeling comfortable in her surroundings.

Linda talked a lot in that first class, and I'd heard most of it before. She took this work seriously, but then, so did we all. I was paying $350 for this class, on top of our fifteen private sessions at $65 each.

Linda gave us each a binder with lesson plans and workbook assignments. Week one listed a skill requirement of attention drills that she would test during week two, with a warning: *This is NOT OPTIONAL. This is REQUIRED work.* She also assigned mandatory reading and written homework, and gave pop quizzes.

Finally, an area of dog training where I could excel! If all it took was reading and acing multiple-choice quizzes, I could definitely carry Isis's weight in this class.

Isis's classmates were Rita, whom I already knew through her owners Sue and Mark; a Doberman mix named Luna, whose picture Linda showed me the day we met, the one who chewed up her owner's arm; a snarly Tibetan terrier named Murphy; and skittish Anita, a white pointer mix with floppy light brown ears.

Rob, seeing that all the other handlers were women (except for Mark), bowed out after the first class and didn't return. That was a funny thing about all our dog-training classes: very few men participated. Even Mark, who always joined Sue when we met at the cemetery, didn't come to every class.

After a few weeks of working with each dog individually while the others rested in covered crates or their cars, Linda invited Isis and Murphy into the 4-H room together, both on leash. Murphy's mom, Janice, brought him in first, and when we were instructed to join them, I flashed back on the intensity of Isis's reaction when Linda tried to bring Duke into this same room. Bracing for the worst, I entered the room and sat down on my appointed metal chair. Isis glanced toward the little white dog, and I clicked as soon as she saw him. She looked back to me, face soft and happy, and I gave her a treat for not barking at the other dog.

She really had come a long way. Maybe I didn't need to carry her weight in class after all.

Watching the other dogs allowed me to observe reactive-dog body language impartially. I saw Isis's stress signals all the time, of course, but rarely had time to analyze them because as soon as she displayed stress, my priority was damage control. In class, I began to understand the difference between a calming signal and a stress signal. Mild signals included things like a head turn, blinking, panting, yawning, sniffing, lip licking, and raising a paw. Sometimes dogs used those to calm themselves down or let another dog know they meant no harm. Medium signals were things like eating grass, spinning, wagging the tail frantically, and staring.

Since lots of dogs did those things every day, I had to learn which behaviors to pay closest attention to in Isis.

With a German shepherd, "staring" was a huge thing to watch out for. I didn't want Isis staring at anything for more than two seconds, because after that, she'd react. For other dogs, "hot zone" behaviors were baring teeth, raising hackles, air snapping, lunging, and barking. Once Isis did any of those things, she was past the hot zone, fully in hindbrain, and I needed to get her away from the trigger as fast as possible.

For the first few classes, Isis didn't have a single reaction, though most of the other dogs did. Then we started working multiple dogs at a time outside with plenty of room between them. Isis had a harder time with that, and took treats so hard my fingers bled. A few times she had full-blown reactions. Even when she held it together in class, she left in a heightened state of arousal.

On the drive home, I liked to stop at a fish-and-chips place. Isis waited patiently for me in the car while I ordered, but once I had my food and got back in the car to eat, she became hypervigilant, barking aggressively at anyone who walked past the car. I decided to turn the fish stand into a training exercise and parked farther away to reduce the number of distractions. On our next visit, I ordered my food and got back in the car to wait until it was ready. Two men passed close by the car, and I clicked and treated Isis for being calm. She noticed them, but did not seem worried. After I got my food and brought it back to the car to eat, I didn't see a couple park behind us until Isis barked like crazy when they walked past.

She quieted only after the couple was out of sight.

I tried not to let frustration spoil my enjoyment of the fish and chips, knowing I'd blown it by not being alert enough to our surroundings. I should have seen that couple before Isis did. When they passed on their way back, Isis went into overdrive, stepping on my lap, smushing my food, and letting loose her serious *Don't mess with us* bark.

"Isis!" I tried to keep my voice cheerful as I waved a treat to lure her attention away from the strangers, but of course she paid no attention. Once their car pulled away, I shoved her off my lap, my dinner ruined.

We'd had a great class earlier, but I drove home feeling defeated. Like there was no end in sight to this training. No permanent cure to Isis's reactive behavior. For the rest of her life, I would never be able to let my guard down with Isis in public.

★★★

When I first met Linda, we outlined three goals:
1. To be able to walk Isis past bicycles and dogs.
2. For Isis never to bite anyone again.
3. To have Isis greet visitors at the door without barking at them like crazy.

So far, so good on the biting, although I credited careful management over any real changes to her temperament. We worked on bikes and dogs nearly every day, but both still challenged us. As for my third goal, we'd trained Isis to lie on her bed while visitors entered, waiting to be invited to say hello. We'd only practiced with two or three people at a time, and the incident the previous spring with my mother had set me on edge. With someone Isis had known since she was a baby, someone she already greeted at the front door and had shared the house with many times, Isis's aggression switch could flip unpredictably.

She didn't bite my mother, but who knew if she would bite someone else?

We had not invited people over in about two years without my being paralyzed with anxiety about what Isis would do. It was time to find out, so we invited some of our martial arts friends over. I planned to keep the front door locked, the cookie jar stocked, and have Isis wait on her bed to greet each person as they entered. I assured myself that Isis was ready to be tested. While she wasn't a hundred percent perfect, she had gotten much more trustworthy.

All I had to do was make sure her attention was on me before I opened the front door.

Several of these friends had practiced door greetings with Isis before, so they knew the drill. The one person of concern was our tall Haitian friend, Manis. The last time he came to our door, Isis got up from her bed and barked at him so ferociously that I shoved him out the front door and put her in the backyard, afraid to try again.

The first to arrive for our party were Shannon and Brittany, a married couple very fond of Isis. I handed them biscuits and Isis waited for my cue before bounding over and jumping up on them. Shannon vigorously scratched Isis's haunches as she wriggled against him.

"Aww, that's a good girl. You're so awesome, Isis."

Isis looked over her shoulder at him, smiling.

Each time the doorbell rang, Isis barked a loud alert and I instructed her to lie down on her bed. She let out a few more high-pitched barks after she'd taken her place, looking at me eagerly, ears pointing straight up.

Who's here now? Let me say hello!

I waited until she settled down before opening the door. If she got up or barked again, I stood my ground until I had her complete attention. Her perky body language made clear that she was not scared of what lurked behind the door, but eager to welcome it in.

About an hour into the party, I heard the front door close. I must have forgotten to lock it after the last person entered. Isis took a few steps toward the front door as Manis rounded the corner. I stifled the "uh-oh" inside me. "Isis, it's your buddy, Manis. Go say hello!"

She didn't bark or rush him, just brushed against his leg and let him pet her before moving on.

"Goooooood girl," I praised.

Isis behaved perfectly the entire night, even taking her Milk-Bone toys to her bed and lying down without being asked. Throughout the evening, our friends petted her and played with her as a major attraction of attending an event at our house. Not only did I surge with pride, but I relaxed more than I had in years with other people around Isis. Isis had an even better time.

Best of all, not one of our friends had any idea that Isis was a "problem" dog.

★★★

On a Saturday in late October, I took Isis with me to a creek restoration project that recently had received a lot of rain. I wanted to get pictures of water flowing through the new channels. Some loose dogs barked at us from a driveway as we walked along the trail to the creek, but Isis didn't bark back. She was happy to be out in the world again. Out for a real nature hike, not just a few controlled laps around an empty asphalt parking lot. I took photos of the creek channels for my job, then slipped off Isis's Halti and posed her against the mountains with blue sky behind her.

The autumn sunlight was so glorious that I took her home and posed her underneath the red-brown leaves of the dogwood tree in the backyard. Beside the retaining wall with a little stone German shepherd statue that Rob got me for my birthday. With the five-foot-tall Buddha statue at the front of the house. I shot dozens of stunning pictures of my supermodel of a dog. Since Rob wasn't home, he wouldn't even know these pictures existed until he saw them on the pages of the Isis Calendar I gave him and his parents every year for Christmas.

Laughing, I remembered that Isis's Halloween costume recently had arrived in the mail. Sadly, no one makes a dog costume of the Egyptian goddess Isis, but I looked for something along that theme, like Cleopatra. I settled on Harem Girl: a pair of sheer genie pants, red bikini top, and little hat. I put the costume on her and snapped several more photos for our Halloween album.

In one of them, the flash caused Isis to close one eye, winking at me with a sly smile under her gold genie hat and red veil.

Of all the pictures that made it into that year's Isis Calendar, my favorite was one I shot the previous spring. She's lying down in the grass, just after rolling her soccer ball to me. She's looking right into the camera, with bright, excited eyes (eager for her ball to be kicked, but you can't tell that in the picture), and her big tongue hangs straight down the center of her huge smile. Her black saddle markings are typical of a German shepherd, but her face is almost entirely golden.

The photo is pure joy.

Later that fall, I searched through older albums on my computer as I assembled the calendar, and stumbled on the photos we took at the seaside park when she was five months old and still learning the command for "down." I remembered that day vividly. How black her fur was. How small she was. Her widow's peak. The green leash and that awful pinch collar. I clicked through the pictures, marveling at a time when our biggest challenge was teaching her to lie down on cue. There's Rob standing beside her. Wrapping his arm around her to encourage her to lie down. Her eyes big and brown, questioning. Her little pink tongue, sticking out between her teeth. Licking the top of her nose. Photo after photo of her licking her own nose.

I remembered pointing it out to Rob. "Why does she keep sticking out her tongue?"

Lip licking. A stress signal. Even someone who didn't know what lip licking meant could see in these photos how scared and confused Isis had been. Rob's body pressing hers to the ground. Her paws splayed. In one shot, she's sitting and Rob is petting her. She's looking at the camera, at me, her forehead knit, black eyebrows tight. Worried.

I regretted using the pinch collar from the moment I started training with Linda, but I had not remembered how we taught Isis to lie down on cue. The technique we learned at Firgrove was not overtly aversive, but it was uncomfortable enough to frighten our little dog. My heart broke to see those photos, a reminder of our early mistakes that might have set her on the path to becoming a reactive dog. I hated myself for being so blind on that day to the depth of her anxiety that just screamed at me from the pictures.

I hated myself, too, for causing that fear.

★★★

The reactive-dog class culminated with a group walk and a celebratory Christmas potluck at Linda's house. Murphy's mom had to drop out because of family health problems, so Isis and I graduated along with Rita and Sue, Anita and her mom Annette, and Luna and her mom Deanna.

Isis wasn't quite ready to walk alongside the other dogs, so we trailed quite a ways behind them as we traversed a ball-field lightly crusted with snow. I watched the three other dogs, all of whom had been working with Linda longer than Isis had, and their owners, bundled in winter coats cinched by the treat pouches around their waists. They walked in a large circle, while Linda tested them by having Dakota approach each dog. The dogs were rewarded when they turned their heads away from the oncoming stimulus. Isis and I stood apart, moving slightly closer and closer until Luna turned and made eye contact with Isis, prompting a barking and lunging reaction from my dog.

I moved Isis away and tried to keep her at a safe distance for the rest of the exercise.

No, Isis wasn't cured yet, but I was proud of our progress. This would be our last class with Linda for the time being. We'd had more than fifteen individual training sessions plus the eight-week class. I felt like I knew enough to keep practicing on my own, with Linda just an e-mail away if I had questions.

After the walk, we left our dogs in our cars while we went inside Linda's house. I was surprised and strangely gratified to see blankets covering all of her couches, just like at my house. Had Linda's perfect dogs torn holes in her furniture, too? We sat down to eat the mixed green salad and garlic bread I'd brought, a polenta appetizer by Deanna, and a spaghetti cake made by Linda. The spaghetti cake was a revelation: eggplant and spaghetti noodles baked in tomato sauce in the shape of a cake. Sue brought a meat lasagna, and Annette provided brownies for dessert. I ate way too much.

I gave Linda a coffee table book of dog photos and a card featuring Isis's photo, thanking her for everything that she had done for us. Isis was a changed dog, and we owed it all to Linda. The rest of us had a blind gift exchange in which I received squeaky tennis balls and dried duck jerky, and Linda had made each of us an assortment of homemade dog treats that looked so good that at first I thought they were for human consumption.

Over our meal, we discussed our dogs' progress. Linda put her dogs in another room and invited Sue to bring Rita inside. Linda's husband accidentally let one of their dogs out and we narrowly avoided a skirmish. Everyone praised Rita for not freaking out at the surprise cameo appearance while Linda scolded her husband for being so careless.

Back at the table, Linda announced that she planned to get a Malinois puppy in the coming year, and asked me if I'd considered getting a little buddy for Isis.

"Actually, I really wanted one a while back, but we thought better of it once we saw how dog-reactive Isis is."

"I think it could be therapeutic for Isis. She's still quite puppylike herself, but her maternal instincts will kick in. Just remember, temperament is everything, and get a boy. Female dogs are always dominant, so if you get a boy with the right temperament, she should do fine."

Linda planted a seed in me that renewed my yearning to expand our family. I used to wonder if Isis might be happier with a friend. I felt guilty leaving her at home most days while we were at work, and hated the idea that she might be lonesome.

I brought it up to Rob that night, as the three of us cuddled on the bed. His first concern was that Isis would feel left out or replaced if we got another dog, but I'd seen her play with Dakota, not to mention all the dog-park dogs before she started becoming aggressive.

"Even after she started getting snarly with little dogs, she played once with a black Lab puppy perfectly well," I said. "I bet that's what she'd be like if we brought one home."

"I don't know," Rob said, reaching down to stroke Isis's head. "I think she likes being an only child."

I frowned. "Don't you think she needs doggie friends? The only time she gets to play with another dog is in these constrained five-minute exercises with Dakota. She only got to do that a couple of times, and now we're not even training with Linda anymore."

Of course I felt anxious, too, about how Isis would respond to a new addition, but living with a puppy wouldn't be the same as seeing a strange dog while on leash. If she were introduced properly and if we picked one with the right temperament, like Linda said, a puppy could be just what we needed. Linda had plenty of clients with reactive dogs that shared the house with other dogs.

There was no reason to think Isis wouldn't be able to adapt.

Rob allowed me to sway him, but he was particular. He wanted Isis's baby brother to be a genetic sibling. "Let's get another dog from Isis's parents."

"Really? There are lots of rescue dogs around here."

"They wouldn't be related to Isis."

"Yeah, but Isis has some, um, problems. Maybe it's not the best idea to get another one exactly like her."

Rob was adamant; he would clone Isis if he could. His rationale was that Isis would be more accepting of a puppy that shared her DNA. That on some level, she would recognize her biological baby brother.

Quin's parents planned to have another litter from Portos in the spring. That gave us some time to prepare emotionally, and I could work harder on desensitizing Isis to other dogs. I had this fantasy of letting Isis loose among the puppies at Quin's parents' house and having her choose the one we'd bring home. But I also lay awake at night worrying about the logistics of driving to Los Angeles with Isis to pick up the puppy and then having to drive back with both dogs. My mother wouldn't love having us stay at her house with

Isis and a new puppy, especially since her shih tzu didn't like other dogs.

The more Rob and I talked about it, the more our hearts got set on getting a puppy. Both Isis and our yard seemed ready. Our backyard studio had been operational for several months, and the landscaping was finished early the following spring. With a brand new cedar fence completely enclosing the yard, Isis romped free on the grassy terraces sculpted by retaining walls. She'd jump five feet high from a standstill to the top of a wall. We encouraged this as one of her tricks, because Linda suggested we improve Isis's confidence with dog agility, a competitive sport popular with owners of high-energy dogs like border collies. We also had some bonafide dog-agility equipment: a set of hurdles and weave poles that Alice gave us for Christmas. Sometimes, Isis got major zoomies after I guided her to weave around the poles and jump the hurdles.

One day, I watched her scamper circles around the yard, with images flashing in my mind of another dog running beside her, a little brother to chase.

"Isis, do you remember playing with other dogs at the park? That was fun, wasn't it?"

Isis froze before racing to pick up her soccer ball and drop it at my feet. *Sure. The park was fun. This is fun, too. Kick my ball now, please.*

I attempted to kick the ball over her head, but she blocked the pass with her chest. "Nice one. Can't get anything past you." I kicked the ball again. "I really think you'd like having someone to run and play with right here in our yard. A baby brother."

Isis stared at me, deflated ball in her mouth. *Just as long as I don't have to share my soccer balls.*

"You know I love you more than anything, Smiley Bird. Maybe you can't visualize what it will be like, but I can. Two doggies playing together. It'll be wonderful."

Chapter 12: Bringing Home Baby

Even though I agreed we would get another puppy from Quin's parents, I grappled internally over the morality of buying from a breeder versus rescuing from a shelter. About a year earlier, I'd heard about a ploy by People for the Ethical Treatment of Animals, where they placed an ad in a well-known dog magazine amid the listings for pedigreed dog breeders. They ran a notice addressing owners of purebred puppies, advertising *Free gift bag!* What the excited owners of new puppies received in the mail was a body bag with a note saying that a shelter dog had to die because they chose to buy a purebred puppy instead of rescuing one. The act really turned me off to PETA, even though it succeeded in making me think twice about buying another dog from a breeder.

But rescuing a dog worried me too. Who knew what kind of behavior problems would come with a dog someone else had given up? Besides, I reasoned, not all breeders were puppy mills. German shepherds had been bred for their brains, strength, and loyalty. Without human intervention to control their breeding, shepherds could lose the qualities that made them such good police dogs and companions. Left to their own mating instincts, dogs everywhere might look like the scrawny street dogs of India.

By late spring, Quin told me that Portos's latest litter had been stillborn and she didn't know when he'd have another one. While disappointed, by then we'd committed to the idea of bringing home a baby brother for Isis. Secretly relieved to cross *Los Angeles road trip* off my list of worries, I found three backyard breeders with available litters, and took a half-day off work one Friday to look at two of them, taking Isis with me.

The first breeder was Jason, a thirtyish man near Seattle who had bred his male dog, Chum, named for one of five Pacific Northwest species of salmon. Chum salmon also are known as dog fish, and I felt an immediate connection to this litter, because of my work in salmon habitat restoration. Chum and his bride wandered free in a woodsy backyard among shrubs and ponds, while their tan pups squawked from an outdoor pen in the corner.

Jason let me in the pen, and I crouched in the dirt and poop to find the boy dog raising the least ruckus. I spent a long time trying to pick out which of these dogs could be

Isis's baby brother, because not one stood out. None had the spark I saw in Isis that let me know the second I laid eyes on her that she was The One. None of them gave off any hint of personality.

Since I already was there and had Isis in the car, I decided not to waste the opportunity to test her with a puppy. We had no way to know for sure how she would interact with a baby brother until we brought one home, but before we made it that far, Isis had to prove she could stand to be in the presence of a puppy at all. I picked the mellowest of Jason's boys and asked if we could introduce him to my dog.

Jason walked beside me as I carried the puppy to my car, which I'd parked in the shade several houses away. I showed the puppy to Isis through the car window. She stood on the passenger seat, ears sharp, and eyed the pup like she wanted to bark at it. I made soothing noises to assure her that he was no threat, and her face relaxed. Handing the puppy to Jason as if I totally knew what I was doing, I opened the car door and leashed Isis, pleased that she didn't disqualify herself by barking and lunging at the strange man.

We followed Jason back to his front lawn, Isis walking politely beside me. When Jason put the puppy down on the grass, miraculously, Isis kept her attention on me. I unhooked her leash and said, "Go say hello."

Isis gingerly stepped forward and sniffed the puppy, behaving like a completely normal dog. The puppy just sat there, not doing much of anything while Isis investigated him thoroughly with her nose, then turned back to me. *What's with the kid?*

Boring in the best possible way. No arousal or spiked shoulder fur. No widened eyes or menacing postures. No tail flicking like an angry metronome. Of course, my fantasy included play bows, licking, and a friendly game of chase, but maybe this puppy was too young to play like that.

The important finding was that Isis was not angry or afraid of the puppy. I considered the moment a huge win. Gone were my doubts that Isis wouldn't accept a new sibling. This could happen! We were going to get a puppy!

We drove another hour south to Puyallup where a woman named Shawna had a litter of five boys and a girl. These puppies were more black than tan, with floppy ears. Each one completely adorable. The family also had horses and goats, and Shawna's sullen teenage daughter filled food and water bowls for the animals while I browsed the puppy selection in the sunny backyard. I let Isis rest in the car, giving her a break after doing so well with the test puppy.

The two parent dogs, Sassy and Santos, each resembled Isis, although nowhere near as beautiful. Sassy had drooping nipples from nursing her pups. I asked Shawna how old her dogs were.

"Three."

Three? Isis was three. And she was just a baby, not a mommy. Linda had said getting a puppy might bring out Isis's maternal instincts, but I hadn't made the connection that Isis was old enough to be her baby brother's mother. We had Isis spayed before her first heat cycle, so in a sense, she never matured into canine womanhood. I simply couldn't picture her responding to a new puppy like a mother, licking him and putting her mouth around his head the way her mother did the day we got her.

The puppies were free to roam the backyard but seemed to prefer sleeping underneath a wooden deck. Shawna had put different-colored collars on the pups so buyers could tell them apart. I played with each and couldn't decide which I liked better between one with a purple collar and one with no collar, probably because I was suffering from puppy overload. While none of Jason's dogs spoke to me, I could have taken any one of Shawna's puppies.

I'd have to enlist Rob's help to narrow it down if we decided to go with this litter, but I didn't think we would. I had extremely high hopes for the third breeder. Her name was Jean, and her website had pages and pages of information about German shepherds, breeding for temperament, and training with positive reinforcement.

The next day, Rob and I drove two hours to Jean's self-titled "ranch" and parked outside a gated driveway. As we walked through the gate, two grown dogs greeted us, trailed by Jean and five adorable puppies who reminded me of Isis at that age. One of the parent dogs jumped up on me, nipping me through my jeans.

"These are my twelve-week-old females," Jean said.

"We're looking for a boy," I reminded her.

"Well, gender doesn't matter at all," she said. "Temperament is what counts."

I rubbed my thigh where her dog nipped me, the sting reverberating as a warning that perhaps Jean's website wasn't a hundred percent accurate. Whether or not gender mattered was not the point. I had told her on the phone we wanted a boy.

While Jean put the twelve-week-olds away, Rob and I peered into a pen housing a younger litter. Several tan fluffballs cried and threw themselves against the chicken wire. I squinted through the wires to assess whether any had the right disposition for our household, but couldn't tell which ones had penises.

"We need a mellow boy," I said again.

"I don't have any of those," Jean said, opening the door to the pen containing the littlest puppies.

As they ran around, we picked them up one at a time, looking for a boy. Not finding one, I asked, "Are any of these boys?"

"Nope, no boys."

No boys at all? Why had we wasted a day driving down here? I gritted my teeth. "Thanks for your time."

Rob and I marched down the driveway where we had to wait awkwardly for Jean to unlock the gate.

The entire ride home, I bitched to Rob about what a horrible human this woman was. An irresponsible breeder! Practically a puppy mill! Her website was nothing but lies. All these declarations about helping people find the right dog for their homes. She had some nerve trying to talk me out of what I specifically said I wanted.

Rob shrugged. "Eh. She's just a kook. I didn't mind driving all that way to play with some puppies."

Having ruled out the kook, we were left with Shawna's puppies. The next week, I took Rob to see them. We were going to a baseball game that night in Seattle, so we didn't bring Isis along. I figured we could bring her the day we picked up the puppy. To help the dogs get used to each other before they met, I brought along two small hand towels. One of them, I rubbed all over Isis to cover in her scent (although anything in the car for more than five minutes would be coated with her hair anyway). The other, I planned to rub on the puppy. I would ask Shawna to put the Isis-smelling towel near our new puppy's bed, and I'd put the puppy-smelling towel near Isis's food dish, so she'd associate it with something good.

When we arrived, Shawna pulled the puppies out from underneath her wooden deck, which made Rob smile. I'd told him they liked hanging out under there. All five boys were still available. Rob liked the purple-collared and the collarless puppy too, and we sat down on the deck to make our decision.

I'd read a lot about temperament testing, since Linda said that was the most important consideration, aside from gender. She said we wanted a dog just like her Dakota: non-confrontational, easygoing, eager to learn, able to turn away and not be offended if Isis reacted. Unfortunately, she didn't tell me how we'd know if an eight-week-old puppy had all those traits, so I turned to the Internet. Temperament testing puppies involved things like rolling them to their backs to see if they fought back, picking them up under their bellies to see if they scrambled to get away, and making loud noises to see if they were scared.

Both puppies responded well when I rolled them to their backs and picked them up under their bellies. They nipped my fingers in an exploratory, not bitey, way. Neither tried to escape my grasp or fought back. As far as I could tell, they were both real go-with-the-flow dudes. I decided I didn't need to borrow pots and pans from Shawna to see if banging them scared either dog.

Rob held the roly-poly collarless one under his front legs and stared him in the face. Black markings encircled the pup's eyes like a bandit, and his ears hung loose on the side of his head. I remembered how Isis's ears pointed straight up when we got her, looking too big for her head.

"He's fat," Shawna said. "He's going to be really big. They all are."

I glanced over at Santos, who didn't look any larger than Isis.

"Santos is unusually small for his litter. All of his siblings are huge."

Still studying the collarless dog, Rob said, "I think this one."

And so, on that mid-June afternoon, our family dynamic changed. Rob pulled out a small digital camera and snapped several photos of our chosen one as he wandered under a wooden bench to lie down and gaze across the green lawn. Waves of excitement washed over me. We found our puppy. While I didn't feel the immediate connection to him that I felt with Isis, he was ridiculously cute. Mostly black with little brown eyebrows and a shorter beak than Isis had at his age.

"You're ours now, little guy," I said.

Not that we could bring him home for at least another week, because we had the baseball game that night and my mother was coming the next day. Mom had been back since the time Isis rushed her, and they seemed to get along fine, but having a brand new puppy was more of a distraction than Mom's visit needed.

Shawna was asking seven hundred dollars for the puppies, which was a hundred dollars more than we paid for Isis, but still less than what a lot of purebreds cost. Shawna said Santos and Sassy hadn't won any dog shows yet, but once they had "Champion" in their names, their pups would go for a lot more.

I started to write out a check for the two-hundred-dollar deposit when she told me it was non-refundable. My hand froze above the signature line. Non-refundable? What if we brought Isis down to meet the puppy and she didn't like him?

Perhaps if Isis didn't like the collarless dog, there would be another one available she liked better. If she didn't get along with any of them, well, I guessed we'd have bigger problems than throwing away two hundred dollars.

★★★

Isis's name came to me long before we met her, so I told Rob he could pick the name for Baby Brother. For weeks before we found the pup, Rob and I ran down the names of every Roman, Greek, and Egyptian god, comic book superhero, as well as martial arts terms and Japanese, Indian, and Thai words (just because we shared an affinity for those cultures). Even though it was Rob's decision, I offered up lots of options.

"Osiris is the goddess Isis's brother. We could call him Siris. Or another Egyptian name. Ra? Ramses?"

After we picked him out, I thought of some very cute names reflecting his size: Colossus, Sumo, Kilo. I really liked Kilo until Rob pointed out that people would assume it was a drug reference. A fan of the *Terminator* franchise, Rob lobbied for Machine, which I vetoed. A few days before we picked up the puppy, Rob suggested Leonidas, after the hero-king of Sparta. Leo for short. Both Leonidas and Leo sounded good next to Isis. Leonidas worked for me.

In fact, I'd already suggested Leo, along with Scorpio and Aries, but apparently Rob didn't like the name until he thought of it himself.

I spent most of Mom's weeklong visit preparing for Leo's arrival: buying baby gates, a new bed, and puppy toys. I intended to wait until after she left to bring him home, but late in the week, eagerness got the better of me. I asked Mom if she wanted to go with me to get him on Friday when Rob had to work. She said yes. Lately, Mom and Isis had relaxed more around each other, with Isis lying down outside the guest room door, and Mom finding this more endearing than intimidating.

The night before we brought Leo home, Isis and I lay on my bed facing each other, our noses touching. Mom passed by the open door and Isis snarled. *Back off, Lady! Don't come any closer.*

"Whoa, Isis," Mom said. "We were getting along so well!"

Isis sat up and looked at the ceiling, panting and twitching her eyebrows.

"Guess you startled her," I said. "Seriously, Isis, she's been here a week. What's your problem?"

Just doing my job.

"Do you really think it's your job to make sure no one comes into my bedroom? She's my mother. She's allowed to go anywhere she wants."

Mom went to her room and I resumed fawning over Isis. "So overprotective. Poor unsuspecting Isis. You don't even know this is your last night as an only dog. You have no idea how much your life is going to change."

Flutters of nervousness filled my chest. How did parents of human babies do this? For more than three years, Isis led a spoiled life as the apple of our eyes, queen of the castle. Beloved and doted upon every single day. How was she going to cope with another critter coming into our home? Would she think we didn't love her anymore? Or that we were trying to replace her? I wished I could make clear that Leo was a gift for her, a playmate, someone who would make her life richer and more fun.

They might not be best friends right away, but no matter what, I couldn't let Isis see Leo as a competitor for our affections.

As I snuggled into bed with Isis and Rob later that night, I assured myself everything would be fine. The positive reinforcement concepts I'd learned from Linda had taught me exactly how to introduce a new dog into our home.

★★★

All of Leo's brothers had been selected and picked up in the week before I came back to get him. I no longer accepted my own logic of bringing Isis along to pick him up. There were no other puppies to choose from, and even if they got along smashingly, the drive home would be long, in a small space, with two dogs and my mother. Better to introduce Isis to Leo under less stressful circumstances. Important to set her up for success.

When Mom and I walked into Shawna's, Leo was roaming around the kitchen, having been upgraded to indoor accommodations. Collarless no more, he wore a thin neon-green nylon band around his neck.

"We named him Leo," I told Shawna. "Have you been calling him anything?"

"Mostly just 'Buddy.' "

I handed Shawna a check and scooped up my little buddy, whose floppy ears had moved just a little bit higher up on his head. On the drive home, Leo wedged himself between the two front seats, lying across the cup holder. He looked happy and alert beside us, not crying after being taken away from the only home he'd known. Mom placed a folded-up blanket under him to make him more comfortable, and I fell quietly in love. Leo was pretty quiet himself, resting his warm head on my leg.

I marveled to Mom as we neared our freeway exit that I hadn't yet heard Leo's voice.

Rob and his parents were waiting at our house for my call. They would bring Isis to meet us in a grassy park a few blocks away, a neutral location where Rob sometimes let Isis off leash to chase her soccer ball. While we waited, I lay on my stomach on the grass and studied Leo, with his pink tongue hanging out. In addition to the tan eyebrow-like markings, he had a tan chest and legs, but the rest of him was black, his face much darker than Isis's when she was a puppy. I slipped off his neon collar and replaced it with a green one with a reflective bone pattern. A black bone-shaped tag dangled from the collar, already engraved with LEONIDAS.

Rob's parents' SUV pulled into the lot. Showtime. Leaving Isis in the car, Rob came over to greet our little boy. We introduced him quickly to Jerry and Alice, everyone eager to move on to the main event.

I had Rob sit down with Leo at the far end of the grass, trying to mimic the positioning when Isis met Jason's puppy on his front lawn. Rob's parents and my mother watched from the parking lot while I brought Isis out of the car on her leash. I planned to walk her parallel to Rob and Leo, but Leo, overjoyed to see someone who looked like his mother, bounced across the lawn toward her.

"Rob, no. Don't let him get to us." I moved Isis behind Alice's car.

Rob retrieved the puppy and again sat down with him. I walked Isis parallel, moving her gradually closer. She pulled ahead of me and whined, seeming more agitated than aggressive. I asked her to lie down and she complied, although not quite as calm as she was the day she met Jason's puppy. I should have waited for her to show complete relaxation, but my impatient side said, *Let's get this over with,* and my prudence escaped me. I moved Isis closer, letting her pull me toward Rob, and I dropped her leash. "Go say hello."

Isis trotted up to the new puppy, sniffed him for a half-second, then reared her head back before unleashing a barrage of snarls. Leo threw himself on his back, wailing as though he were being stabbed while Isis pinned him down, snarling above him. I couldn't read her thoughts when she was in that state. All I felt was her rage, which I knew was fueled by fear. I pulled her off Leo, grabbing the leash and hurrying her back to the car. Rob scooped up the baby, who continued to wail.

My heart twisted as I heard his desperate cries.

I ran back to Rob. "Is he hurt?"

Rob looked him over. "No. She didn't bite him." Lowering his voice he added, "I think he peed himself."

"Oh, sweet Leo," I said, stroking his head. My eyes met Rob's.

Shit. That did not go well. My high hopes dashed, my confidence was shattered. I was a horrible person who put a helpless puppy in an unsafe situation and traumatized him within a few hours of living with me.

Alice strode toward me. "Do you want me to try holding Leo? I don't think Isis would do anything if I were there."

"No," I said. "Let's just go home." I couldn't bear another failed attempt.

Mom turned to Jerry and said in a tone trying to be upbeat, "Looks like you've got a new puppy coming to live with you." As defeated as I felt, I appreciated her trying to make light of the disaster.

Jerry just scowled. "He's not coming to live at our house!"

Rob and his parents took Isis home, and my mother and I got back in my car with Leo.

"So it's going to take a little more time than you thought," Mom offered.

"What did I think? She'd take one sniff of Leo and they'd play like littermates? Okay, that's kind of exactly what I thought. Or at least I hoped." I leaned my head back against the headrest. "This is going to be much harder than I expected."

I had been counting completely on Isis responding well to the puppy. Had I really not come up with a Plan B? Because this was pretty much the worst-case scenario. With my hands on the steering wheel, I tried to bring order to the chaos in my head.

The only thing to do was to keep the dogs separated for now.

We went home and put Isis in the backyard while Leo explored inside. I had put a baby gate across the doorway to the laundry room, creating a playpen where he'd spend most of his time until he could be trusted to roam the house. We set up Isis's old crate in Rob's computer room to create a safe place for Leo when Isis was alone in the house with him.

I took a few deep breaths and reminded myself that we never intended to leave the dogs alone together right away. All was not lost. The first introduction had been a failure, that's all. A devastating failure, but it didn't mean the dogs would never be friends, did it?

I needed a professional opinion. I called Linda at home and on her cell phone, leaving messages both places, before e-mailing her the whole story. Then I closed the gate to the chain-link dog run with Isis on the outside and let Leo onto the back patio. A little "protected contact" experiment.

Too soon. Isis lashed out. *Who the hell are you? You don't belong here! These are my people!*

Leo cowered. I scooped him up and had Rob put Isis back in the house.

Sitting on the edge of the retaining wall, I watched Leo pad around the backyard. I'd been so worried about Isis's feelings in the face of this overhaul to her perfect life. I wasn't prepared for how protective I'd feel of little Leo.

How terrifying for him to see a dog who looked just like his mommy and daddy, and have her attack him. We babied Isis so much, but she was not the baby anymore. She was the big sister and she could not act like this.

My shoulders slumped and I let out a sigh that turned into a sob. What if she never accepted him? She'd told us loud and clear that she did not want him here. I had no idea what to do next. All I could think was: *This is too hard. I can't handle this. It was a mistake. Isis was meant to be an only dog. I have to call Shawna and arrange to take Leo back.*

Baby Leo. I had to give him up. No puppy for us. No best buddy for Isis.

Rob joined me and I pressed my face against his chest as he hugged me. He asked, "What do you think we should do for dinner?"

Dinner? We'd just ruined an innocent puppy's life and he wanted to know what was for dinner?

"I'm not hungry."

"Should we order a pizza?"

"Sure." I kept my face buried in his shirt.

"It's going to be okay," he said.

"What if it's not? I think we should take Leo back."

Here's where Rob and I showed our true characters. For all my diligence in training Isis, I was a quitter at heart. Rob was not.

"What? No! Leo is a part of our family." And Rob hadn't just spent the entire day bonding with Leo on the car ride, like I had.

"You're right," I said. "He's ours. We can't take him back."

Leo's whimpers and screeches rang through the house the rest of the evening. My mother sat at the kitchen table and murmured to him over the baby gate.

"Remember saying you'd never heard his voice?" she asked.

"Yep," I said. "We've sure heard it now."

That night, Rob slept with Leo on the laundry room floor, while Isis slept with me.

★★★

When I took Mom to the airport the next day, I apologized for ruining the last day of her visit. I felt guilty for depriving her of my full attention, bringing on all kinds of dog drama, knowing she was ambivalent about Isis already.

"What are you talking about? Nothing was ruined," she said. "I'm sorry that you have to go through this, but I hope that my being here was of some help."

"You've been really helpful. Thank you for sitting with him last night. Having an extra person really helped. When you come back, Leo will remember you as the nice lady who kept him safe from that scary dog."

Reassured that Mom was happy to have been a comfort to me, I remembered four years earlier when she'd driven to Bellingham in a van loaded up with my things to help me and Rob move. I may have been in my mid-thirties, but she was still my mother. She was there when I needed help, and it felt right that she'd been with me the day we got Leo. She'd been with us when we got Isis, after all.

I worried about Rob with both dogs in the house while I was gone, but he'd figured out to put a second baby gate across the kitchen door to keep Isis from coming nose to nose with Leo through the first baby gate.

That afternoon, we practiced having Leo in the dog run while Isis played in the big yard. Leo showed an interest in what Isis was doing and got braver, moving closer to the fence. A few times, she noticed him and ran toward the gate. At first, I panicked, and so did Leo—he ran back to the house. But Isis didn't bark at him and in fact, came right back to me when I called, running the agility course a few more times. Leo again moved toward the fence, then backed away when Isis came closer. She wasn't acting hostile, just curious. And even though he was afraid of her, he gained courage. I considered this progress and allowed a seed of hope to germinate inside me. I remembered some of Isis's severe early reactions to Dakota. She overcame those. She could overcome her fear and hostility toward Leo, too.

When Linda got back to me, she offered to come over on Monday. I'd already planned to take the next two weeks off work for "puppy leave," so that worked fine. When she arrived, Linda was full of suggestions for what I should have done differently.

"This all should have been done with an X-pen, protected contact, or a playpen so that Isis could be off lead and investigate without doing harm to the pup."

I nodded, wishing she'd laid out the process more clearly in our many conversations before I brought Leo home.

"This doesn't mean Leo is scarred for life, but probably very confused, because all the dogs he's met up to this point have been friendly."

Linda tried to demonstrate an exercise with both dogs, but inside the house, Isis could not be within sight of Leo without barking viciously. "Okay, we'll have to work up to that," she said.

We took Leo to the front yard, where Linda brought out Dakota so Leo could have a positive experience with an adult dog. Dakota settled down on the grass beside

Linda, and I brought my terrified puppy gradually closer. We sat down about ten feet away, and Linda marveled at his temperament.

"You're going to be able to teach this dog anything," she said.

At least I'd done something right. Leo was the right dog for our house. We just needed to convince Isis.

I didn't like the changes I saw in her already. A few days before we got Leo, she was happy to run around in the backyard by herself. She didn't want the door closed on her—occasionally she'd show up at the sliding glass door with her dirty soccer ball in her mouth, asking me to join her—but she was fairly happy entertaining herself out there. After we got Leo, she stopped doing that, needing someone out there to play with her. If I left the door open, she came back inside. At first, she ran right past the baby gate that shielded Leo in the laundry room, as though pretending he weren't there. After a few days, she took more of an interest. She wasn't outwardly aggressive; she didn't immediately bark and lunge at him, or respond at all when he cried. I sat at the kitchen table and Isis lay at my feet just a few feet away from the laundry room. Sometimes she looked comfortable, with her tongue hanging out in a smile. I learned to watch that mouth, though, because if she closed it, a reaction was imminent.

If Isis fixed her gaze on Leo for more than two seconds, she was likely to get up, lunge, and bark at him.

In spite of our dysfunctional situation, I liked being a stay-at-home dog mom and was surprised how fast the first week went, with sunny June days warm enough to spend hours at a time in the backyard with each dog. First I'd let Leo out, play with him, and put him in the laundry room. Sometimes I sat on the floor with him and read a book.

Then I took Isis out. Then, I either took Leo out again, or I showered, or fixed some food. At some point, after I put Leo down for his nap, I walked Isis. Or I ran errands, bringing Isis along in the car. Mother-daughter time with the older child was important. By then, it would be after three o'clock. Once Rob got home at five, he shared in the rotation of playing with Isis outside and bringing Leo out of the laundry room.

We practiced having the dogs on either side of a baby gate. When Isis looked at Leo calmly, I clicked and she whipped her head back to me. *Treat?* Her teeth scraped against my fingers, a sign of stress, although we did manage to end most of these sessions successfully.

Isis tolerated the puppy's proximity as long as there were plenty of treats and a barrier between them.

★★★

At Leo's first vet check-up, Dr. Johnson asked me what sort of training we planned for him. I told her we had a very good trainer who had worked with us and Isis.

"Socialization is the most important thing for puppies," she said. "Wag Academy offers a puppy preschool for free because that's how important it is. Socialization saves lives."

For a second, I thought she was talking about human lives, but she probably meant that improperly socialized dogs wound up in shelters and euthanized. Too bad she hadn't mentioned puppy preschool when we first brought Isis to her three-and-a-half years earlier. Linda blamed poor socialization for most of Isis's problems. We had believed the dog books that told us puppies couldn't go out in public until their vaccinations were complete at four months.

Wag Academy was a doggie daycare and training facility in a big warehouse on the other side of town. Leo would be eligible for their weekly preschool class until he was fourteen weeks old. I led him on leash up the stairs to a large rubber-floored playroom and sat down in one of the chairs lined up on either side of the room. About fifteen other puppies of all breeds and sizes wriggled beside their owners until April, the school's thirtyish brunette owner, welcomed everyone.

Puppies sometimes are scared their first time, she warned, inviting me and the other new parents to unclasp our dogs' leashes first. To my surprise, Leo cowered under my chair instead of running over to greet the other puppies. Exactly one week earlier, on the day we brought him home, he'd bounded eagerly across a field to greet Isis. But that ended badly.

Had living with us already ruined him?

I felt better when April said hiding under chairs was normal and suggested I get up and walk away. If Leo wanted to be near me, he'd have to leave the shelter of the plastic chair.

Rather than follow me, Leo warily watched the other dogs from under the chair. His ears had crept slightly higher on his head, with the tips curled forward, still floppy, but perkier.

Leo may not have wanted to play with the other puppies, but I sure did. Leo's classmates included a teeny Boston terrier, an oafish English sheepdog, a vocal beagle, and various golden retrievers and goldendoodles. Playground friendships already had formed; pairs of dogs rolled around with each other.

Leo's time would come, April assured me, as she instructed me to lift up the chair concealing him. Leo shyly introduced himself to a couple of other dogs, but didn't throw himself into the fray during that first session.

The entire time, April provided color commentary for the puppy play skills on display. "Puppies do not know who they are yet; they do not know their role in the pack. They rely on other puppies to tell them, so they try out different roles with back-and-forth play. They learn how to let the other dog gain the upper hand and allow themselves to be put in their place, as well as what it's like to be the more assertive one. We call this role reversal and it builds confidence."

Toward the end of the class, April tossed toys on the floor for the dogs to share, learning not to resource guard. "Good job, puppies."

I kicked a little rubber ball for Leo to chase until he felt brave enough to engage another dog, the teeny Boston terrier, Ernie Mae.

What a brilliant idea the preschool class was. I could tell April was sincere in offering the class for free because she believed in puppy socialization. On the business side, though, plenty of these people, myself included, would pay for other classes once their dogs outgrew preschool.

My joy at watching Leo play with his peers was tempered by my guilt that I'd gone terribly wrong with Isis. If we'd known about puppy preschool when we got her, could she have grown up without behavior problems? Wag Academy used positive reinforcement, so we never would have used a pinch collar or even a choke chain. I tried not to wallow in despair about all the time I wasted and ways I might have messed Isis up by doing the wrong thing. We had no way to know for sure whether her reactivity was a result of those early aversive training methods, or if she was born that way.

But if we'd taken her to Wag Academy as a puppy, at the very least, I would have learned better skills to deal with it.

I found solace in a Maya Angelou quote I came across when I was learning the intricacies of raw feeding, "You did then what you knew how to do, and when you knew better, you did better."

Chapter 13: A House Divided

The only way our dogs would learn to get along with each other, Linda said, was if we made sure that every time they were together, only good things happened. "Your clicker better be going like a machine gun and the treats flowing like the River Thames for everything each one does right."

The first step, she explained, was "equal deliverance of reinforcement," meaning I'd feed the dogs simultaneously, each of them an arm's length away. I had immediate success with this across the baby gate to the kitchen. Isis sat calmly outside the gate while I sat with Leo on the inside, because I had a bowl of raw chicken hearts on my lap. I dipped my hands in the bowl and hand fed a slimy heart to each dog until the bowl was empty, which took three to five minutes. When I could catch Rob between work and his martial arts class, he helped me feed the dogs dinner this way.

I reported happily to Linda, "We had a great session last night. Rob was on the inside of the gate with Leo in the kitchen. I had Isis on the leash in the other room. We worked for about five minutes."

"Good, but don't rush it or you'll see reactions," Linda said. "I know you want her to progress quickly, but haste makes waste and is dangerous. You have to be so sure by both dogs' body language that there is absolutely no doubt they are ready."

"We're not there yet. We had a small reaction this morning. Isis was lying down, so I thought she was pretty relaxed. I didn't even see what Leo did, but Isis got up and barked at him."

"You didn't see what Leo did? So you weren't supervising?"

"No, I was, but Leo was behind the laundry room gate, so I couldn't see what he was doing. My attention was on Isis."

"So you were staring at Isis? No. You want to look straight ahead, so both dogs are in your peripheral vision."

"Oh, I didn't realize that." I felt unfairly criticized. "Well, after the reaction, she calmed down immediately, but it was one of those things where I got nervous and forgot that I'm allowed to praise her as soon as she behaves appropriately again."

"She shouldn't have to calm down at all, because you should be clicking and marking the right behavior continually, all day, every day. Never give her an opportunity to go into prey mode."

"Okay, got it. Click and treat more."

"Do not let her create drama. These things cannot end in failure. If you expect her to do something wrong, she will."

Cannot end in failure. No pressure or anything. I felt like Linda was focusing on what I did wrong without really listening to me, drawing conclusions that I wasn't sure were true. At least she wrapped up with some encouragement: "Just break everything into small pieces and go for it. That's what I like about you. You work hard and systematically, and you will get results!"

As impossible as the assignment was, my mantra became "Only good things happen when the dogs are together." After two months, Isis tolerated Leo being confined to the laundry room. Most of the time, she'd glance at him nonchalantly when she passed on her way in and out the back door. Other times, there was snarling, lunging, and barking across the barrier.

Not to mention accidental meetings. Once when I was not present, Alice reported that Leo escaped his baby gate and Isis had no reaction at all. Alice said she called Isis away and order was restored, but since I wasn't there, I don't know for sure what happened.

After we'd had Leo about a month, Mom returned for another visit. She and I were on the back patio with Rob's parents when Isis slipped past Jerry through the gate, surprised to come nose to nose with Leo. All was calm for about three seconds until Leo threw himself on his back and wailed. He pinned himself down before Isis did anything other than sniff his belly. Then she devolved quickly into snarling. I scooped up Leo, my heart aching at his anguished squeals that didn't stop even after I held him on my lap.

Once again, he'd peed himself.

I wanted to scream, "I can't do this anymore!"

Mom told me not to be angry with Jerry for letting Isis get by. *Fine*, I thought. *Then I'm angry at you and Alice too. Nobody is being as diligent as I need in keeping these dogs apart.*

How were Isis and Leo ever going to get along when everyone else kept dropping the ball? These incidents slowed down Isis's progress and simply shouldn't happen. They left me discouraged and they were scary. My mother already was afraid of my dog; I hated for her to see the vicious side of Isis. For more than a year, I'd been teaching Isis that it wasn't her job to protect me, that I would keep her safe. Then we got Leo, and I had to keep him safe.

And when Mom was visiting, I had to worry about keeping her safe too.

I felt myself unraveling, losing faith in ever reaching our goal. Rob believed. Alice believed. But I wasn't sure. I'd slump on the couch with Isis on the floor in front of me, Leo in his playpen, and could not imagine a time when both dogs would be in the same room.

I worked exercises with the dogs every day, sometimes with Rob's help. Each regression sent me spiraling into despair. The previous winter, after we completed Linda's reactive dog class, I felt like Isis was in such a good place. We still trained a few days a week, but on my own schedule, without the overwhelming pressure I felt when we first started "behavior modification." With Leo in the house, the pressure was back, along with an ever-present weight of despondence. I really had believed that Leo would be a good buddy for Isis, and that she would play with him happily.

At this rate, I would have settled for her not trying to kill him.

Between sessions with Linda, I put a small video recorder on a tripod and recorded our exercises, e-mailing her the footage: *Here's Leo on the outside of the chain-link dog run. Me in my pajamas bringing Isis forward, clicking and treating for looking from him back to me. Me throwing treats to Leo through the fence.* I could see moments of peaceful curiosity in Isis's facial expression sometimes, even behind her Halti, when she looked at Leo.

She had reactions about twenty percent of the time, but when she did well, I was elated.

When I was at work, Alice worked her own method. She put Isis in the backyard on the outside of the chain link, and let Leo into the small dog run. Alice filled up the blue plastic kiddie pool for Isis to splash around in while Leo watched from the patio. When Isis barked at Leo, Alice told her to stop and alleged that Isis complied. She claimed that the dogs ran back and forth playfully on either side of the fence, but I wasn't convinced she'd read Isis's intentions correctly. A tail wag alone did not mean Isis considered the puppy her friend. In fact, tail wagging could be a stress signal.

I hoped Alice wasn't doing anything to set Isis back.

"I know the dogs are going to be friends soon," Alice chirped one afternoon. "Today while Leo was in the little yard and Isis was in the big yard, they played together with the hose. They loved it."

I cringed. This definitely wasn't part of Linda's regimen, but before I could tell Alice never to do it again, I needed to see this game in action. I sat on a cushioned patio chair while Alice stood outside the dog run with Isis, spraying her with the hose. Isis reared up on her hind legs to a height taller than Alice, pressing her face joyfully into the blast of water. When Alice aimed the spray through the chain link at Leo, he frolicked with slightly less gusto, but increasing enthusiasm. As Leo shook his little black head back and forth, Isis watched with soft eyes and her tongue hanging gently out of her mouth.

She wasn't completely at ease with Leo just on the other side of the chain link, but neither did she seem threatened.

C'mon, Grandma! When's it my turn again?

"Good girl, Isis! Good boy, Leo!" I cheered them on from my chair, careful not to interfere with the dynamic. Both dogs playing with Grandma. Maybe Alice was onto something here. Could it really be this easy? Leo and Isis were engaged in an activity they both enjoyed, each aware of the other, but not displaying any stress or aggression. Just joy.

Sharing the hose, and Grandma, was even better than sharing a bowl of raw chicken hearts.

★★★

Leo got bigger. During the first couple of months, it was easy to move him across the house from his crate in Rob's computer room to the laundry room playpen, because we could carry him. Isis didn't mind his presence as long as he was in our arms; we could walk right past her. By early fall, he was too big to carry, and keeping the dogs separate required more complex choreography. If both dogs had been left at home, when we returned, Isis had to be let into the backyard while we transferred Leo from his crate to the laundry room. After Isis came back inside, we put her on the other side of the kitchen baby gate while we let Leo out back. If they'd been left home a long time, I let Leo out front while Isis was out back, to give him a chance to relieve himself.

I took Leo with me to work as much as possible. When we came home, I brought him through the garage directly into the laundry room. Sometimes, the laundry room gate had been left open and Rob or his parents forgot to close the baby gate to the kitchen, so we had near collisions when Isis tried to greet me at the laundry room door. Very frustrating.

Driving both dogs to our training sessions also was tricky. When Leo was small, he sat on Rob's lap in the front seat, but he had gotten too big for that. I strung bungee cords across the width of my hatchback and draped a blanket over them. To reinforce the barrier, I wedged the plastic floor of Leo's dog crate behind the front seats. I always kept the back seats folded down for the dogs. Leo sat up front with me, and Rob sat on the folded-down seats with Isis. On the two-and-a-half-hour drive to the Island County fairgrounds, Rob complained how uncomfortable he was, but his presence effectively kept Isis from investigating the other side of the curtain.

We drove through Burger King on the way to a session and pulled over in the parking lot to eat. A group of people walked by the car, and Isis erupted in a full-blown reaction.

"Ugh, Isis! Stop." Rob's voice carried irritation that rarely came to the surface. Hearing it directed at Isis wounded me every time. Not only was Isis off to a bad start (revving her reactive engine made her more likely to react to Leo later), now Rob was annoyed at her for lashing out. The strangers passed and Rob got in a few more bites of his burger before someone else went by and Isis started up again.

Rob groaned. "This is not very fun."

Rob's mood didn't get any better when we got to the fairgrounds and Linda started barking commands at him, using terminology I was familiar with, having worked with her for almost two years, but that Rob didn't know.

"Ask and release. Ask and release."

When Rob looked blankly at her, Linda demonstrated the technique of lifting both ends of the lead (the ask) and then letting go (release). Rob was handling Isis and I had Leo about thirty feet away.

"If she gets a bead on him, turn her head away," Linda said.

"What? A bee?"

"A bead. A bead. If she gets a bead."

"A beaddddd," I said from across the field.

Rob was over it. If he was annoyed with Isis for barking from the backseat, he was downright irate toward Linda. Usually, even when he was pissed, Rob was pretty collected on the outside. I'd heard him say to customer service people on the telephone more than once, "I know I sound pretty calm, but I'm extremely frustrated. I don't see the point of yelling and screaming at you, because I know this isn't your fault, but I'd like you to remedy this situation as though I were your most difficult customer." He wasn't doing as good a job keeping cool in front of Linda. His hostility took the form of obstinance. I'm sure she didn't realize his foul mood had anything to do with her. She probably thought he was either simply a rude person or frustrated with his own lack of handling skills.

I wished Rob had even a teeny bit of appreciation for Linda's expertise. He didn't have to like her, but couldn't he just fake a smile and follow her directions? We were making slow progress with her method, after all. I'd even allowed some hope to creep in, since we'd had a period of relative calm where Isis tolerated Leo's proximity.

However, during this session, Linda observed that Isis was not exhibiting any calming signals. "She's practicing avoidance, which is preferable to aggression, but as we've seen, if she gets a bead on Leo, her ears go forward, her body tenses, and without so much as a warning growl, she goes into battle. We want to see her develop some calming signals like a yawn, blinking eyes, or a paw lift that show she's trying to calm herself down."

At home, we set up two octagonal exercise pens (X-pens) in the backyard so I could put a dog in each and click/treat Isis for every single calming signal. This went well because Isis started lying down as a default behavior. After we had several independent successes, which I video-recorded and sent to Linda, she suggested I move ahead to more advanced exercises on my own.

While Isis was in her pen, she lay down and happily looked to me for treats. She still didn't do many of the textbook calming signals I hoped for, but neither did she bark and snarl. After a couple of minutes, I opened her X-pen gate and let her out, dropping her leash as Linda had instructed. My plan was to praise her for appropriate behavior toward Leo, still in his pen.

Isis's first move was to trot toward the back door. *We go inside now, right?* When she realized I wasn't with her, she ran back up to the pen, sniffed Leo, then lunged and barked at him, circling his X-pen.

Leo reciprocated with his baby-boy bark. "Roo! Roo! Roo!"

I chased Isis around the X-pen until I could get hold of her leash, but she kept barking and lunging toward Leo's pen, snarling and vicious. Even with her harness and Halti on, I struggled to muscle her back into the pen. I had her almost to her pen door when my shoulders jerked as she pulled me back toward Leo. As soon as I finally succeeded in shoving her back inside the X-pen, she stopped barking and gave me the same openmouthed "smile" I'd been rewarding as a calming signal for days.

Had she been faking me out, or had I misread her body language? Linda said the problem was "fence aggression," and decided the X-pen was the wrong training tool for our purposes. (Why then, I wondered, had she suggested it?)

We moved on to parallel walking. At our next session, Linda had Rob walk Leo while I walked Isis up and down the length of our backyard. Things went great for a couple of laps before Isis crossed in front of me and threw herself toward Leo, barking with enough force that her jaw snapped the strap of her Halti. Linda scolded me for allowing Isis to get ahead of me. I should have stepped in front and put my hand out flat in her face. But I hadn't and now the only thing to do was to remove Isis swiftly, without drama.

Her "punishment" was to be separated from me. We put her in the house.

"Isis isn't showing any conditioned emotional responses," Linda said. "She is not happy to see Leo and she wants him out of her yard."

As if we needed that disheartening message translated for us.

After Isis had ten minutes by herself to calm down, we brought the dogs out front and walked them a half block down the street. I spotted a dude across the street with two dogs off leash, and used my ninja-like reflexes to move Isis far enough away not to notice them, while still keeping her from getting too close to Leo.

"She is starting to like walking off property," Linda observed. "Isis needs a lot of guidance as to what is expected of her, what to do. It is important to reward everything she does right."

Somehow, that walk redeemed the entire training session for me and Rob, leaving us both feeling encouraged. Rob even said, "It will be fun to work with the dogs this way, walking them together."

Fun. For so long, I'd felt like the only one committed to the training process. Rob's newfound willingness to help overjoyed me.

The rest of that week, unfortunately, it rained and got dark before Rob was available to practice. We only needed to walk the dogs for one to five minutes at a time, so in theory, we should have been able to fit that into our morning routines. Irritatingly, Rob never offered to make time to help me unify our household, and since I found the sessions so stressful anyway, I didn't want to antagonize him by nagging about it. Pathologically concerned with putting him out, I had trouble saying, "Look, I need you to do this exercise with me," which was ridiculous, because he never actually refused me anything that I asked.

Later in the week, we made time after dark to walk them up the yard and back down. The plan was to do that once, and if it went well, do it again. Then end. Isis was obviously stressed after the first lap though, so I said brightly, "Okay, we're going in!"

At which point she growled, barked, and lunged mightily. *Fail.*

I put her in the house for her ten-minute time-out, and then felt too discouraged to try again.

★★★

After he learned the difference between stress signals and calming signals, Rob asked how he could recognize mine.

"My stress signals are very subtle," I said. "I say out loud, 'I'm feeling very stressed and overwhelmed.' "

The only people I ever confessed that to were my mother and Rob. Maybe I didn't give clear visual cues, but the stress signals were there for me to feel. I held my breath, sighed a lot, my head raced, my shoulders tightened, and I felt a weight on my chest. A co-worker once told me she was surprised I never got stressed out or pissed off about anything, but I was pissed off about most things at that job. Apparently I covered it well, giving off the false impression that I had it all together.

Inside, I was just like Isis. We fed off each other's high-strung energy. I seized up when I saw something like a bicycle or a dog that I knew would set Isis off. It set me off before it set her off, thwarting my goal of keeping her calm.

Isis spun and chased her tail when she was excited and overstimulated. She chewed on herself so much that she wound up needing root canals on her other two canines, and wore her smaller front teeth down to nubs. She scratched sore spots on her chest with her hind legs. These behaviors existed before we got Leo, but his presence made them worse.

Linda suggested we put Isis in a stress detox for three days, not letting her see Leo except for brief feeding exercises each day, basically moving us back to square one. We screwed up on the first day and Isis saw Leo a few times. And barked. She heard noises outside. And barked. Not part of the stress detox. The idea was to give her no stimulation at all. No toys. No balls.

She would be forced to sleep for hours and relax.

We renamed the library "The Quiet Room" and I stretched an X-pen across the doorway, draping a sleeping bag over it so she couldn't see out. I sat beside Isis on her favorite couch to help her relax. Even though this was the room where she relaxed eighty-five percent of every day, and even though I was right beside her, she mouthed the couch cushions, spun around, tucked her head under her hind leg, and made her T-Rex "Raa raa" sound.

I stroked her and told her that she needed to try to relax harder.

After Isis's first day of detox, I smiled when I heard Rob ask her how it was going. "Are you having withdrawals from all that barking?"

Rob's calming energy counterbalanced my mania. I understood what Linda meant when she said that Leo could be therapeutic for Isis eventually. Leo, like Rob, was easygoing. At puppy kindergarten, when two shepherds got in a spat over the water dish, Leo just turned away, saying, *I have no idea what those two are fighting about.* How wonderful it would be if Leo could be as soothing an influence on Isis as Rob was to me.

But in October, Leo developed a problem of his own. On our walks, he behaved appropriately for half the journey, then freaked completely out and became uncontrollable. He jumped up and bit our arms hard enough to leave bruises, break the skin, and tear our jacket sleeves.

I knew how to train this behavior away. Click and treat for heeling calmly. Step on the leash (to prevent him from jumping) and ignore the bad behavior. Show him an appropriate behavior that is incompatible with the bad behavior. Practice sits, downs, and stays on the walk. Bring a tennis ball or a toy for him to carry in his mouth. All of that worked some of the time, but he kept returning to the jumping and arm-biting game. So humiliating to think our neighbors might look out their windows to see my six-month-old puppy dangling by his teeth from my arm. We had him using a Halti by then, and I suspected it exacerbated the jumping and biting. He didn't like the pressure of the halter on his face and seemed to be jumping up to beg us, *Get this thing off me!*

During this time period, Isis became the easier dog to walk. On Saturday mornings when there were fewer bicycle commuters on our block, I took her on twenty-minute walks that were downright peaceful. I still had to monitor everything around us to make sure we didn't get surprised by a jogger or another dog, but at least Isis walked calmly beside me, mouth open, tongue hanging out, not pulling her leash like she used to, and not jumping and chewing on my arm like Leo did.

Linda didn't make me feel any better by saying that Leo's biting was a clear result of stress in the home. "He is feeling the effects of Isis's aggression toward him. He is a good dog and deserves a relaxed atmosphere."

Yes, he was, and yes, he did. Was Linda implying that I should give him up? Let him live in a home where he would be treated right, and let Isis return to her perfect life as our only child? I knew that's what most rational people would do, but so far, no one had said so to my face.

I could never give Leo away because I selfishly refused to let another family enjoy the benefits of my perfect puppy. I found him; he was mine. Sure, he was a total nightmare to walk, but everyone who met him agreed that he was a wonderful dog.

A wonderful dog who wasn't getting enough stimulation or attention. When I brought him to work, I had to use my car as a crate for half the day, since he couldn't sit still in my office the whole time. I left him in the car until about ten, when I took him for a short walk that tired him out enough to sleep on my office floor until lunch. At lunch, I took him to a park and tossed a ball for half an hour, bemoaning the fact that I got a puppy for the express purpose of stimulating and exercising Isis, and wound up with two dogs desperately in need of stimulation and exercise because they couldn't play together.

How much longer could this go on? What if they never got along and we had to keep these dogs separated for the next ten years? Linda said the clock was ticking. Leo was six months old, and if the dogs weren't acclimated to one another by the time he was ten months, it might never happen.

I worried about the dogs constantly, sinking into a full-fledged depression about my failure to meet either of their needs. I hated to leave them at home for any length of time because they needed playtime and training. I felt like a terrible mother, starting to believe that Leo probably would be better off in more skilled hands. So would Isis. *I should give them both away…*

With that thought, I related for the first time to those women who drown their children while suffering from post-partum psychosis, having become so distraught over their maternal incompetence.

I was wallowing in this feeling one morning at work when I received an e-mail from Linda in advance of that evening's training session, asking me what progress we'd made since our last session. "How many walks have they had together?"

Uh, none? We were exactly where we left off. Leo was uncontrollable on walks and I had bruises from him all over my arms and legs. I told Linda that all we'd been working on was getting the dogs to tolerate being within sight of each other inside the house.

She responded, "I wish Isis had more dog-aggression work prior to getting the new pup, but that is old news by now. Getting them to a level of tolerance is a critical milestone, otherwise you may be facing some hard questions, such as rehoming Leo (I know that is something that you don't want to hear), but I have to say, the second Isis went for Leo, I would have returned him."

Excuse me, but what the fuck?

I distinctly remembered her saying a puppy would be therapeutic for Isis. She didn't say, "Let's do more dog-aggression work." I'm certain I would have remembered if she had, because I would have scheduled however many sessions she said it would take. When she first met Leo three days after we got him, she said he had such a good temperament that eventually he would be therapeutic for Isis. *Therapeutic!* She said nothing about returning him.

Her e-mail blindsided me. After everything we'd been through. I'd trusted her and followed all her stupid instructions about making Isis wait five minutes before I pet her, and hand-feeding the dogs all their meals simultaneously. I believed her when she said we could bring our dogs together. Now for the first time, I wondered if she had any idea what she was doing. All this time, I'd followed her lesson plans with blind confidence. Frank said I needed to "really listen to her," after all.

Linda talked about writing a book about her method of getting reactive dogs to get along. My rage mounted as I realized we'd been her guinea pigs. Had she just been trying out different methods on us to see what would work?

Livid, I was prepared to call her on her bullshit when she arrived at our house that night. *You said we should get a puppy. You said he would be therapeutic.* But when she arrived, she was contrite, full of optimism and fresh ideas. She carried a tennis ball attached to a red rope—a gift for Leo we could carry on our walks for him to grab onto instead of our arms.

And she said, "I have never suggested this to a client before, but I think you might want to consider putting Isis on Prozac."

Early on, Linda made clear her belief that reactive dogs could be helped without anti-anxiety meds, and of course I'd expected that to be the case with Isis. At the time, something about the idea of drugging my dog didn't sit right, like it would alter her effervescent personality. Perhaps Isis could have lived happily without medication as an only dog, but there was no denying that her anxiety had escalated steadily since we got Leo. The training methods that worked before were not working anymore, and Isis had shown no improvement after the stress detox. Maybe medication was the missing ingredient that would calm her down enough around Leo to make progress.

I was willing to try anything.

But what did it mean that Linda was recommending Prozac for the first time ever? Was she acknowledging that her experimental training method had been a complete failure? I certainly thought so.

I took Isis to the vet to get a prescription for Prozac and have her thyroid retested. Again, her bloodwork was normal. I'd had no idea you could get dog prescriptions filled at the local human pharmacy, and found it extremely amusing to pick up the order for Isis Neumeyer. The clerk asked for the patient's birth date, and I said, "Well, it's for my dog. Do you have her birthdate on file?"

We didn't see any measurable difference on forty milligrams of Prozac. After a couple of months, she still seemed so anxious that we upped her dosage to eighty milligrams a day. I wondered how we would know when we'd hit the correct dosage.

The idea haunted me that she was plagued by continual feelings of anxiety. Leo was supposed to bring joy to Isis's life, but he had compounded her anxiety. How cruel and misguided had we been to bring him into our home?

Looking back at Isis's lifetime of behaviors, I considered how much of it must have been fueled by anxiety. She chewed on her legs a lot, always had. I thought that was just something dogs did out of boredom. By now I accepted that's how she wore away the sharp edges of her teeth. I hadn't thought it possible at the time of our first trip to the vet dentist because her fur was so soft, but there was no other explanation. She gnawed away, grinding her teeth against the hairs, not causing any damage to the fur itself or even the skin underneath. The damage was concentrated entirely on her front teeth, which by this point had eroded all the way down to her gums. Only her flat-top canines were noticeable when she flashed her beautiful smile, but if you lifted her front lip, instead of incisors, you'd see little white islands flush with the surface of her pink gums, top and bottom.

I looked longingly at every adult dog I saw with perfectly pointed teeth.

We always thought of Isis as an extremely happy dog when she wasn't lashing out aggressively out of fear. But her fearfulness didn't evaporate when she wasn't having a reaction. Maybe she was in such a constant state of anxiety that some of the things that we found adorable were really symptoms of something else.

Like when she apologized for farting. Neither Rob nor I remembered when it started, if it predated Leo or not. We'd be sitting around watching TV and smell the unmistakable release of canine flatulence.

Rob and I teased her. "Isis, did you fart?" She quivered up to us and climbed into our laps.

I'm sorry, yes I did. I hoped you wouldn't notice because I didn't want to disturb you. I love you so much.

"Isis, it's okay. We love you, too." We cuddled with her as she lay across us on the loveseat. We cracked up that Isis showed signs of shame that she stunk up the room, having no idea this could be a troubling sign of her neuroses.

★★★

One morning, I was roused by a doggie nose snuffling my face, and smiled at Isis's warm greeting. I stroked the soft dog beak, my eyes still closed, listening to Rob chattering in the bathroom. Who could he be talking to? My eyes fluttered open. Standing at my bedside, about ten feet away from where Isis gave Rob her rapt attention, was Leo.

Good morning. I was lonely over there at the other end of the house, so I let myself out.

"Rob! Close the door!"

At the sound of my voice, Isis alerted to the intruder, fixed her gaze on him, and thundered. Rob's reflexes were fast. He slammed the door before Isis could slip out. Her alert changed frequency from low and menacing to high-pitched, like an anxious car alarm. She threw herself at the closed bathroom door while I got out of bed, slipped a finger under Leo's collar, and wearily led him back to his laundry-room playpen. At times, it felt like animal cruelty, but the playpen was straight from the playbook of puppy behaviorist Ian Dunbar, who advised confining puppies until they could be trusted not to destroy the house.

How sweet Leo's little face had felt against mine. After six months, he had never spent the night with us in our room. (Although Rob had spent a few nights with him on the laundry room floor).

"Back into prison, you go." I closed Leo into the laundry room, where we'd upgraded the baby gate to an X-pen barricade across the doorway. This wasn't our first near-miss; I'd made Rob screw a latch into the door frame because Leo kept escaping. This was our closest call.

Rob released Isis from the bathroom and she crawled back into bed with me while Leo voiced his displeasure, squawking and howling incessantly from the laundry room.

I shouted, "Leo! Shut your piehole!"

Without question, we were a house divided.

★★★

Leo had graduated from puppy preschool and puppy kindergarten, and I'd enrolled him in puppy prep school. Mom suggested I consult his trainers at Wag Academy about our domestic situation. I resisted at first because what could they possibly suggest that we hadn't already tried with Linda? I was embarrassed to tell anyone about the ridiculous arrangement of keeping my dogs separated for months. My shame was validated when I let it slip to Leo's prep-school teacher, Carmen, that we had a reactive dog at home who couldn't be in the same room with him.

She gave me a strange look that left my heart heavy throughout the class. Leo was a superstar in class, and very popular.

I felt like I was bringing him home to an abusive environment.

The best I could do for him was to bring him with me to work most days. The way I saw it, Isis had to be cooped up by herself in the house all day; Leo had to be cooped up most of the time when we were home. Sometimes we confined Isis to the library and brought Leo out for short periods in the house, but we had to keep a constant eye on him, because left unattended he would eat the furniture. I knew this for sure because he had a penchant for chewing the furniture in my office right in front of me. He destroyed both arms of a stuffed chair and also nibbled on my ethernet cable, causing superficial damage.

When I didn't have time to take Leo on a full-fledged walk in the middle of the workday, we had mini play sessions in the long hall outside my office door. (Absent my co-workers, of course.) I'd toss a ball down the length of the office for Leo to scamper after. Once, when no ball was available, I grabbed a stuffed monkey off a coat hook on my door. "You'll like this guy." Sticking my fingers between the caped super-monkey's hands, I stretched back his arms to propel him down the hall.

"Yee-aaaah-haa-haa!" The monkey screamed as he flew through the air.

Back when Isis was allowed to come to work, she had enjoyed retrieving the flying monkey, who sometimes let out an extra scream or two while being jostled in her mouth. However, the monkey did not scream as Leo brought him back. Instead I heard an unpleasant crunching as he chewed the plush material, destroying the mechanical bits inside.

"Five seconds in your mouth, and the monkey screams no more." I took the toy from his mouth and placed it back on its hook. "Nice job, Leo. Let's not mention to Isis that you ruined her toy."

I hoped Leo didn't know how deprived he was. Rob and I tried to find ways to make sure each dog had special experiences. One Sunday, we took Isis to Grandma's house, stopping at Dairy Queen to get her some vanilla ice cream. She played ball with Alice in the backyard and relaxed on the living room floor. Isis didn't look like a dog suffering horribly from anxiety. Her ebullient smile warmed my heart. At home, I spent about an hour outside with Leo. Despite a weather forecast of "miserable," there was some sun and a brisk fall wind. Leo romped and chased a tennis ball. He pounced on a fly. He sat beside me and looked out into the trees with the wind blowing in his face. Seeing him so happy soothed some of my guilt and anxiety.

Instead of feeling heavy-hearted, I decided to adopt the Buddhist notion of living in the present moment. Not worrying about the past or the future. Not dwelling on every setback. Not caring what other people thought. Not fretting about whether the dogs would ever play together.

Live in the moment. Isis was happy. Leo was happy. Today was a good day.

Chapter 14: A New Hope

We were in a holding pattern with Linda. I couldn't forgive her for saying, way after the fact, that we never should have gotten Leo. I wanted to break things off, but we'd prepaid for ten training sessions, so the relationship dragged on.

For our final session, we met Linda on a blustery night in an enormous commuter parking lot near our house. I invited Alice to join us because of her calming effect on Isis and Leo, and because she could provide a second vehicle for dog transportation. She wound up sitting in her car with the heater running for most of the session. Meanwhile, braced against the wind and rain, Rob and I maneuvered the dogs around the darkened gravel lot, depleting the bags of treats stashed in our coat pockets. Our crowning achievement was walking the dogs about thirty feet from each other with Dakota between them. Progress, I supposed, but my trust in Linda had vanished. After working with her for six months, we should have been able to do more than walk the dogs parallel at a distance from each other.

Even thirty feet away from Leo, Isis still showed heightened anxiety.

I'd considered a number of ways to break the news to Linda that we were through. At the end of our session, after the dogs were returned to their respective cars, she gave me an opening.

"I'm going to be out of town for the next couple of weeks."

"Okay, well, I think we know what we need to work on," I said. "We'll just work on our own for a while and touch base if we need to."

Linda nodded, gave us a "Take care," and drove off.

"That was almost too easy," I said.

Rob just shrugged before opening the passenger door to his mother's car, ushering Isis from his seat to the back, and climbing in. I trudged through the stinging rain to my own car where Leo waited for me.

Was Linda secretly happy to be rid of us? I wouldn't blame her; we were a colossal failure. With us on her client list, she couldn't claim to be an authority on bringing reactive dogs together. What she didn't know was that I'd already met someone else: Leo's prep-school teacher.

Compared to our angst-filled training with Linda, puppy prep school was all fun and games. Carmen had a quirky gentleness you might see in a kindergarten teacher who preferred the company of five-year-olds. Linda, on the other hand, taught juvenile delinquents, knew all their tricks, and didn't stand for any nonsense in her class.

Every year, Carmen hosted a Halloween party where costumed canines enjoyed an all-you-can-eat buffet. We couldn't go because we had other plans, but after Carmen invited us, Rob told Isis all about it. Lying on the couch, he stroked her belly. "Did you know that there's a party where there's a special buffet for doggies? They get to eat all the cheese and cookies they want."

I like cookies.

Rob wasn't meaning to rub it in that Isis couldn't go to this party. More like he wanted her to know about the magical world that existed outside our home. In Rob's mind, maybe next year Isis could go to that wonderful party.

After I confessed to Carmen about Isis, she said she'd like to meet her. In addition to teaching at Wag Academy, Carmen had her own facility, Sunny Lane. I drove Isis there on a rainy evening in November. I parked by a well-manicured lawn, and Carmen waved from in front of a small classroom building adjacent to a darling wood-paneled home. Across the lawn, I saw a fenced yard filled with agility equipment—a play area larger than the fenced dog park in Bellingham.

I brought Isis inside the classroom and let her off-leash. She raced around the room, sniffing the corners and drinking from a water dish Carmen set out for her. I was always completely thrilled when Isis didn't bark and lunge upon meeting a new person, but within a few minutes, Carmen said gently, "I think there's something genetically wrong with her."

"Like a birth defect?"

"Not exactly. I just mean that her anxiety and reactivity could be something that she was born with."

That was marginally reassuring. On the one hand, we hadn't done anything wrong. On the other, our baby was defective.

I explained the full history of Isis's behavior problems and subsequent behavior modification training. Carmen thought Prozac was a good idea, but was horrified at the number of sessions Linda had prescribed to treat Isis. "I would never tell someone that it would take fifteen sessions for them to improve a dog's behavior."

Carmen had cultivated a woodsy trail on her property where dogs could roam safely off leash. We flipped up the hoods on our raincoats and led Isis past Carmen's house to the moss-covered trailhead where we set her loose. Isis walked beside me for a short distance before jetting up ahead. She raced out of sight around a bend in the trail, then reappeared, smiling, her ears sharp and alert.

Are you coming?

"Right behind you, sweetheart."

***

Carmen had too full a schedule to take us on as private clients. She taught classes on Saturdays and supervised a doggie play group at Wag Academy on Sundays. She invited us to bring Isis to Sunny Lane some weekend when she wasn't there. A change of scenery seemed like exactly what Isis needed, so we returned to Sunny Lane on a misty Sunday afternoon, this time with Rob, eager to show him the nature trail and play yard. As she had before, Isis raced ahead of us through the trees on the trail and Rob and I smiled, happy to give her a special outing where she didn't have to wear a Halti or struggle to behave around other dogs. This day was just for Isis. Just for fun.

We opened the chain-link gate to the play yard and watched her sniff each corner.

Dog tunnels and hoops had been pushed into the corners, so Rob pulled them out, setting up an agility course. Isis was a pro at the set of weave poles and hurdles at home, and she had learned to jump through a hoop during her training with Linda. She was inexperienced with the other equipment, though. I stood with her at one end of an enclosed tubular tunnel, while Rob stood at the other and called her name. Isis raced through the tunnel to get to him. Next, Rob guided her up the pitched slope of a wooden A-frame and down the other side before heading to the next obstacle: a "dog walk" made of three long wooden planks that were narrower than the A-frame. The center plank was about four feet off the ground, and the other planks led up to it from the ground. I was surprised Isis even attempted it; the plank was so narrow, so high off the ground. But with Rob trotting beside her, she raced up, across, and over the plank again and again.

He ran her through the obstacles like a real agility course, one after another.

"Isis, jump! Through the tunnel! A-frame! Up the plank! Through the hoop! Good girl!"

Isis glowed with pride as she showed off her agility prowess. Since she couldn't play with other dogs, and long walks were challenging, we were thrilled to find a place other than our backyard where she could romp and play, wearing herself out just by being a dog. Rob had a great time as well, given this rare opportunity to play with Isis without my harping on him about his handling techniques.

However, back at home with Leo, Isis regressed. We still were working on having the two dogs in the same room by feeding them chicken hearts and gizzards whenever they were in each other's presence. When we first started this work, I could feed the dogs by myself for up to five minutes with each of them an arm's length away from me, but lately, we couldn't get past two and a half minutes with the dogs on opposite ends of the long TV room. Inevitably, one of the dogs would look at the other wrong, triggering a bout of barking and lunging.

Leo's voice had deepened to what we called his "big-boy bark." Apparently, he'd decided not to take any more crap from his mean big sister, so he started preemptively barking at her loudly and deeply, usually leading to severe reactions on her part. A few times, I managed to move her away fast enough that she didn't bark back, but I could hardly call it a success to force her to retreat from Leo's increasingly masculine trash-talking. We had better luck when Leo faced away from Isis and kept his full attention on the person giving him treats, but since almost every session ended with a reaction, we reduced the time to thirty seconds, working back up to forty-five seconds, then one minute. Only as long as we could go without one of them barking.

Carmen thought that eventually we should bring the dogs together on neutral ground, wearing muzzles to make sure they didn't hurt each other. To prepare them, we practiced slipping black fabric muzzles over their snouts and fastening them around their heads. The process was similar to getting them used to their Halti head collars, and the soft material didn't seem too terribly uncomfortable. They tolerated the muzzles, although they liked them less than the Haltis. Their black noses poked out of a hole at the end of the muzzle, giving them limited access to very small treats.

I didn't expect the muzzles to teach the dogs how to be around each other, but maybe they would help us move one step closer.

One afternoon, in a fit of frustrated whimsy, Rob and I put the muzzles on the dogs at home to see what they did. *What the hell*, we thought. After all, everyone who wasn't a licensed trainer had been advising us to do this for months. All these amateur dog behaviorists insisted that the dogs would work it out on their own, implying that we were somehow sabotaging the unification of our home by keeping the dogs apart.

We couldn't have orchestrated the muzzle experiment worse if we'd tried. We set them loose on each other indoors, near the doorway to the kitchen. Why there, I can't remember. They snarled and barked and went for each other's throats as best they could with the muzzles on. The last time they were this close to each other, Leo was a baby who peed himself and wailed. This time he snarled back, just as ferociously as Isis, only deeper. We separated them, retired them to their corners in separate rooms, and agreed that was a really stupid idea.

I was too ashamed to tell any of the professional dog advisers that we'd tried this at home. We knew we were supposed to start on neutral ground. Carmen said she would help us, but wasn't available until after the winter holidays, so Rob and I took the dogs to Sunny Lane on our own. Rob rode in the back of my car with Isis, shielded by the curtain and plastic crate floor, while Leo and I sat in front. I parked by the chain-link fence and we left Leo in the car where he could watch Isis practice her agility tricks. Once again, she excelled. We put her back in the car and introduced Leo to the equipment. Skeptical at first, Leo let Rob guide him up and over the A-frame and dog walk.

Then Rob leashed up Leo, and I brought Isis out to walk them parallel to each other across the yard. As far apart as they were, Isis lunged and barked at Leo. I executed my well-practiced method of redirecting her attention away from him by turning her head in the other direction. Leo kept pelting us with a barrage of "Rarf! Rarf! Rarf!" Even if I could have taken Isis's mind off the demon at the other end of the field, Leo would not let her forget him.

We returned Leo to the car while we wore Isis out a little more with agility games before trading dogs. I retrieved Leo and muzzled him, while Rob muzzled Isis. We got the dogs lying down at opposite ends of the yard. At the last minute, I worried that if we unleashed both dogs and they got into a fight, they'd be hard to catch up to in order to separate, so when Rob let Isis loose, I held onto Leo's leash. As Isis raced toward us, Leo twisted on his leash, which somehow pulled the muzzle right off his face.

Seizing the advantage, Leo nipped Isis's nose, drawing blood. I let his leash drop and he ran through a tunnel to get away from Isis, who blustered like a wild mustang, heaving breaths through the confining muzzle. Rob grabbed her leash and tried to get her attention with some cooked liver, but she kept lunging at Leo, too far into hindbrain. Not in her right mind.

I caught up with Leo while Rob put Isis in the car. When he came back to me, Rob said he wanted to try again. He didn't say so, but in my head, I heard, *Perhaps this time without you screwing everything up by holding onto Leo's leash.*

"I'm too freaked out. I can't do this." The muscles of my scalp constricted and my shoulders clenched. Of course my dogs couldn't be calm around each other if I couldn't be calm when they were together. "Maybe I should wait in the car."

We put Leo's muzzle back on and locked him in a small caged area in one corner of the play yard. Isis and I traded places, and Rob brought her into the yard wearing her muzzle. From my vantage point, taking deep breaths in the car, Isis didn't show too much interest in Leo when he was in the cage, so Rob let Leo out. A few seconds later, I heard him say, "They're playing! They're playing!"

I could see them running beside each other like regular dogs, so I got out of the car to stand beside the fence. Rob stood confident in the middle of the yard, arms relaxed at his sides, basking in the normalcy of our dogs. For maybe thirty seconds, the dogs did their own things, sniffing around. My heart full of hope, I went back inside the yard and Rob and I praised the dogs for turning away from each other, a calming signal, instead of going for each other's throats.

"Isis, A-frame!" Rob led Isis over the obstacle. But when she came back down, she went after Leo again, snarling and lunging through her muzzle. We separated them and ended there.

On the drive home, we tried to establish whether what just happened had been progress or not. I didn't want to keep inflicting the dogs on one another if it wasn't helping us move toward our eventual goal. Were we helping or making things worse?

"Maybe we could try again, but only have them together for a really short period of time," I said. "Like if we'd ended it right after they were running together, we'd be feeling pretty damn good right now. It's just so hard to gauge when the mood is going to turn."

When I reported back to Carmen, she considered it a minor success. "It might be better next time," she said. "Remember, repetition of behavior creates habit. It they have a couple of good sessions, it would increase the chance for future success."

She offered to be there with us next time, saying, "Don't give up yet."

***

We took two cars to pick out our tree. We were getting two trees anyway; Rob wanted to get a small one for the martial arts studio. Rob and Isis drove in his dad's pickup truck, and I drove Leo in my little Honda. We still preferred a Christmas tree lot about half an hour up Mount Baker Highway. We liked it because they had a machine that shook out the loose needles and they bound the trees in twine for easier transport.

And they allowed dogs. We tried a different tree lot for Isis's second Christmas, but got back in the car when we saw the No Dogs Allowed sign. After that, we always drove as far as Red Mountain Tree Farm.

We introduced Leo to our tradition, trying to get a cute picture of him in front of the smaller tree for the studio. I tied a festive green bandana around his neck, but couldn't get him to smile for the camera. After the first tree was loaded up, we put Leo back in my car and brought Isis out for her turn. She was a modeling pro at this point. I crouched beside her and scratched her chest, getting her to beam toward the camera.

"Who's a good little supermodel? That's my girl."

Looking at the photos later, I said, "Next year, we'll be able to have both dogs in the same picture."

All I wanted for Christmas was for my two dogs to get along. That fantasy felt farther away than ever until Carmen gave me the number of another trainer, Shannon, who was supposed to be the most experienced trainer of reactive dogs in the area. The holidays were such a busy time, I expected Shannon to take weeks to get back to us, but she called back a few days later saying she had time that weekend.

We planned for Alice to drive Leo and Rob in Jerry's truck, while I drove Isis to Shannon's place about forty minutes south of Bellingham. Alice still hadn't gotten to our house by the time I planned to leave and I felt tense about being late, so Isis and I left ahead of them.

I tried to relax my shoulders as I drove south on Interstate 5, nervous about meeting a new trainer. I already told Shannon that rehoming either dog was not an option; we would keep the dogs separated for the rest of their lives if we had to. Naturally, I hoped it wouldn't come to that, but Shannon was our last chance. What if she told me the dogs were a lost cause? What if she thought we were out of our minds to keep hoping?

I knew what to expect from Shannon since she was a positive reinforcement trainer, but my heart always beat a little faster before any training session. Would Isis make progress or regress? Would she be relaxed or stressed? Would I handle her with confidence, keeping her calm by letting her know that I would always keep her safe? Or would I click at the wrong moment, run out of treats, or otherwise fail her, leading to a violent reaction that flooded her with adrenaline and set her back by increasing the likelihood of additional, stronger reactions?

Following Shannon's directions from the freeway to a gravel road, I drove past expansive properties with barns and stables. Shannon met me at the bottom of her driveway. Small-framed and outdoorsy, Shannon had bangs and shoulder-length brown hair streaked with gray. She let me in through a black metal gate, directing me to park near a barn between a small wooded area and a horse corral. When I brought Isis out in harness and Halti, she expressed no interest whatsoever in meeting Shannon, instead sniffing the gravel and glancing nervously at the horses.

Alice, Rob, and Leo pulled up beside me—Alice must have hauled ass on the freeway—and we left Leo in the truck while we took Isis inside the barn. I worried briefly that Leo might chew up the interior of Jerry's truck. We bypassed a large classroom space and crowded into a small heated section of the building, which looked like it was used as a tool shed. We sat on stools while Isis scoped out the space.

Alice described to Shannon what her experience had been with the dogs, and how much promise she saw when they played separately on either side of the dog run fence.

"Isis isn't a mean dog," Alice said. "I know that she and Leo can be friends."

"I notice that she moves around pretty mindlessly," Shannon said, watching Isis flutter from one corner of the room to the other. "Are you familiar with Tellington Touch?"

I told her we were, but that we didn't do the bodywork all that often.

"What have you been doing?"

"We start with the flat hand down her back, then some circles, sometimes working down her tail." I smiled at Rob. "Jellyfish is a favorite of ours."

A few mornings earlier, I woke to hear Rob saying, "Jellyfish massage, jellyfish massage," while placing his fingertips just above Isis's tail and jiggling his hand as he worked up her back. Nothing made me happier than to see Rob embrace one of our wackadoo training techniques.

Tellington Touch was a holdover from our training with Linda, and I couldn't tell whether it worked or not, just like the Prozac. At least doggie massage was fun to do. It did seem that the gentle patterns, named after other animals, helped Isis relax, if only momentarily.

I called Isis over and demonstrated for Shannon a few of the one-and-a-quarter circles that we learned.

"When you do the circles, try using a flat hand, instead of just your fingertips." Shannon demonstrated on Isis, who by then had gotten comfortable enough to slow down in front of the new person. "This is called the 'abalone.' It's more relaxing, especially on her back where she's sensitive."

Shannon also had us try out a Thundershirt, a gray wrap that fastened around Isis's torso and neck. The swaddled effect was supposed to soothe dogs during fireworks and thunderstorms, among other things. We put Isis's harness and Halti over the Thundershirt and brought her outside to show Shannon how she and Leo interacted. Shannon walked with me and Isis into the wooded area while Rob and Alice got Leo geared up.

Isis's face was relaxed until Leo came into view, whereupon she closed her mouth for a split second before roaring in his direction. I tried to move Isis away, and immediately, Shannon noticed a problem in my handling technique.

"With the head halter, you want to redirect her, rather than correcting her." She took the reins from me, walking Isis parallel to Leo. "The key to the head halter is that you look where you are going and take the dog along with you. Being up by their head is much more effective than water-skiing behind them, so if she really pulls, just go for a couple of steps and then stop to help her rebalance."

I flashed back on all the advice I'd ever read about how to keep a dog from pulling ahead on a leash. Usually, trainers said to whirl around and walk in another direction, which effectively got Isis to turn around but never curbed her excessive pulling. Linda had prescribed a handling technique where I was supposed to lift both ends of the two-ended leash and then release.

Shannon clarified this "ask-and-release" technique. "The motion is an up and back motion, rather than just pulling backwards. You have to give the signal and then relax your arms, otherwise you're just back to pulling. It's on the release that the dogs learn self-control. You have to give them that opportunity."

I walked beside Shannon as she handled Isis. Every time the dogs locked eyes for more than a second, one of them barked. The few times Isis could be redirected, Leo spit out his own incessant big-boy bark.

"You're going to want to do Tellington Touch on Leo, too, particularly mouth work," Shannon said. "His stress is starting to show, and it's coming out with that hysterical barking."

We worked a few laps between the trees and a tire obstacle course. By having Shannon handle Isis's leash, a load was lifted off my shoulders, and Rob and his mother were getting practice handling Leo. Shannon subscribed to essentially the same training philosophy as Linda, but Rob was more responsive to Shannon's gentler personality, and her explanation behind the techniques made sense.

At the end of the session, we set up a follow-up at our house.

"I know how stressful this is for you all, so I suggest that you think more in terms of getting both dogs balanced mentally and physically, and teaching them some self-control," Shannon said. "I really liked what you said, that rehoming them is not an option. Since you're already prepared for them to live separated, this isn't a life or death situation. I really commend you for how much work you've already put in and that you're so willing to keep trying."

Rob and Alice drove off with Leo, and I headed home with Isis, on the verge of tears, not from frustration but from relief. For the first time in months, I felt true hope. Shannon understood my struggle. She could tell Isis was a good dog, and she would help us.

I stopped at PetSmart in Mount Vernon to buy some more training treats. Even though dogs were allowed inside the store, of course I had to leave Isis in the car. To celebrate my newfound optimism, I bought each dog a holiday collar from the Christmas display. The soft green material on Leo's came to three points with red bells and was embroidered with the words SANTA'S FAVORITE ELF. Isis's was a furry red bandanna with a white Santa Claus trim. It said HO, HO, HO.

My renewed faith buoyed me through the holiday season. Everything would be okay. Rob had been saying it all along, "They'll be fine. We'll get there." But I'd been carrying around so much doubt and anxiety. What if they never got along? What if my doubt and anxiety made the problem worse? Now I convinced myself that all I had to do was believe. Visualize them playing together someday. Visualize an immediate goal: Leo and Isis coming nose to nose on leashes without Isis having a reaction. A calm, happy look in Isis's eyes.

***

Before our next session, Shannon asked if I believed in animal communicators.

"What, like a pet psychic?"

Shannon laughed. "I know, it's pretty out there, but I've had communicators come up with amazing results." She described a horse that acted strangely until a psychic, without even seeing the animal, told her the horse had a pain in its ear. When Shannon took the horse to the vet, indeed there was something wrong with its ear. She explained that pet psychics don't have to touch or even meet an animal in order to communicate. All they need is a picture. I couldn't imagine how that was possible and as a rule, didn't subscribe to that kind of hocus pocus, but Shannon was no space cadet.

I was curious what a pet psychic might tell us.

"I guess I don't *not* believe. I'll try anything."

I e-mailed her a smiling picture of Isis in front of the Christmas tree, cropping myself out. A few days later, Shannon called to report what the animal communicator said Isis had said to her.

"I wanted to tell you on the phone, instead of e-mail. It's sort of hard to hear."

With a sinking heart, I pushed my computer keyboard away from me and reached for a notebook in case I needed to write anything down.

"Isis says she has trouble breathing, that she feels like she has a weight on her chest," Shannon said, her voice thick with emotion. "And this is the part that makes me want to cry. She said, 'How come I wasn't enough?' "

Heartbreaking words indeed. But I wasn't completely convinced they came from Isis. "What did you tell the communicator about our situation?"

"All I told her was that you had a new puppy and Isis didn't get along with him."

Even that was too much information. I wished Shannon hadn't told the psychic anything. I don't claim to be clairvoyant, but if I had to guess what went on in the mind of a jealous sibling, *How come I wasn't enough?* seemed pretty obvious. I'd be really impressed (and more devastated) if, based on nothing more than the photo, with no other information at all, a psychic intuited that my dog wondered why she wasn't enough.

Knowing the psychic had been given a hint kept me skeptical of her other feedback as well. Trouble breathing? A weight on her chest? Maybe Isis felt that way, but I doubted it. Isis had been to the vet recently and had nothing wrong with her. Beyond that, how could I validate these statements? Was I supposed to have her chest X-rayed? Run respiratory tests? All I could do with this information was file it away and continue loving Isis as best I could. How else could we help her understand that getting Leo had nothing to do with her being enough?

Of course she was enough. She was more than enough. We loved her more than the world.

Looking back, perhaps I was supposed to hire the pet psychic to communicate these feelings back to Isis. But the first psychic connection, included in Shannon's fee, hadn't made me a believer. I didn't need to shell out more money to retain the services of a medium.

When I reported back to Rob at home that night, he agreed with me that while the psychic's words weren't necessarily complete crap, we had no reason to believe them either. We lay across the bed with Isis between us, fawning over her.

"We don't need some psychic to help us understand you, Isis," Rob said.

True enough. Maybe I hadn't been able to cure Isis's anxiety, but I'd been communicating with her since the day we brought her home. I pressed my face against her beak.

"We read each other just fine, don't we, Smiley Bird?"

★★★

Alice joined us again for our session with Shannon at our house. Shannon stood between us as Rob and I each handled one of the dogs, telling us when to move the dogs toward and away from each other while clicking and treating for good behavior. Alice acted as a buffer. Leo's Halti seemed to be the wrong size, so Shannon went out to her car to see if she had a smaller one. Rob and Alice took Isis inside and I sat with Leo for what seemed like a really long time. Finally, Shannon came back out.

"I found something in my car that we could try on Isis," she said. "It's called a Calming Cap and the idea is that it reduces visual stimuli by filtering a dog's vision. I held it up to my eyes and you can still see through it, but it just makes things kind of indistinct."

Rob came outside smiling. "Isis looks like a superhero."

When I followed him back in, I found Isis lying on the area rug at Alice's feet, happily taking treats while wearing a stretchy bright blue mask over her eyes.

"Too bad they don't make a Thundershirt in bright blue," I said. "She'd have a full costume."

"Play around with it," Shannon said. "Try having her lie on her bed wearing it while you walk Leo past her."

Between the Thundershirt, the Calming Cap, and perhaps also the Prozac, Isis did well during these exercises at home. My mother gave me a second Thundershirt for Christmas, which we wrapped around Leo, even though he didn't quite fill it out. Rob sat with Isis on her bed while we paraded Leo past a few times, clicking and treating both dogs for being calm. We didn't have too many outbursts, but I don't know if you could call it progress, because we'd reduced the time to such a short period.

The dogs could be in the same room for one minute and forty-five seconds. We were a long way from integrating our household.

When we tried working them together for longer periods, Leo's hysterical barking continued to be a challenge. Given their history, I could hardly blame him. Shannon suggested we bring Isis down to her place without Leo, so she could build her confidence working with Shannon's dog, Kinsey.

I put plastic bags of greasy cooked chicken hearts and gizzards in my coat pockets and filled the treat pouch for Rob to wear around his waist. Just in case we ran out, I had another whole Tupperware container full of treats and some string cheese as a backup (although Rob ate a couple of those on the drive down).

With Isis geared up in her pink harness, black Halti, and blue leash with two points of contact, we waited by our car while Shannon prepared Kinsey. I put up the hood of my black parka, shivering in the January cold. Isis fixed her gaze on Shannon's horses in an adjacent gated field. Great. All we needed was for Isis to start off on the wrong foot with Kinsey because the horses freaked her out. I kept Isis in motion, moving her behind my car and trying to keep the horses out of her line of vision.

Shannon approached with a dog about Isis's size on a leash. Kinsey was brown, black, and fluffy. Rob and I walked on either side of Isis toward the small woodsy patch next to Shannon's house. I held the leash and operated the clicker. Rob was supposed to administer treats every time he heard me click. Clicker training was so much more efficient with four hands. The harness/Halti method alone required two hands to steer.

With my hood up, I couldn't hear Shannon's instructions. I paused, tilting my head to let the sound travel between my ear and the down parka and asked her to repeat.

"Walk to those tires and then wait there," Shannon said. Our goal was to get Isis to walk parallel to Kinsey at a distance, but first we had to get them within sight of each other.

My distracted pause to listen to Shannon gave Isis a chance to make eye contact with Kinsey, and the switch flipped. Isis let out a series of staccato barks in the strange dog's direction: *I don't know who you are, and I don't know what you want, but you're not coming any closer.* She didn't lunge though, so the reaction measured low on the intensity scale.

Shannon held her ground and when Isis took a breath, I used the Halti to turn her head and move her in the direction of the tires.

"Good," Shannon said. "That's exactly what you want to do, reward her by moving her away when she's calm."

We had a few more reactions like that before Isis settled down. Each time, I said, "Rob, Rob, Rob," in my own staccato bark, trying to get him to read both my mind and Isis's, so he could use a treat to lure her gaze from Kinsey at precisely the right moment. I started using treats from my own stash, then refilled Rob's pouch when his supply dwindled. We went through the treats quickly, "making it rain" by throwing treats on the ground when Isis caught glimpses of Kinsey, so she would associate strange dogs with cooked meat falling from heaven.

Between the two of us, we figured out how to keep Isis feeling safe as we walked closer and closer to Kinsey. Isis started whipping her head back to us of her own will, happily taking a bite of gizzard or chicken heart. *Oh, you want me to ignore that other dog? And as long as we keep moving forward, you'll give me treats. No problem, I can do this.*

After several minutes, we successfully got Isis and Kinsey trotting parallel to each other at a distance of only about ten feet. It helped that unlike Leo, Kinsey didn't bark back. We walked to the end of Shannon's dirt driveway and back.

Isis's smiley face was soft and relaxed, and she showed such calm body language, Shannon suggested we try something more advanced: a protected greeting. She and Kinsey stood on one side of the black metal driveway gate, the dog facing away from us. Rob and I walked Isis nearly to the gate, letting her get a good close sniff of Kinsey's butt, then guided her away, heaping praise and treats upon her for behaving like a normal dog and not a vicious beast.

She looked up at us, eyes bright and fur smooth against her back, not remotely threatened by that other dog.

"Okay, let's end there," Shannon said. "We don't want to push her too far out of her comfort zone."

We went into Shannon's small living room to wait while she put Kinsey away. I unhooked Isis's leash and Halti and let her investigate the couch and coffee table, taking in all the new smells. I liked being in other dog people's homes, where fur covered the couches and giant dog beds took up available floor space. I exhaled for what felt like the first time that day and realized that Isis had relaxed too. The hard part was over.

We'd made it through our training session and ended on a high note.

"Isis really was a star today," Shannon said when she returned.

Isis wiggled up to all three of us, basking in our approval and smiling like an eager puppy. *I'm a superstar! What a fun walk. Hey, a football!* She pounced on a rubber football in Kinsey's toy basket, clenching her teeth around it and shaking her head back and forth.

"You know, my dogs don't play with that football. You can have it," Shannon said. "Isis deserves a reward for doing so well today."

Rob took hold of the football and played tug-of-war with our Smiley Bird.

"She's really proud of herself," Shannon said. "And she can tell you're proud of her too."

Not only was I proud of Isis, I was proud of us! At home, when I handled Isis and Rob worked with Leo, we were on opposing sides. When one of the dogs barked at the other, someone had to be to blame. To Rob's great exasperation, I needed to dissect every failed exercise to determine exactly what had gone wrong. Rehash every detail. Without this precision, how would we ever make progress?

But that day, we were a team. We got back in the car with our new football, the three of us beaming with pride, feeling well on our way. If Isis could be that calm and happy around Kinsey, getting her to accept Leo in our home was within our grasp.

Chapter 15: Heart Dog

Certain dogs hold the top spot in one's heart. I find the expression "Heart Dog" to be a little cloying, but I relate to the sentiment, preferring to think of Isis as a "Once in a Lifetime Dog." Prolific dog author Jon Katz describes a lifetime dog as one "we love in especially powerful, sometimes inexplicable, ways. While we may cherish other pets, we may never feel that particular connection with any of the rest."

I loved Leo dearly, and wouldn't give him up for the world, even when finding him a new home may have been the kinder, more rational thing to do.

But for my sweet Isis, I would have given the world.

Through the month of January, I felt energized by my optimism that my two dogs were getting closer to being friends. Isis really did seem to be doing better. Everything was going great all around, actually. I had enrolled in a writing class through the nearby university's continuing education program. I felt happy, motivated, and secure in my job. Rob had just celebrated his fortieth birthday over Thai food with a large group of friends from both his work and martial arts club.

Plus, Shannon had one more suggestion that might alleviate Isis's anxiety: Chinese herbs. She referred us to a holistic vet named Dr. Donna, whose office was on the ground floor of a small building that also housed a massage therapist, about a block away from the Lighthouse Mission. When we pulled up to the office for the first time, a shaggy homeless man passed by on the sidewalk, so I had to wait for Isis to finish barking at him before letting her out of the car. Probably Dr. Donna could hear the barking right outside her window.

After Isis quieted, I led her through the building's glass doors and into an empty waiting room. Dr. Donna had no receptionist or other means to check in, so I just sat down on the single chair and slipped the bright blue Calming Cap over Isis's beak.

Voices murmured from the other side of a closed door. Not knowing what sort of animal was in there, I worried what Isis would do when it exited past us.

Isis sat beside me and let me stroke her head around the Spandex cap. I remembered how before the Calming Cap, she would have needed to walk to the end of her leash in all directions, nervously inspecting every corner of a new environment. At Dr. Donna's, she squeaked out a few high-pitched German shepherd whines, but stayed safely out of full panic mode.

"Maybe these herbs will be the missing ingredient, Smiley Bird," I said, realizing that I'd said the same thing about Prozac.

The muffled voices continued several minutes after my scheduled appointment time. I heard the door start to creak open. "I have Isis here. What kind of animal is coming out?"

Dr. Donna peeked out. "It's a cat. She can carry it."

The other patient left without incident, and I walked Isis into the sparsely decorated exam room. The wide wooden blinds on the window were closed, blocking out the view of the street, and a door was open to a large closet filled with glass jars of herbs. I took off Isis's leash and superhero mask and let her catch a whiff of all the animals that preceded her.

"I'm really impressed that you're here on time," Dr. Donna said. "Compared to the patients I see in Seattle, I've noticed that people in Bellingham tend not to be too concerned about arriving on time."

Dr. Donna was probably in her mid-forties, sweet-faced, with a long braid over one shoulder. Isis allowed her to do a physical exam, looking into her ears, and checking for abnormalities in her joints and skin.

I recapped the situation at home. "She just seems so anxious. She chews on her legs all the time."

Dr. Donna nodded. "It's probably allergies."

Could it be as simple as that? Isis's coat was perfectly glossy from her raw meat diet, and she didn't have the flaky skin that many German shepherds suffer from, but chewing incessantly on her legs was an obvious sign that something itched.

Dr. Donna asked, "Are you familiar with muscle testing?"

I was not.

"It's the most 'out there' thing I do, but it really works. You act as a surrogate."

Dr. Donna had me put one hand on Isis and hold the other arm up in the air. Isis sat calmly while Dr. Donna put a hand on my free arm, and used the other to touch small vials of likely allergens: pollen, birch, beef, chicken, grains, dairy. When Isis had an allergy to something Dr. Donna touched, my arm involuntarily yielded to the pressure she placed on my arm.

It was in fact "out there," but the muscle testing was consistent. Somehow Isis's sensitivity to allergens passed through me. I couldn't see which vials Dr. Donna touched, but my arm weakened for the same allergens each time.

Apparently Isis was allergic to yeast and "nonessential amino acids," which Dr. Donna said could be beef or pork. She explained that she would use acupuncture to "clear" the yeast allergy. I knew about dog acupuncture because Barney, my mother's Lhasa apso, had back trouble a number of years earlier, and acupuncture had helped.

Dr. Donna strapped a Velcro collar around Isis's neck and attached a small vial of yeast. "Isis will have contact with the vial for twenty minutes while receiving acupuncture. This will energetically change her immune system's reaction to the yeast, and can permanently cure the allergy."

Isis shot me a worried glance, her ears flat against her head, but she didn't mind when Dr. Donna inserted the small needles behind her ears and along her legs. "The needles by her ears will help Isis relax," Dr. Donna said. "The points on her legs are immune gates."

Isis settled into a down position and yawned. *Don't mind me. I'm just gonna take a quick nap.*

"Good girl, Isis." I stroked her head while the acupuncture took effect.

Dr. Donna gave me an exhaustive shopping list that felt as overwhelming as when I first switched Isis to the raw diet. Dr. Donna was a believer in feeding dogs raw meat, but she did not agree that dogs were carnivores who did not need vegetables. She told me to give Isis only chicken as a protein for a couple of weeks and add detoxifying vegetables like burdock root, kale, carrots, and parsley.

I was pretty sure Isis wouldn't go for the veggies. We tried feeding her carrots before and she just spit them out, which at the time I considered further proof she was carnivorous. For added mineral nutrition, Dr. Donna advised me to get a food processor and grind up raw almonds, Brazil nuts, sunflower seeds, and cashews, sprinkling a tablespoon or two into every meal. She also sold me an expensive shampoo that was supposed to get rid of the yeast on Isis's skin.

Oddly, Dr. Donna didn't prescribe any herbs, which was the reason we went to see her in the first place. But if she was right, and allergies were causing Isis's anxiety, maybe we wouldn't need the herbs at all.

"I'd rather see if the changes to her diet work first," Dr. Donna said.

Once again, I was left with the feeling that I'd failed Isis by misdiagnosing her illness. Was it possible that itchy skin had been the root of the problem all along? That Isis was uncomfortable in her own skin and that's why she lashed out at Leo? In my heart, I knew Isis's problems were more complicated than that, but we had made progress in so many other areas, I hoped allergies would be the last hurdle to overcome.

On the way home, I stopped at the food co-op and bought all the veggies Dr. Donna prescribed, including the strange, stick-like burdock root, which I'd never heard of before, along with coconut oil, fish oil, and a calcium/magnesium supplement. Alice bought us a food processor at Goodwill, and I ground up the veggies with boneless chicken breast and plopped the mixture in Isis's dish.

Isis barely sniffed the bowl before walking away.

"Hey, Isis, what's with the hunger strike?" I wanted to believe that she was simply rejecting the unusual texture or the added vegetables, but when I stopped to think about it, she'd been snubbing her food for a while now. Had she done that before we got Leo? Not since we started feeding her raw meat, as far as I could remember.

The previous summer she threw up her entire dinner a few times, but I thought that was because I fed her too fast during our training exercises with Leo. As with our earlier treat-based training, I was afraid to let enough time pass between mouthfuls of food to give her a chance to react. After she barfed up a meal of raw pork and beef heart, she lost interest in those meats for a few days. She sniffed and licked it in her bowl, but left it. Ground turkey still appealed to her, and gradually she started eating the heart and pork again.

Now, I wondered if the lack of appetite was related to a medical problem. I'd have to ask Dr. Donna next time we saw her.

"Isis, come here." I balled up a glob of raw chicken, parsley, burdock root, and carrots, and held it out to her. She ate it out of my hand. Glob by glob, I hand-fed Isis her entire meal.

★★★

We had a big snowstorm in mid-January. I stayed home from work in anticipation because it was supposed to start coming down at two in the afternoon. The forecasters adjusted their prediction to later in the day, but the snowfall didn't really start until after dark. The weather guys also said it would be gone by morning. When Isis woke me up in the middle of the night, like she did every night, I let Leo out first, then grabbed my camera. I expected Isis to race around in the drifts when it was her turn, putting her paw in every inch of the snow, like she used to.

Instead, she stood outside the back door, looking at me.

"Is that the best you can do?" I snapped her picture anyway, capturing her as she licked a snowflake from the side of her mouth. The flash bounced off the snow, making her eyes glow green in the photo.

Are you coming out with me or not?

"If you're not going to play in it, let's go back to bed."

Leo let out a few cries from the laundry room as Isis and I snuggled back under the warm covers next to sleeping Rob. "Poor jealous Leo," I murmured. "Maybe someday he can sleep in here too."

We were a long way off from having both dogs sleep in our bed, but I felt like we were getting there slowly. Isis was adjusting to her new diet, and we'd been back to see Dr. Donna a few times to clear her other allergies. We still hadn't cracked the two-minute mark with the dogs in the same room. In our latest attempt, I had Leo facing the opposite direction, so he wouldn't bark, while Rob and Isis sat on her bed, Isis wearing the Calming Cap. With fifteen seconds to go, Isis stood up.

That's all she did, but it was enough to make me end the exercise out of fear that an eruption was brewing.

Maybe the dogs hadn't made actual progress at all, but the change was in me, because I could finally picture a unified household. One night in early February, Rob left me a message while I was at writing class, saying that Isis was in her quiet room and he planned to play with Leo for a bit before running out to pick up some dinner. Rob's car was not in the driveway when I got home, so I knew Isis was loose in the house and Leo was in his playpen. I saw Isis watching me through the window, and when I opened the front door, I had a vision of what it would be like to have two dogs greet me. What if Leo came running from one side, while Isis came from the other?

I set my purse on the floor, basking a moment in what felt like my wildest dream.

Isis stuck her face in my purse, pulling out a red-caped monkey. *Hey, I love this guy!*

I laughed. "That's quite unlike you. You never go into my purse."

How come he isn't screaming?

"I wasn't going to tell you, but Leo munched him so he doesn't make noise anymore." I'd recently purchased a replacement monkey for the office, so I brought the broken one home for Isis.

When Rob got back, we flung the monkey across the room over and over. Each time, Isis scrambled after it, paws skidding across the floor, as happy as I'd ever seen her.

"She went a little crazy earlier when I had Leo out," Rob said. "He got too close to the quiet room and she started barking. After I put Leo back in the laundry room, she just cowered under the table, shaking."

"Isis? Are you okay?"

She walked up to me, carrying the monkey in her mouth with its legs hanging out like a dead bug. I stroked her face. I hated when she had reactions to Leo in my absence. Since I hadn't seen her outburst, I didn't know how bad it was. While I felt mildly frustrated that Rob let Leo get too close to the gate, my larger concern was that Isis was still so anxious.

Even on Prozac, she'd worked herself into enough of a tizzy that Rob thought it was worth reporting to me.

Isis dropped the monkey. *Throw him again, please.*

When I headed to bed that night, Isis was lying down with her head resting on the monkey. "You little monkey stealer, I love you so much. So much," I crouched beside her and pressed my face against the top of her head. "I will always love you, more than you could ever know. You are my most special girl and I will love you for the rest of your life. Longer than that, actually. Good night, Smiley Bird."

★★★

The next day was freezing but sunny. Since my work got pretty slow during the winter, I took the rare clear day as an opportunity to take Leo along on some field visits. We drove to a restored estuary in the Skagit delta where my stated goal was to take pictures of new fish and wildlife habitat. My pictures of Leo were better. We practiced "stay" while I posed him in front of a tangled mass of a rootwad, with bare winter trees reflecting upside down in the still estuary water behind him. At nine months, he didn't look like a puppy anymore. His tall ears and pointed muzzle formed the points of a long triangle.

His face retained most of his black markings, but his chest and front legs had faded to a golden tan, and his body was long and lean.

He hadn't reached Isis's level of supermodel-dom. Sometimes when I said, "Leo! Leo!" or made a kissing sound with my mouth, he'd look at the camera happily. Other times, he'd break from his stay and ruin the picture by walking toward me. I got a few good shots by the estuary, and also photographed a pair of eagles side by side in a tree, icicles defrosting noisily into a pond, and Leo with his front paws up on a hunting shelter.

My overactive imagination spun a nightmare fantasy of a hunter mistaking Leo for a bear and shooting him. Following the thread of my own macabre vision, I knew that by expecting the worst, I was preventing anything truly terrible from happening. On the drive south from the Skagit delta toward Marysville, I imagined that I hadn't fully shut the tailgate of the company's Ford Explorer. What if the hatch flew open and Leo went tumbling out onto the freeway behind him? At another restored estuary, we walked a suburban trail looking for wildlife. All we saw were several dogs barking at us from behind the wooden gates of their backyards. What if one of them burst through a loose board and attacked us?

Maybe nine-month-old Leo could defend himself, or maybe not. I might have to kick the other dog in the head and run.

Shaking off the bad juju in my head, I reveled in spending the day outside with my puppy. As much stress as Leo brought with him, he was a delightful work companion, and I was lucky to be getting paid to hang out with him. I remembered how much fun I'd had walking Isis, not yet a year old, after my company picnic at Twanoh State Park, before she was aggressive. For all I knew, Leo would develop problems as bad as Isis's once he reached two years old, but for now, he'd outgrown his habit of nipping my sleeve when we walked.

He smiled at me sweetly as we walked and bounded clumsily yet energetically into the back of the Ford Explorer when it was time to head to the next location.

Back at the office, Leo slept on the floor for about an hour while I edited photos. He woke up pesky, nipping at my knees and pulling papers off my desk, so I put him in the car and went back inside to get a little bit more work done.

My cell phone rang with Rob's mother's ringtone. "Where are you?"

"At work."

"When are you coming home?"

It was a little after four. "Five, I guess, but I could leave whenever."

"Can you come now?" Her voice sounded strange; she was crying.

"Why? Has something happened to Isis?"

"Just come home. Come home," she sobbed. "But drive safe."

On autopilot, I picked up my purse and left without shutting down my computer. My mind swirled, but my heart felt numb. Nothing bad was supposed to happen. I'd protected myself by always anticipating the worst-case scenario.

With an enormous weight in my heart, I knew there was only one reason Alice would call me crying and then refuse to tell me why.

Isis was dead. I could hear it in her voice.

What could have happened? If Isis had gotten out and been hit by a car, Alice would never forgive herself. If she'd choked on the broken mechanical innards of the screaming monkey, I'd never forgive myself.

Leo sat beside me as I drove the thirty miles home. He rested his chin on my knee, so well behaved compared to his bratty attention-getting moves in my office. I stroked his soft dark head remembering how Isis did the same thing when she rode shotgun. I kept my hand on the gearshift to prevent Leo from bumping the car into neutral.

My cell phone rang again with an unfamiliar number.

"It's me," Rob said. His boss was driving him home and he was calling from her phone. "Did my mom call you?"

"Is Isis dead?" I heard the pleading in my voice. Don't let this be true.

"That's what she said. She wouldn't tell me at first, just told me to come home. But I told her I couldn't leave work without a reason. She blurted out, 'Isis is dead.' " He sounded as stunned as I felt.

As I drove, I watched myself from the outside, ashamed that I didn't look like a girl whose dog had just died. I was supposed to be struggling to see the road through tears, but my eyes were dry, my emotions wound tightly and encased in shrink wrap. I couldn't cry because I didn't believe it yet. This could not be the end of the story. After raising Isis for four years like she was a human child and loving her more than I'd ever loved anything. Doing every single thing to make sure she lived as long a life as a German shepherd possibly could.

Wanting most of all for her to be well adjusted and happy.

I wasn't crying because I always expected the worst. Rob dreamed she could live forever. Once, we cuddled up on the bed with her, long before we had Leo, and Rob said, "I don't want anything to happen to Isis. Ever." He was choked up when he said it, as though even the idea of her death was more than he could bear.

I pulled off at my exit, wishing the drive had taken longer. Wanting time to slow down as I made the last few turns. Alice had said, "Drive safe," like I'd rush home so recklessly I'd get in an accident. But I was in no hurry. If I never arrived, I wouldn't have to face my worst fear. Isis would still be alive, romping in the backyard.

I scanned my street. Isis's body wasn't lying in the road. That was good. My breath caught in my chest as I pulled into the driveway. Not knowing what I was going to find, I dreaded getting out of the car and walking into the house.

Leo sat up eagerly when I turned off the car. Isis could be anywhere, and I couldn't have him going near her. "You're going to have to wait here a minute, little buddy."

I stepped carefully through the front door. "Hello?"

Was she dead on her favorite couch? On the floor somewhere? No one answered. They were outside. Alice walked in the back door as I came through the kitchen. She reached for a box of Kleenex on the kitchen table.

"Where is she?"

Alice pointed up toward the back of the yard where I could see Rob kneeling on the ground beside a large holly tree. When I started to walk toward him, Alice grabbed my arm. "She's dead, Kari! She's dead!"

"I know! I get it!" I snapped. Did she expect me to cry about it with her before I even saw the body?

Isis lay on her side next to a young cedar tree I'd planted and some stepping stones shaped like feet, which I'd decorated with symbols to represent the footsteps of Buddha. Rob was beside her, still in his black corrections-officer uniform.

He was crying. In seven years, I'd never seen him cry.

★★★

Alice hadn't noticed anything out of the ordinary when she arrived at our house that day. Isis was her usual happy, energetic self and Alice had gone outside to throw the soccer ball. Isis sat beside the retaining wall and pushed the half-deflated ball down the hill with her nose. A few times, Isis got impatient and raced down the gravel hill to snatch it back. When she held out long enough for Grandma to throw the ball, she leapt in the air, caught it, then ran a few circles around Alice to receive congratulatory strokes before dropping the ball at her feet.

Alice went inside the house for a couple of minutes. When she came out, Isis wasn't waiting by the back door with the soccer ball in her mouth. She wasn't perched on the hill by the retaining wall.

"Isis!" Had she gotten out? Alice opened the wooden side gate and looked for her in the front yard, calling her name, growing more worried. Isis sometimes played tricks by tucking herself behind bushes, but Alice didn't see her in any of her usual hiding places.

Isis wouldn't have crawled under the chain link at the back of our yard and run onto the freeway, would she? Alice looked up the incline of our lawn toward a patch that once had been thick with blackberry bushes. When we built Rob's martial arts studio, we'd cleared those bushes and put a picnic table back there, covered by a gazebo beneath a canopy of cedar trees that curtained our property from the view of passing freeway motorists. My footsteps of Buddha led away from the picnic table to the edge of our property.

Finally Alice saw, partially blocked by the holly tree, Isis lying down next to one of the stepping stones.

"What are you doing, little girl?" Alice walked the length of the yard to find out. When Alice reached her, Isis didn't get up.

"Isis!" Alice's first panicked thought was that Isis had been shot. At eighty-five pounds, Isis was too heavy for Alice to turn over. Alice felt underneath to see if there was any blood. There wasn't.

"Isis!" Alice attempted chest compressions. How could this happen? Young, healthy dogs didn't just keel over and die.

Crying, Alice pulled out her cell phone and called both me and Rob. She didn't want Isis to be alone, so she sat with her until Rob arrived. Then she went down into the house to get a flannel sheet. Wrapping the wine-colored sheet around Isis, Alice sobbed, "I don't want her to be cold." Next, she looked up the vet's phone number to ask what to do. They told her we could bring Isis in any time before six.

★★★

I trudged up the hill to where Rob sat beside Isis, his eyes looking so lost. Sitting in the dirt with Isis between us, I shivered in my fleece sweatshirt. Rob and I looked at each other in disbelief, and seeing him cry, my tears came, streaking my face as I rested my head on Isis's still-warm black-and-gold fur. She smelled like Isis, that comforting doggie scent that reminded me of warm biscuits. Her eyes stared, but didn't look dead. She could have been resting, except for the tongue. It hung lifeless and strangely dark from her mouth, which still wore a smile.

Rob kept saying in a choked, pleading voice, "Her tongue shouldn't look like that." He wept. "She would never leave us if she could help it."

The heartbreak I felt at the loss of my baby was compounded with the pain of seeing Rob so devastated.

"I'm never going to get over this," he said.

"You don't get over it. You just get used to it." In the past few years, I'd lost my iguana Emerald. I'd lost Barney. My love for those animals was nothing compared to what Isis meant to me, but the quality of grief was at least familiar. Even before her body was cold, I knew that someday it wouldn't hurt this much. Rob wasn't convinced.

"You're not going to go to work tomorrow, are you?"

I read the true meaning in his eyes. *Don't leave me.*

No, of course I wouldn't go to work the next day.

The sky started to darken, and Rob's father arrived, turning the focus to logistical concerns. Whose car to take to the vet? Not mine, I insisted. If my car were the hearse, I would always associate it with transporting her lifeless body.

Suddenly everyone wondered where Leo was.

"I left him in the car."

"I'll get him," Jerry said. "Alice, give me your keys, I'll bring your car around to the side gate."

The four of us had to carry Isis down the slope of our backyard and out the side gate via a narrow walkway flanked on one side by the dog run fence and the other by the retaining wall and about a dozen weight machines Rob kept outside. I couldn't count the number of heavy, awkward things the four of us had carried up this same hill. Wrestling mats. Exercise bikes. The gazebo. A refrigerator. Things that exceeded eighty-five pounds. Rob could lift more than eighty-five pounds by himself, and his sixty-five-year-old, five-foot-tall mother was freakishly strong herself. But we four struggled under Isis's weight, carrying her down that hill. The heaviness of our grief sapped our strength and we were terrified of dropping her. No one wanted to set her down, but we had to at the bottom of the hill, where Isis's soccer ball still lay.

We took a moment before lifting her again and making the sharp left past the dog run. I could see Leo in the kitchen, jumping up with his paws against the sliding glass door. Just a baby. Did he know what we carried in the flannel sheet? Did he know the mean dog who ruled the house was gone?

I moaned, hating myself for feeling the slightest relief that my struggle to bring the dogs together was over. Was this the only possible resolution? Did Isis have to die so that Leo could have the life he deserved?

Jerry had put the seats down in the back of the SUV. We put Isis inside and I crawled in with her. Burying my face in Isis's fur, I wailed, no longer trying to be strong for Rob. I wanted to curl up there with her forever.

Isis, how could you do this to me? I can't lose you.

I felt Jerry's hand on my arm, trying to pull me out of the car, and I shrugged the hand off, refusing to move. I didn't know if he wanted to comfort me, or force me to move where there was a seatbelt, but I intended to hold Isis until the last possible moment. Rob rode in the front seat with his mother and Jerry stayed home with Leo.

At the vet, two young female techs had no trouble carrying Isis on a stretcher from the car to an exam room. A vet I'd never seen before, Dr. McCarthy, came out to speak to us. There was no outward sign of trauma that explained how or why Isis had died.

Did we want to do a necropsy? Yes.

Did we want to have her privately cremated? Yes. Actually, I didn't care. She was dead, it didn't matter to me what happened to her ashes, but Rob wanted them. Did we want to see her body one last time? Alice said yes, but Rob said no. I was too numb to have an opinion. I stayed with Rob in the waiting room while Alice said goodbye.

"That's why I wanted to stay with her so long in the yard," Rob said. "That's where I want to remember her."

Dr. McCarthy said she probably wouldn't have any news until the next day. The receptionist was exceedingly sympathetic, telling us, "Blessings, blessings," as we walked out the door. We went home where Leo greeted us at the door and Jerry sat in a recliner reading. Rob's parents went home almost immediately, which surprised me. They just left us Isis-less and not knowing what to do with ourselves.

Even though the lights were on, the house felt dark. We ordered a pizza.

I had to call my mother. She answered cheerfully and I asked her if she had a minute to talk, just in case she was on the other line or in the middle of dinner or something.

"Isis died." I stretched out the second word. Died.

"What?" Her voice a shocked gasp. I told her what happened.

"Oh, Kari, I'm so sorry."

"I know," I whimpered. Not much else to say.

Less than an hour after we got home, Dr. McCarthy called, saying she knew we'd want to hear news as soon as possible. I lay across the bed as she told me she could not tell the cause of death based on a visual necropsy, but Isis had an enlarged heart.

"It could be just that she's such a big dog, but it also could be symptomatic of something, like a clot or even a growth."

Did we want to send the heart to a specialist who might tell us more? Yes.

I got off the phone and told Rob, "She says that Isis had a very large heart. I think from loving us so much."

Her heart. I remembered the pet psychic. *I can't breathe. I feel like there's a weight on my chest.*

★★★

For the next several days, Rob and I were like two planets dislodged from our orbits, feeling aimless as we went through the motions of life. We took Leo to the dog park and to his doggie class, pretending to be normal dog owners in public and then crying on the way home. I wept into my pillow at night and gasped for breath while sobbing in the shower. I made it through my writing class without melting down, fighting the temptation to blurt out, "My dog died!"

Grief weighed heavily on Rob, who calculated how much he missed Isis after two days, multiplying that times the number of days that he'd have to go on living without her. After twenty days, he expected to hurt ten times more. After two hundred days, it would be a hundred times worse.

A week later Dr. McCarthy called with the specialist's results. Isis died from bleeding in the thymus, an organ near the heart, likely caused by one of three things: trauma (of which there was no other evidence), aneurysm, or rat poison. I got hung up briefly on the rat poison possibility. What if someone put rat poison somewhere in our yard, deliberately to kill our dog? Was Leo in danger? But rat poison tends to cause dogs to bleed from more than one organ, and Isis didn't eat random things. Even if someone had thrown the most delectable filet mignon over our fence, I'm not convinced she would have eaten it.

That left us with freak aneurysm. Something that would have killed her that day no matter what we did differently. Maybe Isis was meant to live only four and a half years; maybe her death was predetermined by her DNA. Maybe she had a medical condition this whole time (like Carmen said: "something genetically wrong with her"), which contributed to her anxiety and aggression.

Unless it was the other way around.

"Could an aneurysm be caused by anxiety?"

Dr. McCarthy said she didn't think so.

I released my held breath, not wanting to believe that we'd killed Isis by bringing Leo into our home. Not wanting to believe that eighty milligrams of Prozac a day could give a dog an aneurysm. I didn't think her death was caused by either of those things, but what if I'd taken Isis to the vet and told them a pet psychic said Isis's chest hurt? Would they have found something wrong with her heart? Could we have done anything to save her? We'd never know, and that was just as well. Knowing wouldn't bring her back and would only make me feel worse.

I already felt cheated out of a lifetime of happiness.

Most of our friends and co-workers were kind, because they understood how hard it was to lose a pet. Even those who couldn't relate knew the depth of our love for Isis.

My wise mother warned, "The sympathy runs out before the grief does." She was right. After a week or a month, people forgot that Rob and I were walking around with Isis-shaped holes in our hearts.

Alice told us again and again the story of the day Isis died. Tempted as I was to cut her off and tell her it was too painful to relive, I listened. I already felt overwhelming guilt for snapping at her in the backyard when she told me Isis was dead. She couldn't have known that I'd figured it out. I'm sure she was trying to protect me from the shock. She was in shock herself. I couldn't be selfish with my grief; Alice loved and missed Isis too. Worse, she'd lived the trauma of being there when Isis died. As much as I ached for Alice's pain, I was grateful she had been there, because neither Rob nor I had to find the body. How harrowing it would have been for any of us to come home and find her, not knowing whether she suffered, and thinking we could have could have saved her if only we'd been there.

I reassured myself that she went quickly. Isis had been playing happily with one of her most favorite people just before she died. We didn't have to make any difficult decisions about how much money to spend on medical treatments to keep her alive, or when the right time was to put her down. With dogs that die of old age or cancer, the grieving starts while the animal is still breathing. Your last moments together are painful because you know what's coming.

The last time I saw Isis alive, I'd come back inside the house to get something before leaving for work with Leo. "I love you, sweet girl," I told her. "I'll see you when I get home."

At the same time, I resented not getting to make those difficult decisions, because given the choice, we would have kept Isis alive as long as medical science would allow. We would have traded anything to have her back. Maybe even Leo.

Some people have been surprised to hear this. "Really? As much trouble as she was? Isn't life easier without a reactive dog?" Yes, really. In retrospect, my biggest regret was wasting half her life agonizing over modifying her behavior.

True, neither Rob nor I wanted to spend the next ten years living with two dogs who couldn't be in the same room together. But imagine if a dog trainer had told us before we got Leo, "Look, Isis can never be around other dogs or small children. Whatever you do, don't get another dog." We could have lived with that. We happily would have arranged our lives around our beloved reactive dog who was absolutely perfect in controlled situations. But that's not what happened. We had a trainer tell us it was in Isis's best interests to get a puppy.

Despite my remorse over subjecting Isis to Leo during the last months of her life, I believe it was meant to be. Before Isis died, I beat myself up constantly, worrying that getting Leo was a terrible mistake. I'll never know whether Isis would have lived longer if Leo hadn't come into our home, but I doubt it.

Leo joined our family for a reason. We got him so we wouldn't have to come home to an empty house after Isis died.

There was truth in my initial guilty feeling that Isis's death was the best thing that ever happened to Leo. Now he had our full attention and didn't have to be banished to the laundry room. We moved his crate to a more prominent place in the TV room, and put him there whenever he started chewing on the furniture. With Isis gone, he learned pretty quickly how to behave if he wanted to spend time with us outside of the cage.

We adored Leo, but he didn't fill the void. Rob couldn't enter the house through the front door anymore, because Isis wasn't there to greet him. He missed feeling the weight of her walking beside him from one end of the house to the other. He even missed her budging his hand off his computer mouse. Rob took it harder than I did. He was inconsolable. His face wilted with grief when he talked about her.

We clung to each other, lying on the gold couch together, my head resting on his chest, tears soaking into his shirt.

We enshrined Isis's ashes in a wooden box displaying my favorite photo of her frolicking on the beach. Rob had a painting made of his favorite photo of her on the couch, waiting in the spot. I had her name engraved on a stone and tattooed on my foot. I placed the stone by the spot where she died. The tattoo I keep with me always.

We tried to transfer our affection onto Leo, but he wasn't the snuggler that Isis had been. His bright eyes didn't shine with intelligence. He didn't climb on top of us in bed and lick our faces. He didn't wait for Rob on a special place on the couch and wriggle with delight as we fawned over him.

When Rob reached out for him, Leo nipped at his hands.

"See? It's not the same!" Rob's voice cracked, prompting a fresh wave of tears. I tried to remind Rob that Isis used to nip at his hands and feet too, but he didn't believe me.

"Leo is a great puppy," I said. "He's going to be a wonderful dog someday. He's just not there yet."

We both felt lucky to have Leo to get us through our heartbreak.

But Isis was our first love.

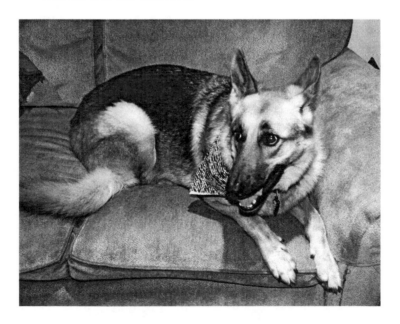

Author's Note: Because of Isis

Everyone hates it when a dog dies in a book. But the truth is, the dog always dies. Usually before the owner. Nobody wanted more than I did for Isis's story to have a happier ending.

As it turned out, we did get a happily-ever-after with two dogs in our home. Sadly, neither dog was Isis. Four months after we lost Isis, we were asked to give a home to a female German shepherd whose owners had moved away and left her behind. Mia hopped into my car like she owned the joint and became the big sister to Leo that I hoped Isis would be. Mia doesn't bark at bicycles or joggers and only sometimes at other dogs.

I'm learning for the first time how to walk a dog that isn't reactive. A normal dog.

Because of Isis, I don't take that for granted.

I feel ashamed of how naive I was, thinking I could just love the puppy and follow the advice of training books and everything would be great. I made so many mistakes and followed so much bad advice.

Because of Isis, now I know better. Because of Isis, I will always have a dog in my home. At least one.

I will stand up for force-free training and against the aversive techniques that I believe exacerbated the neuroses of a dog with a genetic predisposition for anxiety.

The length of a life is not equal to its importance or its lasting lessons. Whether Isis lived to be four or fourteen doesn't change the value of her life or the sadness we felt when she died.

We treasured every minute we spent with Isis, and she brought us joy beyond measure. And if you asked her, I know that Isis would tell you that her life was filled with an abundance of love and happiness.

Acknowledgments

Having consumed books my whole life, I thought I knew all the ingredients, but I didn't really have the recipe until I took Laura Kalpakian's fiction and memoir classes. Laura taught me about scenic detail and narrative weight, among other key aspects of the writing craft. Through Laura, I met writer buddies Tele Aadsen, Jolene Hanson, Pam Helberg, Linda Lambert, Cami Ostman, and the rest of the Red Wheelbarrow Writers, including the members of the Working Title Critique Group: Sean Dwyer, Susan Tive, Susan Chase-Foster, and Ruth Baker.

I am grateful, too, to all the trainers whose names I've changed. I know you meant well and each of you helped me in your own way. Thank you, Shannon Finch, Carmen Williams, and Kerry Mitchell, for seeing what we saw in Isis.

Thank you to my first readers, Louise Lewis, Rick Neumeyer, and Carol Boyd, and my editor Jim Thomsen, for your encouraging and validating feedback. And to Ian Dunbar and Nicole Wilde, whose work in dog behavior I've long admired and who so generously took time to read my book before publication.

Thanks to Andy and Quin Neumeyer for introducing us to Isis.

I don't have words to express my gratitude to Alice Eis, who loved Isis as much as Rob and I did, and who was there in her last moments. And to Jerry Eis, for being the most devoted dog grandpa there ever was.

Thank you, Rob Eis, for your endless support and love, and for our little dog family.

Finally, thank you to Kathy Neumeyer, my first writing teacher and a model mother.

About the Author

Kari Neumeyer has a master's degree in journalism from Northwestern University's Medill School and has worked for news outlets in Washington state and the Czech Republic. She grew up in Los Angeles, graduated from the University of Southern California's School of Cinema-Television, and worked in the film industry before graduate school.

In 2006, she and her beau, Rob, settled down in Bellingham, Washington, where they started a dog family.

In her spare time, she volunteers teaching an adaptive martial arts class to adults with developmental disabilities at the Max Higbee Center; fostering a love of creative writing to Whatcom Young Writers; and walking shelter dogs at the Humane Society of Skagit Valley.

She blogs about dogs at KariNeumeyer.com.

CPSIA information can be obtained at www.ICGtesting.com
Printed in the USA
LVOW06s1548150115

422984LV00003B/144/P